Marriage
From Roots to Fruits

Marriage
From Roots to Fruits

Understanding
God's Design
for
Growing in
the Good Soil

MATT PAVLIK, MA, LPCC-S
BRINGING YOUR POTENTIAL TO LIGHT

Christian Concepts
New Reflections Counseling, Inc.
Dayton, Ohio USA

Marriage from Roots to Fruits

Copyright © 2015 by Matt Pavlik

All rights reserved. No part of this publication may be reproduced, stored in a retrieval system, or transmitted, in any form or by any means, electronic, mechanical, photocopying, recording, or otherwise, without the written permission of the author.

Published in the United States of America by Christian Concepts (christianconcepts.com), an imprint of New Reflections Counseling, Inc. (newreflectionscounseling.com).

The author offers Internet addresses as suggested resources but does not guarantee the validity of the content. Because of the dynamic nature of the Internet, any links may have changed since publication and may no longer be valid.

Some of the examples are composites from several situations. Details and names have been changed to protect anonymity. Any resemblance to persons alive or dead is purely coincidental.

This book is not intended to be a replacement for professional counseling.

Library of Congress Cataloging-in-Publication Data

Pavlik, Matthew Edward, 1971-
    Marriage from Roots to Fruits: Understanding God's Design for Growing in the Good Soil / Matt Pavlik.
    p. cm.
    ISBN-13: 978-0-9863831-0-6 (softcover)
    ISBN-13: 978-0-9863831-1-3 (kindle)
    ISBN-13: 978-0-9863831-8-2 (epub)
    1.   Marriage—Religious aspects—Christianity.
    2.   Interpersonal conflict—Religious aspects—Christianity.
    3.   Developmental psychology—Religious aspects—Christianity.
    I. Title.
    BV4596.M3 P38 2015
    248.8'44—dc22

Unless otherwise indicated, all Scripture quotations are from the ESV® Bible (The Holy Bible, English Standard Version®), copyright © 2001 by Crossway, a publishing ministry of Good News Publishers. Used by permission. All rights reserved.

Scripture quotations taken from the Holy Bible, NEW INTERNATIONAL VERSION®. Copyright © 1973, 1978, 1984 by Biblica, Inc. All rights reserved worldwide. Used by permission.

Scripture quotations from THE MESSAGE. Copyright © by Eugene H. Peterson 1993, 1994, 1995, 1996, 2000, 2001, 2002. Used by permission of Tyndale House Publishers, Inc.

Publishing History

2015 04 29 --- First Edition (print)
2018 12 31 --- Changed font for title, subtitle, blueprint space;
                 Removed italics from quote attribution
2018 12 31 --- First Edition (kindle)
2018 12 31 --- First Edition (epub)

Dedication

To my wife Georgette, a true Proverbs 31 woman and love of my life.

CONTENTS

Foreword ix
Preface xi
Acknowledgements xiii
Introduction 1

Part I – Spiritual Foundations 5

1. Abundant Fruit Begins with Good Soil 7
2. Paradise Lost 13
3. Paradise Found 15
4. God is Our Source 17
5. God's Design for Growth 21
6. Investing in Growth 25
7. Balanced Growth 29

Part II – Individual Growth 33

8. Focus On What You Can Control 35
9. Increase Self-Awareness 37
10. Become an "I" 41
11. Develop Secure Attachment 45
12. Learn Your Limits 49
13. Bring Your Core Longings to Jesus 53
14. Believe Lies or Truth 57
15. Discover Your Unique Identity 61
16. Recognize Your Gender as a Strength 65
17. Play Your Position 69

Part III – Marital Growth 73

18. God Creates Marriage 75
19. Living Your Gender Identity 79
20. Headship and Submission 83
21. On Becoming an "Us" 89
22. The Storming "Us" 93
23. The Norming "Us" 97
24. The Performing and Adjourning "Us" 101
25. Your Past Affects Conflict Resolution 105
26. Intentional Communication 109
27. The Four Languages of Love 115
28. Healthy Sexual Intimacy 119
29. Productive Conflict 123

30. Two are Better than One 127
31. Healthy Expectations 131
32. From Conflict to Harmony 135
33. Optimal Decision Making 139
34. Pursuing the Win-Win 143
35. Embracing Conflict Realities 147
36. Biblical Conflict Resolution 151
37. Biblical Confrontation 155
38. Deep Betrayal 159
39. Restoration 163
40. Repentance 167
41. Finding Complete Healing 171
42. Surviving an Offense 175
43. A Forgiving Heart 179
44. A Reconciling Heart 183
45. A Trusting Heart 187
46. Divorce Prevention 191
47. Divorce Decisions 195
48. Divorce Recovery 201
49. Is My Partner Abusive? 205
50. Is My Partner Addicted? 209
51. Grieving Traumatic Loss 213
52. Time to Endure and Enjoy the Journey 217

Supplemental Material 221

More Help for Your Journey 223
Appendix A – Cinema Therapy 225
Selected Bibliography 227
Index of Scriptures 229

Foreword

As I read through Matt's book, *Marriage From Roots to Fruits*, I felt hopeful. I thought of all the couples I have met along the way who looked at their relationship, present and future, with a sense of futility and hopelessness. The author gives details of God's design for a healthy relationship, with very practical tools, filled with real life examples to encourage them along the path of healing and living victoriously.

The author uses his many years of experience as a gifted Christian licensed professional clinical counselor. To share ways of how to make a relationship work, the author explains God's definition of marriage and how deeply God knows, understands, and cares for the struggle that can come with marriage. The author shows how God offers a path of healing, when we are able to find greater intimacy in Him.

The application of each chapter makes it easier for couples to understand God's love for them, offering a path of healing and how to find that greater intimacy with each other and with Him along the way.

I have not read a book (manual) like it before. I believe it will help couples who are at the point of hopelessness and emotional pain to truly heal. I also feel it is very applicable for married couples who feel good about the relationship they have but want to have a stronger and deeper relationship with God and with themselves. Matt designed the book to be a tool for pastors and counselors, to use as a guide for premarital counseling, and to help hurting marriages. I feel that this book is a must-read for all caregivers.

I am genuinely excited about this book because I work with so many people with broken relationships. I will be using this book with my clients. It represents unique counseling insights with strong biblical applications, and the author does a wonderful job in expressing those ideas in a way that is understandable and applicable for those who are in need.

Will W Alejandro, M.Div. MA
Doctoral Candidate
Director/Formational Counselor,
Joshua Recovery Ministries Inc.

December 2014

Preface

Measure Once

I've been married once and engaged twice. I married my wife Georgette in 1999. What happened before I met Georgette? Back when I was engaged the first time, my motto could have been, "Measure once, cut twice."

After I graduated from the University of Illinois in 1993, I moved to Austin, Texas to start my career as a software engineer. Not too much later, a friend from college introduced me to a friend of hers. We developed a long-distance relationship based on our mutual interest in spiritual and emotional growth.

Around November of 1994 I figured out I wanted to return to school for a counseling degree. To do this I needed to leave Texas, so I quit my job. I asked her to marry me; she said yes.

A few months before the wedding, I moved to her location. Even though living close by was good for us, we ran into some potholes. We attended counseling together for a couple of months, which helped our relationship, but doubt lingered in the back of my mind. As we approached the wedding day, my mood shifted from excitement to alarm.

In hindsight, my first engagement was more of a logical choice rather than a realistic one. Back when I was still in Texas, I went to individual counseling. This moved me from being too cautious to the opposite extreme: too careless. My choice to be engaged was more of an overzealous reaction to my counselor's advice. Under these circumstances, discounting the signs and red flags was too easy for me. For example, I overlooked her inability to separate from her mother in an emotionally healthy way. As you will see later in this book, this says as much about me as it does her. I can see now that my need for emotional connection overshadowed the reality that the decision to marry deserves our utmost respect.

I was not ready to be married and/or this was not the right woman for me. Fortunately, I realized my mistake before it was too late. Unfortunately, breaking the engagement one week before the wedding cut it a bit close. I learned first-hand that marriage is not something to jump into with both feet without due diligence.

Born Twice

In college, I majored in computer science and worked with a professor as an undergraduate research assistant. I appreciated working with him and even took his independent study class.

However, my first two years of college were difficult. I felt lost. My high school friendships faded. I attempted to make new friends, but no one seemed to understand me. To make matters worse, I was robbed while delivering pizza, which led me to quit my job.

During this time, God used my relational emptiness to draw me to Himself. I became a Christian in July 1991. I remember to this day what it was like not having Christ in my life. The contrast energizes me: one day I was antagonistic toward the idea of God existing, and the next God enabled me to believe in Him.

The final project for the independent study consisted of me building a small finite state machine (logical computer chips containing "and" and "or" gates wired together so they remember to turn on the same lights in each state, plus a switch to trigger the next state). My professor was impressed with my effort, "Most computer science people have their heads in the clouds, but you actually built something out of computer chips that works." That feedback increased my confidence. It was exciting to learn that I am able to make the abstract understandable to others.

A few months later, my professor announced he was leaving the university because he accepted a position in Austin, Texas. He called me before I graduated and said he'd like to hire me.

Ecclesia

In Texas I connected with a dynamic group of Christians. I felt at home with them because we shared an intense desire to grow and learn. The youth pastor named the group Ecclesia 546 (*Ecclesia* is Greek for church and we met at 5:46pm). This group is the best church experience I've had to date. I am thankful to have had the experience and regret it lasted only one short year.

God called the leader away from our church. God called me away, too. This group further influenced my desire to return to school to study counseling.

Married Once

Cancelling the engagement was difficult but for the best. I spent the summer pondering and recovering from the broken relationship. Then in the fall, I moved to Columbus, Ohio to start working on my counseling degree at Ashland Theological Seminary.

Two years later, I met my wife Georgette. We met in the context of a church group, which I believe helps make the decision process more straightforward and safe. Also, I was wiser because of my previous experience. Two years later we married. Georgette and I have had our ups-and-downs, but I am grateful God brought her into my life.

Measure Twice

Most of my life, I've felt five to ten years behind my peers emotionally. In my twenties, I had the maturity of a teenager. In my thirties, I was more like someone in their twenties. I suppose this could describe many people, but for me it's been a blessing and a curse.

Becoming a Christian, knowing God and His love, attending my own counseling, marrying Georgette, and counseling others have helped me catch up emotionally. Some days I still feel like a child—but now I know I am God's child.

I've had a career as a software developer and I currently work as a professional counselor. With this book, I am a published author.

My love for learning grows every day. Being behind emotionally has taught me the value of growth (emotional and spiritual), psychology (the study of the soul), and philosophy (the love of wisdom). Actually, God gifted me with understanding and gently nudged me into the counseling field when I became a Christian. I feel alive and filled with purpose today more than ever.

Finally this Book

I actually started writing this book in 2007. I've started it three times. The first two times I lost my sense of direction with it. Finally I've finished what I started! I didn't understand why at the time, but I understand now that I simply didn't know all of what God wanted me to put into it.

Marriage is a calling that we must first enter and, once married, re-enter daily by faith. Knowing everything about your fiancé or marriage partner is impossible. However, we can enter marriage with due diligence. Working through this book will prepare you for your upcoming marriage, or if you are already married, it will help you navigate to a place of health.

This book contains the best of everything I've learned about marriage both personally and professionally. You will learn how to build your marriage from establishing the roots (a strong foundation) to producing fruits (emotional intimacy, children, fruit of the Spirit, and eternally lasting ministry).

Acknowledgements

Thanks to God who loves me and who empowers me to complete His work.

Thanks to my wife Georgette for her steady support, encouragement, willingness to help, and belief in me.

Thanks to my parents for their dedication to pray as I follow God's calling.

Thanks to the many teachers and mentors in my life who helped me grow.

Thanks to my clients who teach me every day how to be a better counselor.

Thanks to my editor Johnnie Alexander for her above-and-beyond effort, suggestions, and encouragement while reviewing and correcting my writing.

Thanks to Will Alejandro, Melody Shaw, Brenda Moore, and Rick Crain for their honest feedback and encouragement, which helped me improve what I want to say.

Introduction

By wisdom a house is built, and by understanding it is established.
—Proverbs 24:3

Unless the LORD builds the house, those who build it labor in vain.
—Psalm 127:1a

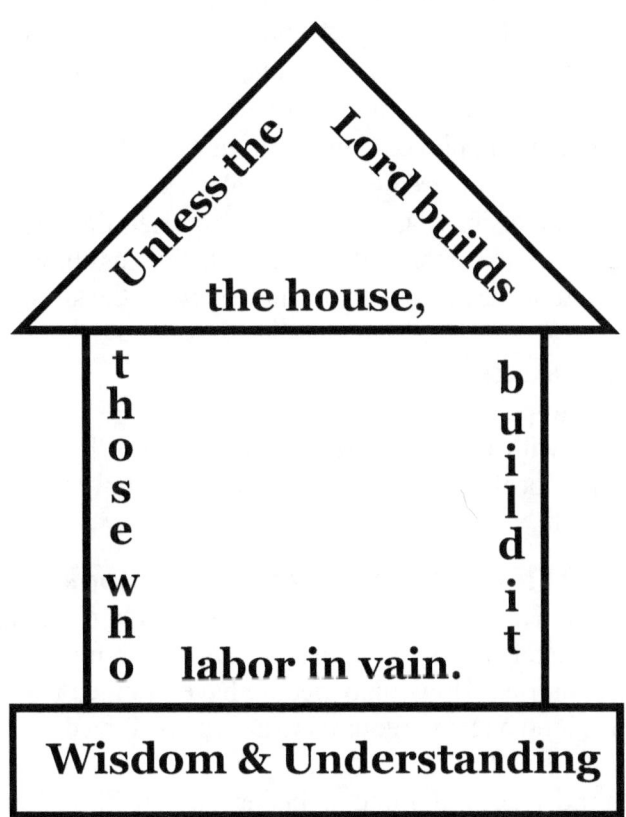

The Lord, with wisdom and understanding, builds and establishes a marriage.

About This Book

What I believe about Marriage

Marriage is God joining together a man and a woman, loyal to each other for life, who each contribute distinct but equally important abilities towards the completion of a fruitful mission greater than can be accomplished apart.

- The relationship between husband and wife reflects the relationship between Christ and the Church.
- God intends marriage to be a lifetime commitment, with sexual relations reserved between only one man and one woman who are married to each other.
- God hates divorce and there are natural, negative consequences for it. But God forgives and restores those who divorce as He does every time we miss His ideal for our lives.
- God made man and woman as equals, but they are not equivalent; of equal value, but not interchangeable. God intended both genders to be essential as each provides a distinct contribution, and they have specialized roles in marriage and in life.
- God made man and woman so that any man and any woman can fit together to form a one-flesh marriage. Yet God in His sovereignty knows exactly whom you will marry.
- No one marriage will be everything—like no one person can be everything. Just as a person has limits and personality, so does a marriage.
- Each marriage union forms a unique relationship that no other two people can replicate.
- Every union has a unique set of strengths and weaknesses.

Difficulty in marriage is not a sign that someone has married the wrong person. All marriages have difficulty. Challenges are an opportunity for growth just as they are in other areas of life. Therefore, the hard work of marriage is to activate and energize the strengths of a unique marriage while:

- Improving upon the weaknesses when possible; and
- Tolerating them when impossible.

This means being flexible with and accepting of a partner's healthy individual preferences while being firm and patient with unhealthy choices. A marriage will only be as strong as the individual health of the husband and wife.

Who will Benefit from this Book

Unfortunately, a marriage license does not mean we are ready or competent enough to marry. If we continue to think and feel like a single person, we will remain single on the inside even though, outwardly, we are married. How many people have plunged ahead into marriage without a clue? What would happen if no one was required to pass a test for a driver's license before getting behind the wheel?

I wrote this book with individuals in mind. Whether you are single, engaged, single-again, or married, this book is for *your* personal growth. As you complete the reading and exercises, share your insights and questions with your trusted friends, fiancé, partner, and/or counselor. You can even use this book in group discussions (if you are brave enough). This book is especially for you if you:

- Are struggling with how to make your relationship work;
- Like to understand how things work—how each part functions in relation to the whole;
- Want to learn the details of God's design for relationships;
- Like to reflect in order to gain understanding;

- Want a full-brain (left and right) learning experience;
- Appreciate visual diagrams to gain understanding;
- Learn best by seeing principles and ideas in their simplest form;
- Want to apply the appropriate principles and ideas to bring about positive change; or
- Want to make the most of your time in counseling.

How to get the most out of this Book

- Read the chapters in the order presented. If you haven't already done so, read the Preface. While each chapter can stand alone, most chapters build upon previously developed ideas.
- Expect further insights with each chapter you read.
- Have fun with this! You are about to embark on a full-scale learning experience.
- Use the checkboxes (□) in the Next Step sections to mark when you've completed the exercises at the end of each chapter.
- For the movie exercises, be sure to use the questions in Appendix A and review the comments and cautions (some movies are rated R).
- Journal your thoughts and feelings while reading each chapter.
- Draw images that represent your learning experiences. This will engage your right brain.
- Use the Blueprint Space to journal and draw.
- Share your insights with your partner and others with whom you share a close relationship. Ask them questions about what you are reading.
- Seek counseling to address those topics that identify one of your tender spots.
- Use this book as part of your counseling.
- When making tough, life-changing decisions, allow one or more trusted advisors or counselors the opportunity to offer their perspective (Proverbs 15:22). I've made every effort to be clear and accurate, but even the inerrant truth of the Bible can be applied incorrectly.
- As you work through the material, it will stretch you and some of your emotional baggage will surface. You may feel encouraged but also uncomfortable. This is by design. Pursue the material at a pace you can manage, but don't give up. Those who push through will benefit the most.

Editorial Notes

- See the copyright page for disclaimers.
- I often use the plural pronouns "they" or "their" instead of the more awkward "he or she" or "his or her."
- I alternate between "he" and "she" except where the example naturally calls for one gender over the other. While each gender has their own strengths and weaknesses, either gender can, at some point, struggle with just about any problem. The use of a particular gender in an example doesn't mean I am excluding the other.
- Marriage is a partnership. I am intentionally choosing to use the word "partner" instead of "spouse." When the context is marriage and you read *partner*, think *marriage partner*.

How this Book is Structured to Help Your Marriage

This book has 52 short chapters that you can easily read in one sitting. Each chapter has a primary principle to help your marriage. The three main sections correspond to the three main developmental areas:

Part I   Chapters 1–7   Spiritual Foundations for Individual Health

Part II   Chapters 8–17   Individual Growth needed for Marital Health

Part III Chapters 18–52 Marital Growth needed to keep your marriage growing for a lifetime

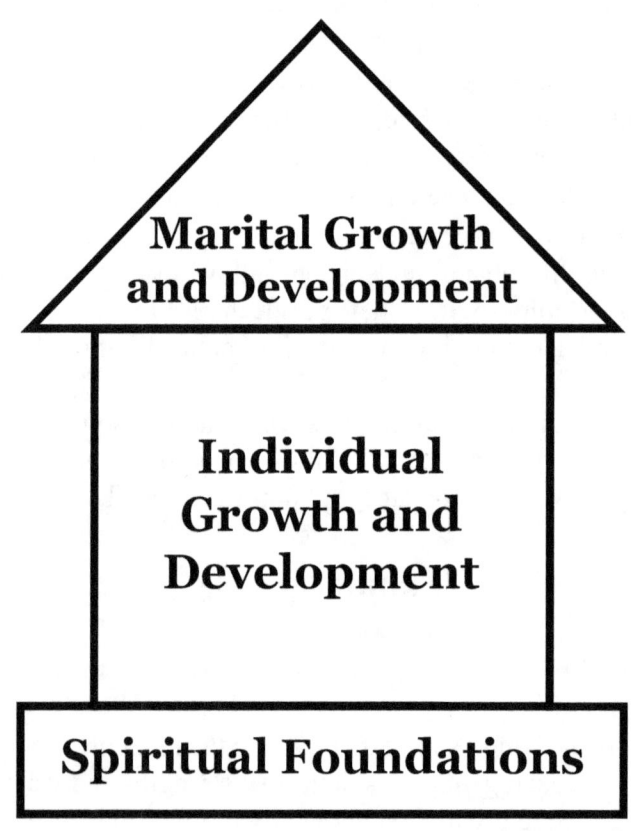

Part I – Spiritual Foundations

Chapter 1　　　　　Achieving a Fruitful Marriage

Chapters 2–4　　　Finding God Amidst the Chaos

Chapters 5–7　　　God's Design for Growth

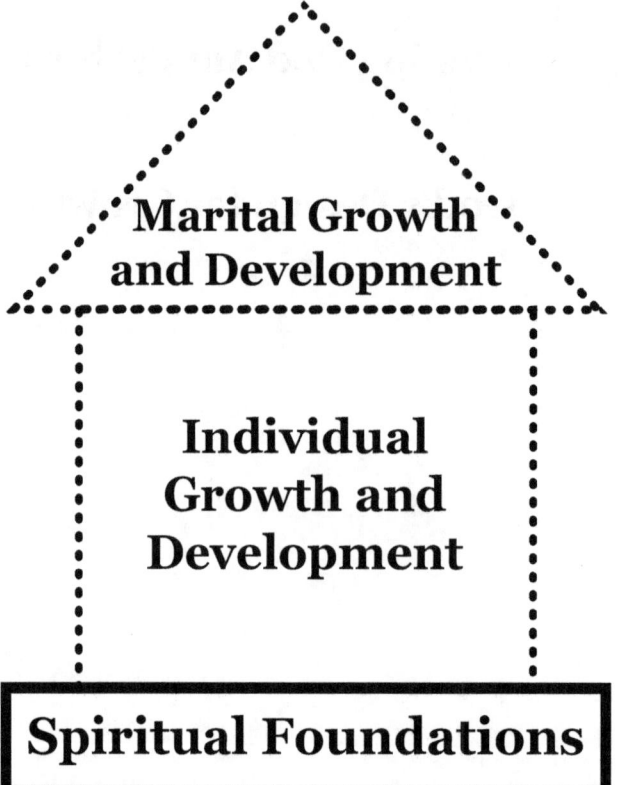

Chapter 1

Abundant Fruit Begins with Good Soil

And he told them many things in parables, saying: "A sower went out to sow. And as he sowed, some seeds fell along the path, and the birds came and devoured them. Other seeds fell on rocky ground, where they did not have much soil, and immediately they sprang up, since they had no depth of soil, but when the sun rose they were scorched. And since they had no root, they withered away. Other seeds fell among thorns, and the thorns grew up and choked them. Other seeds fell on good soil and produced grain, some a hundredfold, some sixty, some thirty. He who has ears, let him hear."
—Matthew 13:3–9

The Four Types of Soil

Jesus uses the Parable of the Sower to speak about our receptivity to God's words (Matthew 13:3–9). Let's consider how the parable also applies to marriage. The four types of soil in the parable match up with four types of relationships. From least to most desirable, these are Path, Rocks, Thorns, and Good Soil.

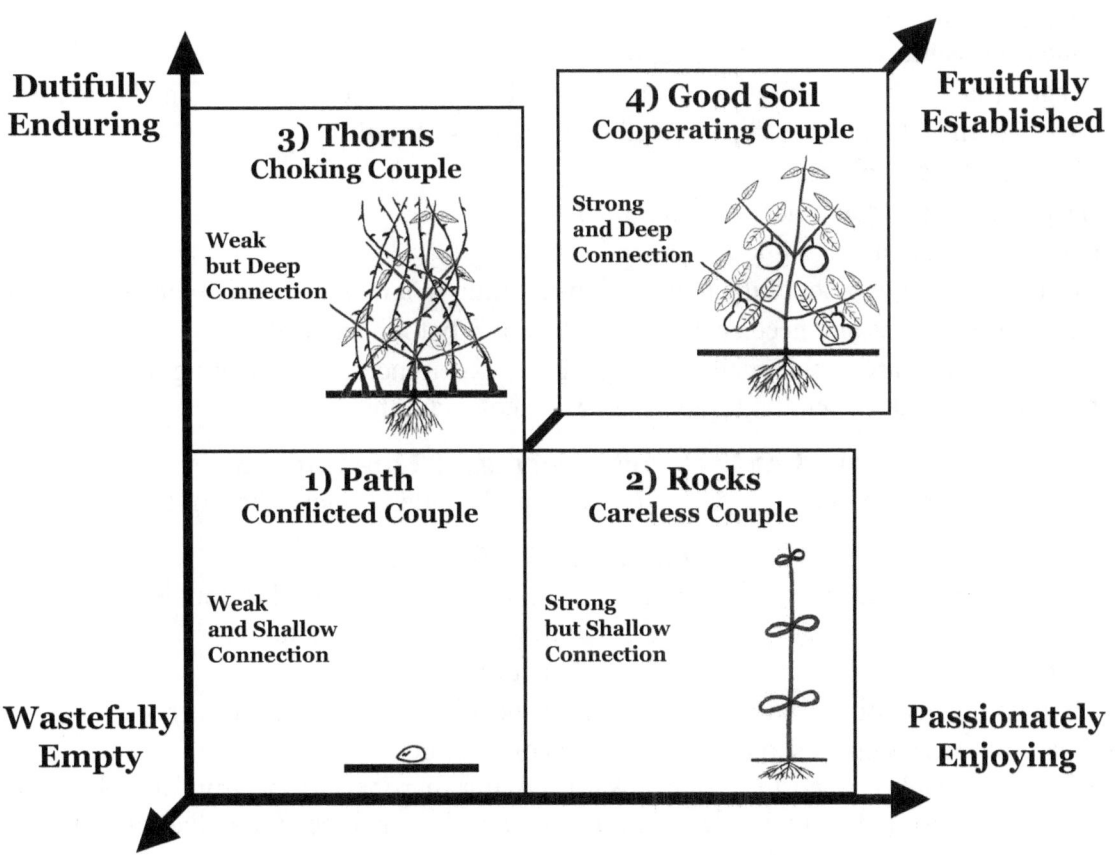

1. The Path or Conflicted Couple alternates between extreme behaviors of intense fighting and extreme feelings of distance; they cannot begin to build a positive connection.
2. The Rocks or Careless Couple relies superficially on short-lived positive experiences; they cannot experience contentment with their connection.
3. The Thorns or Choking Couple has a history together, but are stuck in a rut; they fail to pursue a passionate connection.
4. The Good Soil or Cooperating Couple has endured both highs and lows; they experience closeness and distance without losing a positive connection.

The typical inexperienced couple begins as either Conflicted or Careless. Along the way, every couple experiences being Conflicted, Careless, and Choking before making it to Cooperating.

1) On the Path: The Conflicted Couple is Oblivious

Jesus makes it clear that the hardest place to be is On the Path. In marriage, when both partners' hearts are hard, look out! They will either tear each other apart or be so disengaged that no relationship exists. Either way, the result is an empty, unfruitful relationship.

Jesus says the seed sown along the path is like someone hearing the words but having no understanding. He equates understanding with fruitfulness. The ground is so hard the seed cannot penetrate. When growth cannot begin, a couple loses the opportunity to be a source of light in a dark world. They may be together only by habit and convenience. If they have not already given up, they are in danger of separation, divorce, or some type of extra-marital affair.

A conflicted relationship consists of either extreme conflict (battling for the last crumb) or extreme disconnection (not speaking for days). The path represents immaturity—being oblivious to how to make the relationship work.

<u>Couple Characteristics</u>
- Intense frustration, anger, and loneliness;
- Regular unresolved conflict with defensive self-focus and hurtful words and behaviors;
- A stubborn lack of ownership coupled with blame-shifting;
- All or nothing thinking;
- Dependence on each other for contentment;
- Confusion from a lack of definition and direction;
- Rare, if any, enjoyment of the relationship resulting in a lack of positive memories; and
- High expectations and needs along with a low ability to meet needs.

A couple who lacks relational skills, positive experiences, a validating history, and an understanding of God's intention for marriage will feel a tangible hopelessness.

Another Way to Understand This Couple

The couple has an unreliable, inexpensive car, but they blame each other for lack of a Porsche.

Adjustments for Success

An On the Path relationship has few assets and many liabilities. This couple needs patience because improvement may take a while. But the Conflicted Couple can:
- Accept the current deficit by lowering expectations;
- Be intentional about creating success because positive momentum breeds hope; and
- Focus on small steps to experience positive connection.

Reading this book is a positive step toward moving marriage to the fruitful soil. Also, this couple can invest in studying marriage, attending counseling, and receiving other outside help.

2) On the Rocks: The Careless Couple is Impetuous

The Careless Couple's relationship starts quickly (received with joy) and may even appear to be thriving (shoots up quickly). This is possible because they avoid conflict, and consequently, they lack experience in successfully resolving conflict. The pressure to be liked by one's partner results in behaviors that avoid failure and rejection.

The couple acts too quickly without considering if they can finish what they started. They tend to seek the benefits of marriage before they've built a foundation to sustain those benefits. This impatience may show up, for example, as a financial crisis (debt) or pregnancy before marriage. The discovery of personal and relational weaknesses threatens to wither the relationship. The shocked reaction is too often, "Oh, no! Did I choose the wrong person?" Complications, which may only be a normal rite of passage, become a crisis of doubt as the couple questions whether they can overcome their obstacles.

Couple Characteristics
- The honeymoon effect: extreme highs followed by shock, fear, and disappointment;
- A one-dimensional, superficial focus on excitement;
- A lack of genuineness: compromising values to create the illusion of being one;
- Conflict avoidance, along with denial of difficulty;
- Dependence on pleasure now: all that matters is this moment;
- Creation of emotional debt by recklessly borrowing against future happiness;
- A strong temptation to give up when difficulty surfaces; and
- Fear and intolerance of conflict, separation, individual space, differences, preferences and opinions.

The primary danger is that the Careless Couple believes good relationships are easy. Relationships begin easily because of chemistry. They last by learning how to accept the bad with the good.

The couple lacks the understanding that can only come from a history of overcoming doubts and difficulties. Their above-the-ground focus neglects root development and threatens their future together.

The Careless and the Conflicted Couples have in common a lack of understanding about marriage. They build the relationship on the benefits they expect to receive then can't cope when those benefits are lacking. Without the maturity to accept that the relationship is incapable of meeting all their needs, they try to experience the best aspects of a relationship without appreciating the time and work involved.

By keeping conflict to a minimum, the Careless Couple receives some benefit from the relationship. However, without conflict resolution, the couple neglects to build a strong and lasting marriage. If the couple does not establish something deeper than a "love is all we need" mentality, any new growth will wither and die.

Another Way to Understand this Couple

The couple is driving a Porsche but does not have the money to maintain it properly. They feel a need to cover up their insecurity.

Adjustments for Success

This couple must face reality by exploring and accepting each other's differences while maintaining their heartfelt connection. They need to spend time working on communication and conflict resolution. Successful relationships have both:

- Feelings and experiences of oneness, togetherness, peace, and unity; and
- Acceptance of differences and weaknesses with a plan to navigate them.

3) Among the Thorns: The Choking Couple is Dutiful

This couple endures hardship responsibly because of their high regard for marriage. But intimacy between them is blocked because they are distracted by the worries of this life and the deceitfulness of wealth. The thorns represent a distraction away from what is most important.

While their potential for marital success is high, too many weeds demand their attention. The relationship is last on a long list of other things they consider more interesting or more urgent.

<u>Couple Characteristics</u>
- ☐ Emotional distance: a lack of expressiveness and passion;
- ☐ Growth that has slowed or ceased altogether;
- ☐ Emphasis on separate, individual pursuits;
- ☐ A focus on responsibilities (productivity, money, kids, etc.) more than on the relationship;
- ☐ So busy they are ships passing in the night and feel like roommates or strangers;
- ☐ A sense of "I am no longer in love"; and
- ☐ An unhealthy stability.

Another Way to Understand This Couple

The couple can afford to maintain the Porsche but leaves it sitting in the garage. Their money goes to other individual interests.

Adjustment for Success

God is creator and master designer; He doesn't make mistakes. He intends for us to live a balanced life that has room for both work and fun, as well as both individuality and closeness.

This couple has learned from experience that their relationship will not provide all they need. But their acceptance of reality doesn't keep their passion lit. Their workload keeps them unhealthily separated and disconnected.

They can revive their relationship by spending more time enjoying each other in the moment. Fully realizing this involves:

- Remembering what initially attracted them to each other;
- Reviewing their purpose for being together; and
- Experiencing activities that blend attraction and purpose together.

4) In Good Soil: The Cooperating Couple is Established

Good soil allows a healthy root structure below ground and a healthy branch structure above ground, resulting in quantities of fruit many times more than the other soils. In the same way, the established couple develops a healthy endurance while maintaining a healthy passion resulting in a thriving and intimate marriage.

The journey to an established relationship begins with keeping the passion while learning how to endure. A couple needs wisdom to balance these two nutrients in the Good Soil. Marriages aren't born with this wisdom, but it comes as the couple experiences their lives together.

Couple Characteristics
- ☐ Resolution of conflict resulting in a win-win;
- ☐ Acceptance and tolerance for their partner's shortcomings;
- ☐ Balance enjoying the relationship (excitement) and working on the relationship (stability);
- ☐ Realistic expectations;
- ☐ Their emotional needs being met often by their partner;
- ☐ Their emotional needs being appropriately met by others;
- ☐ A reflection of God's love to their children and others they know; and
- ☐ A sense of a legacy.

Another Way to Understand This Couple

The couple has the Porsche, can maintain it, and regularly enjoys taking it out for a spin. The couple did not achieve their success quickly but developed it over time.

For Reflection

1. As no person is perfect, no marriage is perfect. No matter which soil condition most closely describes your relationship, you can decide to grow a godly marriage by cultivating the path, clearing out the rocks, pulling out the thorns, and planting in the good soil. When you do this, you will be well on your way to yielding fruit one hundred times what was sown.
2. Conflict is not bad; not resolving conflict in a healthy way is bad. Learn to see conflict as a doorway to engagement and engagement as the pathway to an established relationship.
3. Conflicted Couples are stuck in a negative conflict pattern. They experience emptiness that results in an imploding relationship. With little experience of a healthy bond, they need help lowering their expectations of the relationship and learning how to bond to each other.
4. Intimacy includes both enjoying positive experiences and overcoming negative experiences.
5. Careless Couples enjoy positive experiences but fail to endure negative ones. They need help pushing through fear and doubt to reach confident competence.
6. Choking Couples endure negative experiences by disconnecting but lose sight of enjoying positive ones. They need help reconnecting and keeping their bond active.
7. Both Careless and Choking Couples avoid full engagement. Avoiding any part of intimacy eventually produces distance and decay of the relationship bond.
8. Marriage is a calling. Marriages don't just happen. Would you go to a doctor who believes they are called to be a doctor and, because they enjoy the idea so much, they skip any training, learn as they go, purchase a cheap certification, and start the following week?
9. Often one partner is more work-oriented and the other is more play-oriented. Growing a fruitful marriage means finding ways to have these valuable personalities cooperate.

Next Steps

- ☐ Review the couple characteristics and check off the ones that most closely resemble your relationship. Which couple type most closely fits your marriage? Considering what you learned about your type, write out a description of your relationship's strengths and weaknesses. Weaknesses are growth areas. Keep these in mind as you read the rest of the book.
- ☐ Review these resources:
  - ☐ Movie: *The Notebook* (review Appendix A before watching)

☐ In your Blueprint Space, write out the first few words that come to mind when you think of marriage. Then review each couple description and decide which type they are.

Blueprint Space

Chris and Brittany are in their twenties and have been married for four years. Chris is working 60 hours per week to secure a promotion. Brittany wants to have children but cannot imagine raising children with Chris gone so much. Brittany feels lonely and regularly communicates this. Chris is getting too close to a female co-worker. Brittany suspects but Chris denies everything. They fight all the time over the small amount of time they spend together. Emotions are high and Brittany is feeling desperate. She's starting to think she made a mistake marrying Chris.

Ryan and Nicole are in their thirties and have been married for nine years. Ryan is younger than Nicole by four years. They have three children. One is 15 years old and is Nicole's from a previous marriage. The other two are six and four. Nicole is getting too close to a male co-worker. Ryan has struggled with employment at times.

Josh and Emily are in their twenties and have been married for two years. If you ask them, they say they get along fabulously. They spend a lot of time away from home visiting family, spending time with friends, eating out and seeing movies. Josh would like to be home more, but he hasn't gathered up the courage to tell Emily.

Dave and Samantha are in their thirties and have been married for seven years. They have two young children. Both work outside the home. They work hard and play hard, keeping busy most nights watching their kids and with church and sports activities. Samantha is finishing up her master's degree. They keep busy, but neither seems to mind.

Bob and Karen are in their fifties and have been married for twenty-five years. They have three grown children and two grandchildren. Bob retired last year and hopes to start a new career. Karen returned to school for nursing. They have plans to travel but disagree on the timeframe. They feel comfortable with each other. Bob also has a 30-year-old daughter, Julie, but Karen doesn't know about her. Julie recently contacted Bob because she wants to restart their relationship.

Mike and Amanda are in their forties and have been married for fourteen years. They have five children ages thirteen, ten, eight, seven, and four. They adopted their seven- and eight-year-olds six years ago, and then had another child. Their first few years together went well, but they spent four years trying to get pregnant. During this time, they felt extremely distant because of communication problems. But they finally worked through their issues a couple of years ago. They feel close today and feel relatively confident about the future.

Chapter 2

Paradise Lost

Then the eyes of both were opened, and they knew that they were naked. And they sewed fig leaves together and made themselves loincloths. And they heard the sound of the LORD God walking in the garden in the cool of the day, and the man and his wife hid themselves from the presence of the LORD God among the trees of the garden.
—Genesis 3:7–8

I will greatly increase your pains in childbearing; with pain you will give birth to children. Cursed is the ground because of you; through painful toil you will eat of it all the days of your life.
—Genesis 3:16–17

The Reality of Death

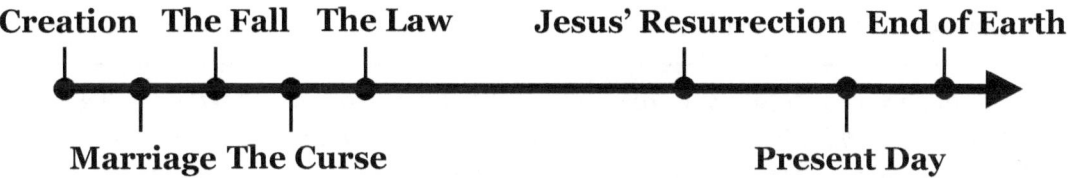

God told Adam, "You will die when you eat of the tree of the knowledge of good and evil" (Genesis 2:17). Then God created Eve. God or Adam must have told Eve because she knew at least a distorted version of God's command (Genesis 3:3). Adam and Eve lost paradise when they chose to trust in themselves over dependence upon God. When they disobeyed Him, they died spiritually and lost their secure connection with Him. Encountering fear and shame for the first time must have been brutal. Preoccupied with grief, they were unaware of the depth of the problem. Little did they realize they were powerless to undo the mess they'd gotten into.

> **Thankfully, God knew what to do. He altered how the world works through divine correction, cursing what is external to us to be a constant reminder of our internal disorder.**

Even though the external disorder makes life extremely difficult, the alternative is ignorant bliss on the road to destruction (hell). By increasing our awareness of the reality of death, God highlighted our helplessness and need for Him:
- The Fall: We died spiritually resulting in shame, fear, doubt, and pride. As a result, we feel the need to be self-sufficient. In this state, we are vulnerable and weak (Genesis 3:7–8). We cannot please God by our fleshly efforts (Hebrews 11:6).
- The Curse: Life is now difficult and issues such as illness, death, and suffering provide concrete reasons to doubt God's goodness. Perspiration and pain continue to be familiar experiences, even while pursuing good works (Genesis 3:16–17).

- The Flesh: A real desire for evil instead of God leads to choosing our own way, blame-shifting, and idol worshipping (Genesis 3:12–13). We no longer look to God as our source of life but become dependent on what He created (Romans 1:25). The flesh provides real temptation to sin (Matthew 26:41).
- The Presence of Evil: Our enemy, in the realm of our flesh and the earth under the curse, is stronger than we are (Romans 7). Evil seeks to increase our fear and suffering and desires to destroy us (1 Peter 5:8).
- The Law: God instituted the law to make it obviously impossible for us to achieve perfection through our own efforts (Romans 7).

How the Fall Affects Marriage

The Fall tainted every aspect of life. God did not make marriage an exception. The Curse hits at the heart of who Adam and Eve are as male and female, which adds pressure to marriage.

Because of our flesh, we miss a fully satisfying connection to God. This leads to an irresistible temptation to make marriage an idol. We tend to project our desire for perfection onto marriage. This projection is the cause of most marital conflict. Marriage will never take the place of God. Nor will it, by itself, fulfill all your deepest needs. Aspects of marriage may be disappointing for a long time, perhaps even a lifetime.

Yet God is merciful. Eve can still give birth and Adam can still produce food. The human race survives. Hope for marriage is alive. Marriage is ripe with potential more than any other relationship. Through marriage, we get an up-close and personal taste of God's love for us. Patiently pursue its fullest potential.

For we know that the whole creation has been groaning together in the pains of childbirth until now. And not only the creation, but we ourselves, who have the first fruits of the Spirit, groan inwardly as we wait eagerly for adoption as sons, the redemption of our bodies. For in this hope we were saved. Now hope that is seen is not hope. For who hopes for what he sees? But if we hope for what we do not see, we wait for it with patience.
—Romans 8:22–25

For Reflection

1. How does the Fall affect marriage?
2. What is the purpose of the Curse and the Law?
3. Only one marriage exists in Heaven—the marriage between Christ and all believers. What does this tell you about marriage on Earth?

Next Steps

- ☐ Read Romans 7. What is the purpose of the Law?
- ☐ How do the Fall, the Curse, and the Law affect *your* marriage?
- ☐ What are your hopes for your marriage? Why do you suppose you have those hopes?
- ☐ What are you expecting from marriage? Have you made marriage an idol? In what ways are you expecting too much? In what ways are you expecting too little?
- ☐ What would patiently pursuing your marriage's potential look like?

Chapter 3

Paradise Found

Christ redeemed us from the curse of the law by becoming a curse for us.
—Galatians 3:13a

And those whom he predestined he also called, and those whom he called he also justified, and those whom he justified he also glorified.
—Romans 8:30

Redemption means Christ saved us from our sin for eternity; Sanctification is the Holy Spirit removing a little more sin today.

The Reality of New Life

Fortunately for us, Jesus' resurrection cancels the effects of spiritual death. As Christians in the world we live in, we are in the process of escaping the negative effects of the fall. We are caught in the middle between death and life, curse and blessing. We live with the pains of a broken world (past reality) and the promise of a perfect life (future reality). Present reality is a time of transition—a letting go of death and an embracing of life.

In present reality, we both suffer and have hope in a future without suffering. Spiritual rebirth results in a new reality of hope and life. We feel the effects of death's reality while we live as broken people in a dark world. We wonder how God can allow such suffering but we also taste perfection communing with God the Holy Spirit. The Holy Spirit's renewing presence within us empowers us to overcome the realities of death:

- The Fall: The resurrection provides us the opportunity for spiritual life (John 11:25). New birth re-establishes our connection with God (John 3:3). Faith is stronger than doubt.
- The Curse: The effects of the curse remain for the most part but as old news. We know they will be passing away. As believers, we have hope by tasting the first fruits of eternal life (Romans 8:23). In Christ our yoke is easy and our burden is light (Matthew 11:29–30).
- The Flesh: Our flesh remains a struggle, but sin is now a choice instead of being inevitable (1 Corinthians 10:13).

- The Presence of Evil: The enemy hasn't changed. We've changed, and we know he is defeated (Revelation 20:10). With Christ, we are now stronger than our adversary (1 John 4:4).
- The Law: Our flesh may contend with the law, but we are under grace not the law. The law brings death; grace brings life (Romans 5:20–21).

Redemption is Complete and Permanent

Redemption is both an event and a process (Romans 8:22–23). Jesus' death and resurrection sufficiently disempowered sin once for all time (past, present, and future). Before His sacrifice, people looked forward in faith and were saved (Hebrews 11). After His sacrifice, people look backward in faith and are saved. God's grace reaches every place and every time.

Has Jesus' sacrifice sufficiently wiped out sin and reversed the curse? Yes. Does suffering remain while we learn and understand our redemption? Yes. Does this ever mean we are in danger of condemnation again? No, Jesus' work is finished and complete. We can be sure of our salvation, but we have not yet experienced the redemption of our bodies. We are not completely free from the effects of sin while we are connected by our flesh to this world. Marriage will be a struggle.

How Redemption Affects Marriage

Jesus has redeemed us, is redeeming us, and will redeem us. Redemption provides a way to experience true intimacy. Love overcomes shame, hope overcomes fear, faith overcomes doubt, and grace overcomes pride. When we rely on Jesus as our source, we have everything we need to win back our marriage.

For Reflection

1. How are you doing with grasping the reality that life as we know it is passing away?
2. How much have you experienced redemption, and how much of you still needs redeeming? From what specifically is Jesus saving you?
3. Reflect on the Scriptures mentioned in this chapter. What is the difference between redemption and sanctification?

Next Steps

- ☐ Read Hebrews 9:25–26. Jesus' sacrifice covers all the sinning you have ever done and ever will do. Use this reality for good by focusing on the positive as much or more than the negative. God's goal for us is not simply to stop sinning. He wants us to develop into the person He created us to be. Part Two of this book will help you discover your identity.
- ☐ What in your marriage appears to be doomed? Ask God to redeem your sins and mistakes. Continue asking even if little change is evident. The benefits of redemption are yours.
- ☐ Review these resources:
    - ☐ Movie: *The Passion of the Christ*

Chapter 4

God is Our Source

The God who made the world and everything in it, being Lord of heaven and earth, does not live in temples made by man, nor is he served by human hands, as though he needed anything, since he himself gives to all mankind life and breath and everything.
—Acts 17:24–25

We can submit and surrender ourselves to anything, treating it as a source. Some sources are life-giving and some are life-stealing. Most of our sources will fail us in one way or another. They may be excellent sources with natural limits, or they may be horrible substitutes for fullness of life. God is the only true and trustworthy source that will never run out or fail us.

Marriage Needs God

God is the only inexhaustible source of power and love in all of existence. He is self-sustaining and doesn't need us so that He can continue to be God. He didn't need us to form the universe nor does He need us to keep it running. We can take great comfort in this because we can let God be God. He has everything under control. We need not worry.

We can see in Acts 17 that everyone depends on God for "life and breath and everything." Nothing survives without God. You and I cannot. Our marriages cannot. A husband and wife cannot manufacture enough power and love for each other to survive.

If God does not need us, does that mean we are disposable, unimportant, or redundant? Absolutely not! Some things are disposable and some are not. God does not need us for anything *but what He made us for*. If God made us common, then we would be redundant. If God found us defective, He could replace us with someone else; however, love does not operate this way.

Marriage Dies Without God

God is available to supply our needs. When a couple puts marriage into practice according to God's design, they create a shelter that protects them. But when a couple seals themselves off from support and other help, they create a "tomb" that suffocates them. Having no fresh air to breathe makes it hard to be rational and leads to more conflict. This happens despite the fact that God creates us and loves us perfectly. Couples at this point have a marriage in a closed system.

Marriages die when we leave God out of the equation. Then, because no earthly parent's best effort can come close to God's, we transfer the responsibility of our unmet needs from our parents to our partner (the only other person with us in the "tomb"). Marriage becomes a place of friction and agitation without considering God as the source. The next logical step is to blame each other for the failure to love.

A couple becomes hopelessly stuck in a depleting cycle when the pain of their relationship cannot escape and can only be passed back and forth. The scarcity of resources leads to a tug-of-war.

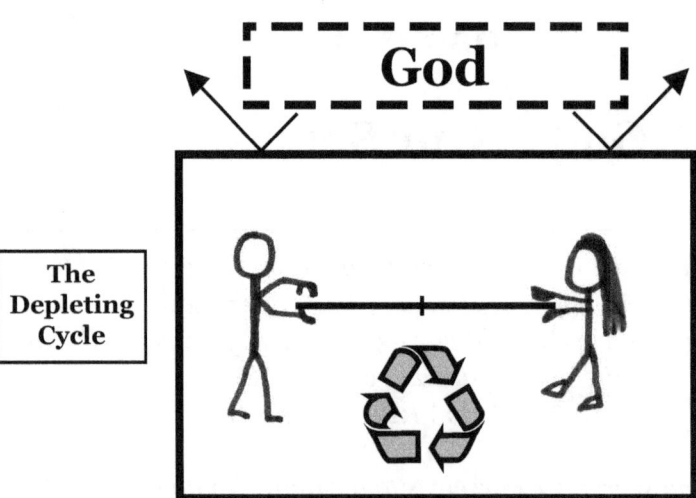

When difficulties surface and emotions take over, crisis and panic ensue. The couple becomes less patient and less rational with each other. As anxiety increases, fear increases and creativity decreases. The couple lacks the ability to think outside their box. They do not consider outside help. Thoughts become discouraging:
- "I must survive this at all costs."
- "This is intolerable! I have to solve these problems now!"
- "He is the problem." "She is the problem."
- "I don't know how to make this work."
- "This is either going to work right now, or I will have to throw out the box (the marriage) and start over (with someone else)."

Facing the evidence that we are not enough for our partner is painful. Being unable to love our partner can lead to feeling insecure. Actually, this is a good sign because God never intended for us, on our own, to have all it takes to fulfill our partner.

When we fail, we rationalize while in our box, "If I do not have the energy, ability, skill, strength, or maturity to get this marriage working again, then the only hope is my partner. Therefore, my partner must have the ability to make up the difference—or else survival is hopeless." That is why it is so easy to blame our partner for the failure.

We think we would be better off if our partner was more mature. But nagging and ultimatums don't work well. The pace at which our partner changes is out of our control. Pushing our partner to change faster than they are capable of often only escalates the situation.

Marriage Lives With God

Marriage is not supposed to be "the two of us alone in this together." A couple in a closed system will eventually deplete their resources. A marriage thrives when both individuals connect to the source, receive God's love, and soak it in so that it flows out to the other. Everything we have comes from God first.

> **God is the source. God is love. God is the source of love. God initiates love. When we let God empower us, marriage enters an energizing cycle.**

We can reproduce only what we have experienced (if not directly from God, then indirectly through others).

Chapter 4 - God is Our Source

I am the vine; you are the branches. Whoever abides in me and I in him, he it is that bears much fruit, for apart from me you can do nothing.
—John 15:5

We can only genuinely love others with the love we have already received. We cannot manufacture love apart from God. If we are not very good at loving, we need to open ourselves to receiving more of God's love. Expanding our capacity to love takes time. Fortunately, in an open system, both partners can receive directly from God.

For Reflection

1. Has your marriage become no more than something you must survive?
2. If you are struggling in your marriage, could you be expecting your partner to be your source instead of God? Are you trying to be sufficient apart from abiding in Jesus?
3. Are you looking to someone else to be your source? While we all have important roles to play, Paul warns us to stay focused on God as our source.

I planted, Apollos watered, but God gave the growth. So neither he who plants nor he who waters is anything, but only God who gives the growth.
—1 Corinthians 3:6–7

---

4. Our intense desire for affirmation is one of the strongest forces that attract a man and woman together. Of course, character, physical beauty, and personality play significant roles too. But needing to feel appreciated and valued is a powerful desire you should not underestimate. The more the need for affirmation was not met in childhood, the more we bring this need to our partner. To the degree our need is greater than our partner's ability to meet it, our marriage is set on a collision course. At one time or another, all marriages will experience this simple, yet disrupting reality. How much does this describe your marriage?

Next Steps

☐ Spend some time thanking God that He is self-sustaining.
☐ Who/what are your sources?
☐ We can love our partner because God loves us first (1 John 4:19). To what degree have you truly experienced God loving you?
☐ Ask God to be your source and to meet your need to be valued and significant.

☐ In a closed system, we cannot repeat the exact same behaviors time and time again and expect different results. How many of us act out this in marriage? What can you do differently to get unstuck? In your Blueprint Space draw a picture (or use words) that represents your marriage as it is and another as you want it to be.

Chapter 5

God's Design for Growth

Then he told them a story: "A man had an apple tree planted in his front yard. He came to it expecting to find apples, but there weren't any. He said to his gardener, 'What's going on here? For three years now I've come to this tree expecting apples and not one apple have I found. Chop it down! Why waste good ground with it any longer?' "The gardener said, 'Let's give it another year. I'll dig around it and fertilize, and maybe it will produce next year; if it doesn't, then chop it down.'"
—Luke 13:6–9 (The Message)

A Blueprint for Growth

God provides growth instructions for every living thing, but we can easily take for granted the miracle of how things grow. When God creates us, He puts inside of us a set of instructions like a blueprint.

From the moment we are born, our bodies follow a biological plan to reach maturity. We cannot (or at least should not) change our developmental blueprint (our God-given identity). When we are born spiritually, we follow a plan to mature spiritually as guided by the Holy Spirit. As the biological plan results in a physical identity, the spiritual plan results in a spiritual identity.[1]

Spiritually, growth is a step of faith. When we cooperate with our internal blueprints, we grow and bear fruit. Jesus' parable of the barren tree includes all three necessary ingredients for growth:
1. Plan: the detailed instructions which explain how, when, where, and what to grow into;
2. Power: the nourishment to fuel the growth; and
3. Patience: the time (grace) to reach full maturity.

In the parable, the owner, compared to the gardener, lacks patience, is quick to judge, and seeks only results. The gardener suggests adding fertilizer and allowing more time. If this tree is going to bear fruit, it has everything it needs. The owner represents God (His coming judgment), the gardener represents Jesus (His intercession), and the tree represents us.

> **Accepting grace shifts our focus from daunting self-reliance to partnering with God. Mercy allows us to avoid sin's distraction and instead receive power for growth.**

As God is intentional about growth, we should be too.
1. God provides the plan; we seek to know the plan by increasing our self-awareness.
2. God provides what we need; we need to know our needs.
3. God is patient with us; we need to be patient with others and ourselves.

---

[1] See chapters 13–15 for more details about your identity.

Change is Barren and Growth is Fruitful

Growth includes change, but change happens all the time without growth. Though change can be positive or negative, growth is always positive.

Change is a poor substitute for growth. It stirs up everything, but the dust settles without any substantial difference. For example, quitting our job or divorcing our partner is change, but we could end up worse off for our efforts.

Often, we will come out ahead by directing our energy into making improvements. In the midst of life's busyness, we need to make sure we are not simply changing our circumstances, but that we're growing within this change. Growth requires thought and effort such as the decision to return to school and pursue a newfound calling. Superficial change requires little effort. Impulsively quitting a job because we don't like our boss probably isn't a good idea. Likewise, quitting our marriage because we don't feel in love anymore doesn't resolve the problem.

Intentional Growth

Developmentally, teenagers desire to experience life rather than have someone tell them what to do. For the less serious aspects of life, this works sufficiently well. But some consequences to our decisions seem to be more than we can bear in this life.

You may like to listen to loud music, but may not realize your actions could result in permanent hearing loss. A sun-tanned body is more pleasing to the eye at first, but later in life, there may be more wrinkles or even worse, cancer. Prevention of such serious mistakes is worth our efforts.

The attitudes and beliefs we develop early in life stay with us throughout adulthood, unless we work to improve them.

Jumping in without knowing what will happen is exciting. God made us curious, and He provides guidance through parents and other mentors. Yet, we must pursue growth for ourselves that goes beyond what others alone can teach us. We can do this because we have the Holy Spirit to guide us.

Growth Means Greater Capacity

God's model for life is developmental. This means we do not start out with everything God created us to be, but we discover, develop, and receive our identity over time—over a lifetime. Sometimes God heals us instantly, and sometimes He leads us through the pain. We grow because of, or in spite of, the pain. The process is sometimes short, sometimes long, and sometimes it takes a lifetime. No matter how long, He is with us every step of the way.

As a tree grows, its ability to carry nutrients increases. Growth means capacity has expanded (for example: more patience, loving-kindness, tolerance, or wisdom).

Change could mean no change in capacity, a simple change in circumstances, or even a loss of capacity. Growth means we challenge and push ourselves beyond our current capacities.

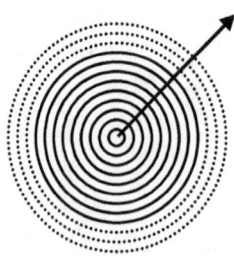

A marriage, the commitment of two developing people, must also develop over a lifetime. Can a one-year-old achieve what a ten-year-old can? Can a ten-year-old achieve what a thirty-year-old can? A couple who has been married ten years hopefully understands and is more skilled at marriage than a newly-married couple. Of course, this is not always true because we can choose to remain immature and less developed. Hopefully, we can avoid the big mistakes, but no one, no matter how mature, knows what it's like to be married until they experience it firsthand.

For Reflection

1. What do you call a marriage that has lost its ability to grow?
2. Love is patient. God is love. Therefore, God is patient.
3. Growth is maturity, learning, positive change, thriving, improvement, and expanding of one's capacity to hold more of God's truth and love.
4. God made everyone different, so everyone will need a different combination of "nutrients" to grow.
5. Growth is God's will for you.
6. You will pursue growth when the pain of staying the same is greater than the pain of growing.
7. True growth results in a greater capacity to tolerate another person's shortcomings.
8. If you are truly growing then growing apart is impossible—instead you will be maturing in love and this will keep you together. So when you are "growing apart" can you really say you are growing?
9. *Jehovah-Jireh* means "The Lord will provide." This is also the name Abraham gave to the place where the Lord provided a sacrifice in place of Isaac (Genesis 22:14). God will supply all you need to grow.

Next Steps

☐ Review your past five significant decisions. Are you growing (working through challenges) or merely changing (running from challenges)?

☐ What are Jesus' role and your role in the growth process?

☐ Judgment is looking only at the product and not the circumstances. Expect apples from an apple tree only if you know it has everything it needs to produce apples. Are you giving yourself a fair chance? Are you expecting more from yourself or others than can possibly be accomplished?

☐ You grow by God's grace. Do you have everything you need to grow? What do you need?

☐ If you agree and understand that God's model for life is developmental, how does that change how you view yourself and marriage?

☐ Your marriage is only as good as the work you put into it. Some people have more of a head start than others, but all marriages need work because all people need work. Developing takes time. In what areas do you and/or your partner need patience?

☐ Use your Blueprint Space to talk to God about your plan for growth. What do you hope for? Ask Him for the power and the patience to see it come to fruition.

☐ Review these resources:
  ☐ Movie: *The Truman Show*
  ☐ Book: *How People Grow* by Cloud and Townsend

Blueprint Space

Chapter 6

Investing in Growth

Therefore, since we are surrounded by so great a cloud of witnesses, let us also lay aside every weight, and sin which clings so closely, and let us run with endurance the race that is set before us, looking to Jesus, the founder and perfecter of our faith, who for the joy that was set before him endured the cross, despising the shame, and is seated at the right hand of the throne of God.
—Hebrews 12:1–2

A problem is an opportunity for growth. If you know God is partnering with you, then you can face problems head on and become stronger as you find your way through them. God can use any problem to help you grow. Look beyond your problems to the bigger goal God has for your life.

Develop Long-Term Vision

The purpose of *marriage* isn't to be conformed into God's image. God's purpose for *life* is to be conformed into His image. Marriage just happens to be one way this can happen. If we never get married, God will find other methods to accomplish His purposes for us. Therefore, marriage is not the problem. The problem is an inability to maintain steady growth for the long haul.

Some growth is easy and happens without much effort. Our human nature puts off or avoids the hard character growth hoping that problems will go away on their own. But they won't. Wanting an easier way is normal. Even Jesus asked for an easier way before his crucifixion. If God denied His request, God will deny ours sometimes too.

> **Eventually we have to face the challenge. Are we going to grow up or give up?**

Seeking instant gratification requires little if any sacrifice and therefore does not provide lasting pleasure or hope. The emptiness of a one-sided, receiving-but-not-giving lifestyle eventually becomes evident. Each of us, in our own timing, realizes there is more to life than selfish gain. Making changes to stop living for short-term gains requires determination and a high tolerance for postponing the fulfillment of our desires, but it is also the surest approach to experience fulfillment.

Growth Results in Hope

God plans our growth. When we activate it by our faith, we gain hope. But just because God has our growth planned that doesn't make it easy for us. Growth is challenging, but the struggle has its reward. If we end the struggle prematurely, we miss the reward.

When we endure growth, the result will be hope. In Romans 5:3–5, Paul describes a progressive growth that leads to an eternal hope:

> *Not only that, but we rejoice in our sufferings, knowing that suffering produces endurance, and endurance produces character, and character produces hope, and hope does not put us to shame, because God's love has been poured into our hearts through the Holy Spirit who has been given to us.*
> —Romans 5:3–5

Remember that growth is evidence we are alive.

Identify Your Attitude Toward Growth

If all you have is a tiny cup, you can still quench your thirst, but it takes several fill-ups. When you invest in developing a larger cup, quenching your thirst will be easier. Invest in a giant cup, and you cannot only quench your thirst, but also the thirst of others. These larger cups indicate a commitment to growth.

We can measure our attitude toward growth using a five-category scale. The five stages of growth from least to greatest are: No Interest, Interest, Committed to Action, Active Growth, and Integrated.

No Interest

I'm not growing. Perhaps this is because I don't want to grow, don't know I need to grow, or don't know growth is possible. But the thought of doing more than existing is exhausting. I only want to do what will bring me immediate satisfaction. I would rather keep filling up a small cup than invest in a larger cup. I would rather drink dirty water than invest in finding clean water.

For example: I eat junk food and I don't care that I am gaining weight.

Interest

I realize that seeking immediate gratification does not bring lasting satisfaction. Whatever I do to feel better wears off quickly, leaving me with all the same problems. Regardless, most of the time, I self-medicate. Using the same cup, I drink the same water.

For example: I eat junk food even though it bothers me that I'm gaining weight.

Committed to Action

I am finally tired of living with my limitations. The effort to improve my situation is now worth the cost. I am ready to go for better water and a larger cup, but I don't know how to make that happen. I will do what it takes to grow. I will learn what I need to know. I will ask for the help I need.

For example: I can't tolerate gaining weight any longer, and I'm committed to losing weight.

Active Growth

I have changed, but I still have to think about how to navigate the new process. I am pursuing growth for myself and I am able to help others. I want a cup big enough to help others.

For example: I joined a weight loss group and have lost ten pounds.

Integrated

The new process has become second nature. Because I now trust that God will provide the cup and water I need, I can pour some of what I need into others. I am ready to start again at stage one with a new goal.

For example: I have been close to my ideal weight for two months. What was a new diet has become my standard diet.

Don't Give Up

In a perfect world, growth would occur without any setbacks. In our world, sometimes going backward actually moves us forward more quickly. When we are stuck, retracing our steps is often helpful. Even if we have been stuck for a while, a breakthrough can come at any moment. Resistances we face may not mean something is wrong with us but that God is challenging us so we can become stronger.

Learning something new requires an investment, which means we take one step back before two steps forward. In the diagram below, we can see that D-C-A is a short but impossible route. The only way to get to A from D is the more roundabout D-C-E-F-B-A. Stepping backward allows us to build enough momentum to move forward. When we pursue growth, sometimes life gets worse before it gets better. That's normal. The old way of doing something might be easier but no longer works well. The best way forward might be investing the effort to learn a new approach.

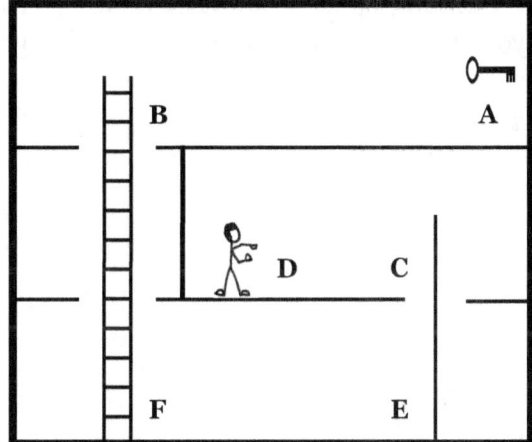

Having a teachable spirit and a determined attitude matters more than the exact growth stage you've reached. The right direction is more important than speed or location.

Wise Evaluation Before Marriage

Luke 14:25–33 teaches us to estimate the cost of a project before committing to it. All couples seeking to be engaged and married need to heed this advice. If we are not willing to give our all to our partner, we should reconsider marriage. We should be willing to examine ourselves and fully consider our partner before marriage.

For Reflection

1. A mature couple was asked, "How did you manage to stay together for 60 years?" They replied, "We were born in a time when if something was broken we'd fix it, not throw it away."
2. When marriage does not seem to be working well, check your attitude towards growth. How important is growth to you? How purposely do you pursue growth?
3. Sometimes growth occurs quickly, sometimes slowly, and sometimes by going backwards first. Don't stop trying. Whatever your struggle, take it head on.
4. Hope thrives on growth. If nothing ever changed (in a meaningful, positive way) there would be no hope.

5. Marriage is a journey, not a destination. Marriage is a marathon, not a sprint. Running less often but faster doesn't work very well. Pace yourself accordingly.
6. Marriage is efficient. It will expose your weaknesses and shortcomings in record time. You should not have a growth area shortage.
7. When you choose a particular person as your partner and they return the favor, you are each choosing an equal. Don't forget that during the times your partner is not pulling their own weight. Finish what you start.
8. A point in life or marriage doesn't exist when you will be done with growing.
9. God made marriage to last a lifetime for a reason. We need a lifetime (or more) to get love right.

Next Steps

- ☐ If you are single, read Luke 14:25–33 and put together a plan to make sure you've considered the cost of marriage.
- ☐ Are you actively pursuing a specific growth area? If so, what stage are you in? What do you need to move to the next level? If not, are you aware of where you most need to grow? Ask God to show you where you are growing and where you need to grow.
- ☐ Review these resources:
  - ☐ Movie: *Life is Beautiful*

Chapter 7

Balanced Growth

Every branch in me that does not bear fruit he takes away, and every branch that does bear fruit he prunes, that it may bear more fruit.
—John 15:2

Remove far from me falsehood and lying; give me neither poverty nor riches; feed me with the food that is needful for me, lest I be full and deny you and say, "Who is the LORD?" or lest I be poor and steal and profane the name of my God.
—Proverbs 30:8–9

Why Balance is Needed

Because marriage is a long-term effort, being sensitive to our pace is essential. Pacing provides balance so we don't become so burned out or bored that we take our eyes off the goal. Proverbs 30:8–9 indicates we are better off having what we need, but not too little nor too much.

Extremes are rarely useful for long periods of time. Outdoor plants receive nutrients under variable conditions rather than at predictable intervals. This results in uneven growth. All rain and no sunshine for a day is useful. But for a month it's not. Plants cannot drink a season's worth of rain in one month.

When plants grow too quickly they spend energy where it does not need to be spent. This is why a gardener prunes the excess. When plants grow too slowly, the gardener invests extra effort to stimulate growth and, when necessary, cuts off any dead leaves or stems.

The seasons, in their variety, balance each other. In the springtime, rapid growth establishes the plant in time to have fruit during harvest. In summer, plants stabilize and pour energy into maturing fruit. Following harvest, plants die and the ground rests.

Each stage has its purpose. Spring is no longer valuable when plants need summer conditions. We need all stages of growth to reach maturity and bear fruit.

Likewise, the conditions of life and marriage are highly variable. But God opens and closes doors in our lives to encourage purposeful growth. He made us to thrive on a mixture of many good nutrients received over time. In marriage, couples need both seasons of growth and contentment. In this context:

- Growth means rejection of the status quo and includes: efforts, trials, work, and looking at the truth; and
- Contentment means acceptance of the status quo and includes: rest, peace, enjoyment, and receiving God's grace.

Challenges provide a cure for boredom, but they eventually leave us weary. Because of this, an environment of unconditional acceptance, love, and care supports effective growth best. The growth process finishes during times of rest by integrating new understanding with old understanding. Without the rest, we don't learn as well. A season of contentment provides stability, a position of strength, and a means for further growth.

God loves us exactly as we are and does not need us to change. Paradoxically this accepting love compels us to become all He made us to be. Marriage flourishes with the same balanced love.

Balance keeps our lives simple enough to allow us to focus exclusively on what is most important.

Knowing when it is time to catch your breath and when to stir the pot is as much art as science. Learn both skills so you can choose the appropriate time to:
- Accept the status quo to increase unity and decrease the vulnerability of your marriage; or
- Push for growth to expand your marriage into all it can be.

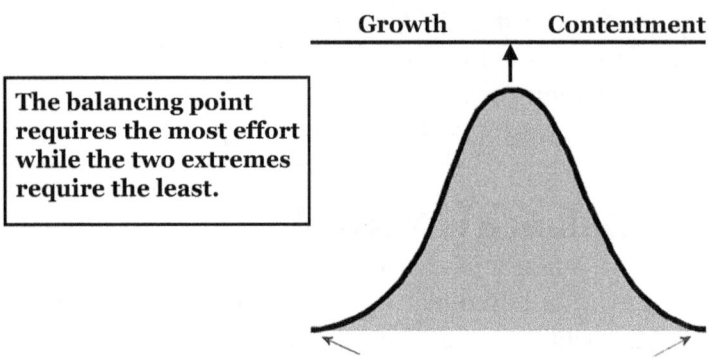

Keeping Your Balance

Growth should not be perpetually overwhelming nor the only important aspect of life. To slow down a time of growth, choose one or more of the following options:
- Acknowledge that you have been working hard. A break can actually help you be more efficient.
- Make time to reflect on where you have been, where you are, and where you want to go. Then prune your schedule of what you do not need, and do more of what you do need.
- Remind yourself that God has given you enough time and enough grace for today. You can resume growing tomorrow. Chances are no one will die if you slow down and take a break.
- Be intentional about being content and thankful in the current moment.

If you want to expand your capacity, or if you are bored or not producing enough fruit, then the time has come to take action to encourage growth:
- Focus on action over waiting. Do not spend a lot of time trying to decide what to do. Be decisive.
- Do something new and different. At first, you do not have to know exactly why you are choosing a particular activity. You may not know the value of an experience until you are in the middle of doing it.
- Spend time daydreaming about what you want and then go after it.
- Talk with someone about what is going on inside of you.

For Reflection

1. Contentment without growth leads to death. Growth without contentment leads to burn-out.
2. In a relationship, pushing for growth without contentment leads to division. The person pushing for growth sees the other person as merely a means to an end.
3. On average, men are better at initiating action (charging ahead) and women are better at maintaining stability (nesting).
4. Repeated attempts to delay growth indicate an emotional immaturity—a defensive approach to life.
5. Maintaining balance means denying yourself the easy way out. In conflict, the easiest way out is one of two extremes: either relief from being done (divorcing) or relief from avoiding (maintaining the status quo). Instead, love is tough and requires self-denial.
6. We all have to start somewhere. If we waited until the perfect time to get married, have kids, go back to school, etc., no one would ever start anything new. We can find a balance by sometimes choosing the short-term "best effort possible right now," and, at other times, choosing the long-term "make a certain aspect of life easier forever" investment. For example, parents can learn how to raise a child by having a child (best effort now), but they can also study parenting books and attend seminars (parents invest in the future by taking time away from their children to improve their skills and also recharge their batteries).
7. A tennis match between two equally skilled players is much more enjoyable to play or watch. Similarly, a successful marriage takes two people committed to self-growth. However, you can always practice your skills even when your partner does not want to play.

Next Steps

- Read Proverbs 13:11. Growth is strongest when we have the time to understand why we are growing. Sometimes we remember the hardest lessons the best. Rushing skips the necessary steps to sustain long-term growth. Take the time you need and you will prosper.
- Answer these questions while considering your marriage:
  - Where is your relationship along the Growth-to-Contentment continuum?
  - Are you stuck in one season, seemingly unable to move on?
  - What does your relationship need most right now?
  - Which one of you is better at growth? Which one is better at stability? Can you use your natural gifts to create a seasonal rhythm in your relationship?
  - How balanced is your life? Are you over-focused on some aspects and neglecting others?
  - Are you living a life opposed to or in agreement with your true values and priorities?
- Our individual choices are supremely significant. The next time you are deciding whether to do something, or not do it, consider how your decision will affect all those involved. To organize your thoughts, start with you and the people closest to you, and move outward until you are considering the decision's global impact.
- Review these resources:
  - Movie: *The River Wild*
  - Movie: *Jerry Maguire*
  - Blueprint: Complete the Balance Wheel (next page)

Step 1: Evaluate Your Life

The life balance wheel has ten areas with each representing an important aspect of a balanced life. Rate your level of satisfaction in each area on a 0–10 scale. Then, for each point, fill in 10% of the wedge (each circle represents 20% or 2/10 points). This is your satisfaction right now. Feel free to change any category name to what fits your life best.

Step 2: Determine Specific Improvements

Next, prioritize the things you want to improve and make an action plan to get you moving. Some support will be helpful. It could be formal (counseling, coaching, groups) or informal (friends, family). Support from others can dramatically increase results.

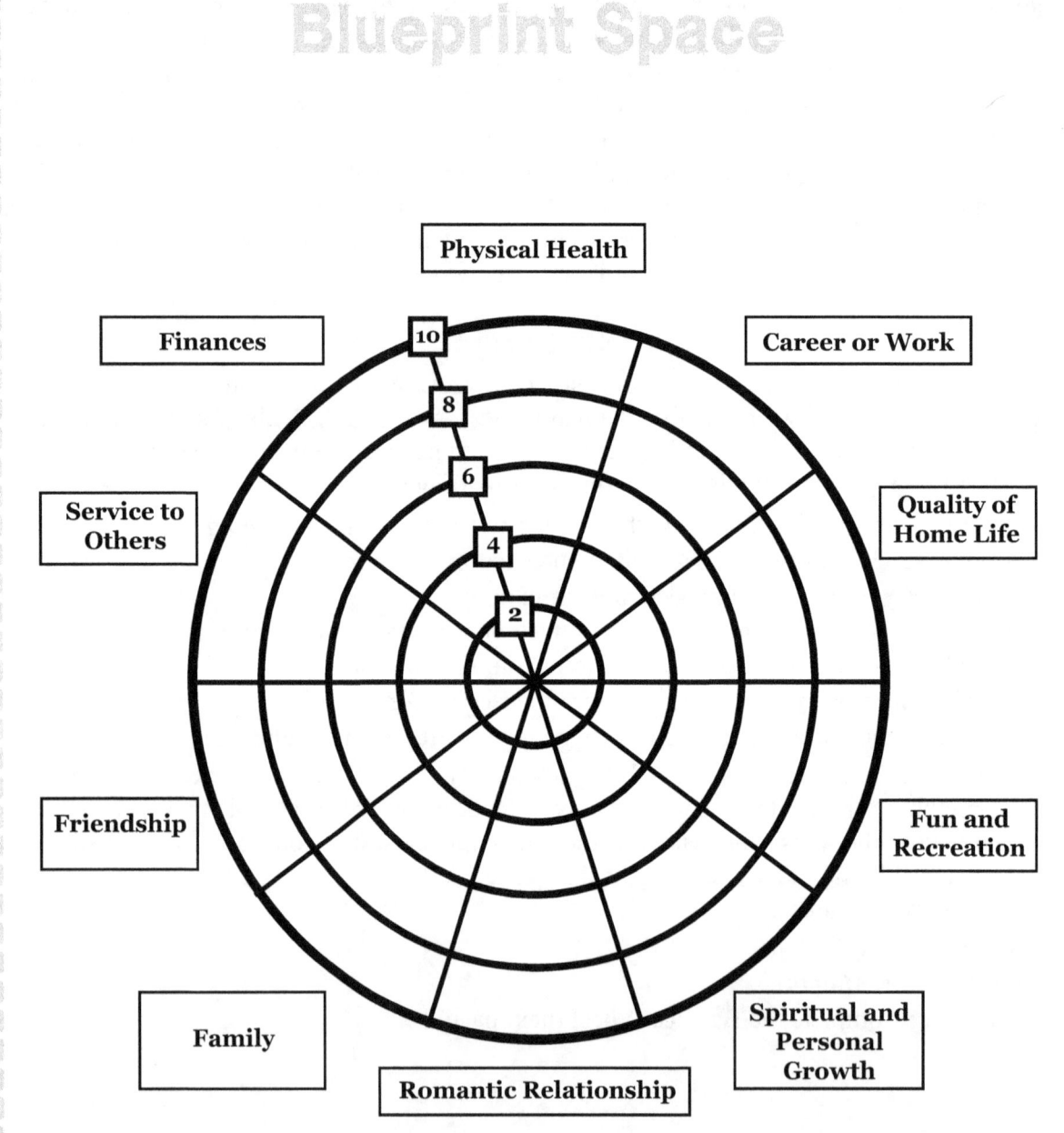

Part II – Individual Growth

Chapters 8–9   Focus on You

Chapter 10   Developmental Overview

Chapters 11–12   The Child Years

Chapters 13–15   The Teen Years

Chapters 16–17   The Young Adult Years

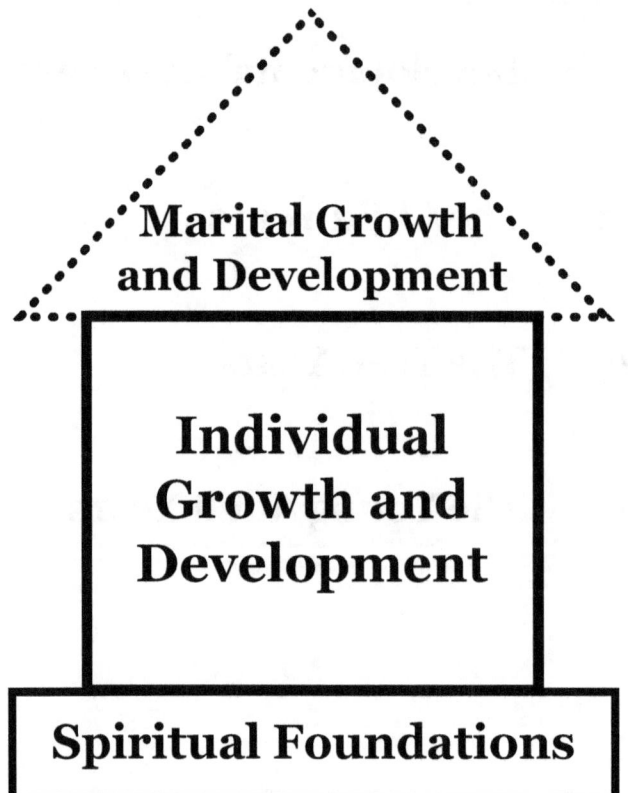

Chapter 8

Focus On What You Can Control

Why do you see the speck that is in your brother's eye, but do not notice the log that is in your own eye? Or how can you say to your brother, 'Let me take the speck out of your eye,' when there is the log in your own eye? You hypocrite, first take the log out of your own eye, and then you will see clearly to take the speck out of your brother's eye.
—Matthew 7:3–5

*And so it criticized each flower, this supercilious seed;
Until it woke one summer hour, and found itself a weed.*
—Mildred Howells

Charge Your Batteries

Most marriage advice says to focus on your partner. I say spend twice as much time on yourself as you do your partner! For every moment you spend addressing the faults of others, you should spend at least two moments examining yourself. Why? Because you need time to:
- Examine yourself, develop and mature; and
- Recharge your batteries by pursuing your interests.

Then, you will have something substantial to offer your partner.

Our partner is here with us to relate to, encourage, and challenge in love, but not for us to demand they change for our purposes. God expects us to accept our partner as they are, graciously receiving what they have to offer. Then we are to go to God for whatever else we need.

Remove Your Logs

Why does Jesus say things like, "first take the log out of your own eye" and "let he who is without sin be the first to cast a stone?"

- Your weaknesses are blind spots. Attempting to correct others without seeing clearly causes more harm than good. Who wants a surgeon with poor eyesight?
- Self-examination and growth are easier said than done—make sure *you've* tried it first.
- Self-control is a fruit of the Spirit; other-control is not. You can influence your partner, but you have complete control over yourself with the Spirit's help (Galatians 5:22–23).
- If you have considered your own shortcomings and made sincere attempts to address them, the result will be fruit: compassion that brings comfort and healing to the hurting.
- By the time you've addressed your concern (the log), the problem might be gone. And your growth experience means you have wisdom to share with your partner.

In the diagram below, the "log" on the left creates a sizeable blind spot.

Be Yourself

Nothing is actually more freeing and fruitful than when we give up hiding and find God totally accepts us. He sees the worst of us and knows when we feel shame. He is interested in helping us become all He intends us to be rather than bringing condemnation (Romans 8:1).

Focusing on ourselves brings a natural humility that eases the pressure we might feel to demand our partner to behave differently. The result can be unexpected: we realize God is in control, and we will be okay even if our partner doesn't change. Even better, we realize with God's help we can change and nothing can prevent this. Nothing can separate us from the love of Christ—not even our partner (Romans 8:38–39).

You are the only one beyond God who knows exactly what it's like to be you. Find a way to be content within yourself no matter the outside circumstances:

- You don't have to be more than you are. Stop trying to please others. This only moves you away from your identity—the center of who you are.
- You don't need to settle for less than you are. Stop neglecting yourself—you are worth the investment to develop and grow.

For Reflection

1. Be who God made you to be even if, at first, no one seems to appreciate you.
2. Not being happy with your circumstances is less concerning than lack of fruit.
3. You can choose for yourself and let your partner choose for their self.
4. You don't have to change or leave your partner when you are not happy. The growth of your partner is beyond your control. Increasing your tolerance level is always within your control.
5. Confronting in truth and love is caring when done with humility after self-examination.
6. Does your life feel out of control? The hardest part of developing momentum is getting started. The first step to regaining control is to take a step.
7. Controlling people don't exist—only people you give control to.
8. You cannot control the wind, but you can adjust your sails.
9. With God, all things are possible and God is the master of making the most of our experiences. No matter how poorly you think your life has gone, God is the winning ingredient that can cause everything to change in an instant. Think of Joseph becoming in charge of Egypt (Genesis 41:41).

Next Steps

- ☐ Marriage thrives when we know how to adjust to circumstances beyond our control.
  - Search online for the Serenity Prayer attributed to Reinhold Niebuhr, which starts with "God grant me the serenity to accept the things I cannot change…" Read the full version of the prayer.
  - Make two lists: 1) everything you can control and 2) everything you can't control.
  - Pray and ask God for insight into how you can refocus your life.
- ☐ Review these resources:
  - ☐ Movie: *Back to the Future Trilogy*
  - ☐ Book: *The Law of Happiness* by Henry Cloud
  - ☐ Music: *God is in Control* by Twila Paris

Chapter 9

Increase Self-Awareness

Search me, O God, and know my heart!
Try me and know my thoughts!
And see if there be any grievous way in me,
and lead me in the way everlasting!
—Psalm 139:23–24

The purpose in a man's heart is like deep water,
but a man of understanding will draw it out.
—Proverbs 20:5

Benefits of Self-Awareness

Self-examination is difficult because it requires vulnerability. Naturally, no one wants to see their own weaknesses; however, self-awareness is essential for many important aspects of marriage:
- Communication;
- Intimacy (spiritual, emotional, and sexual);
- Conflict resolution and negotiation; and
- Forgiveness, reconciliation, and trust.

As we grow in self-awareness, we become increasingly conscious of our:
- Motives and desires that reside in our heart;
- Feelings in the present moment;
- Identity, including gifts and abilities; and
- History, including access to past memories.

Roadblocks to Self-Awareness

The two roadblocks to greater self-awareness are ignorance and self-deception. The cure for ignorance is education. The cure for self-deception is more complicated.

Self-deception is the process of denying or rationalizing away significant, unsettling information so that a favorable conclusion is attainable. It's also a way to avoid responsibility. The cure involves exposing what we've hidden. At best, this means gentle confrontation. At worst, our recovery requires increasingly more difficult consequences. Often these consequences come as the rude awakenings or trials of life.

For example, consider Mike and Amanda who have been married for 14 years. Mike starts spending more time at work. When he is home, he is distant and avoids sharing what is happening in his life. When he and Amanda attempt to communicate, he:
- Raises his voice;
- Monopolizes the conversation by speaking rapidly and non-stop;
- Interrupts her when she starts to talk;

- Speaks in generalities instead of specific examples; and
- Switches subjects multiple times in the same few minutes.

What does your gut tell you about what is going on with Mike?

When asked how he is doing, he says, "I was down a few months ago, but I am doing great now." When told he is nearly incomprehensible, he becomes irritated. When Amanda tells him that he sounds angry and out-of-control, he says, "You are trying to make me look crazy. I forgave you a long time ago. I am doing great."

What do you think now?

Mike lacks self-awareness, and Amanda avoids conflict by lying to him. She's lied to him for years, and only in the last few months has she shown any signs of improvement. Understanding this, his behavior makes more sense.

But Mike's behavior is making the communication worse instead of fostering reconciliation. He is not only in denial about his hurt but is completely unaware of his dysfunctional communication style. Reconciling the relationship is not likely until he gets a handle on his deep anger.

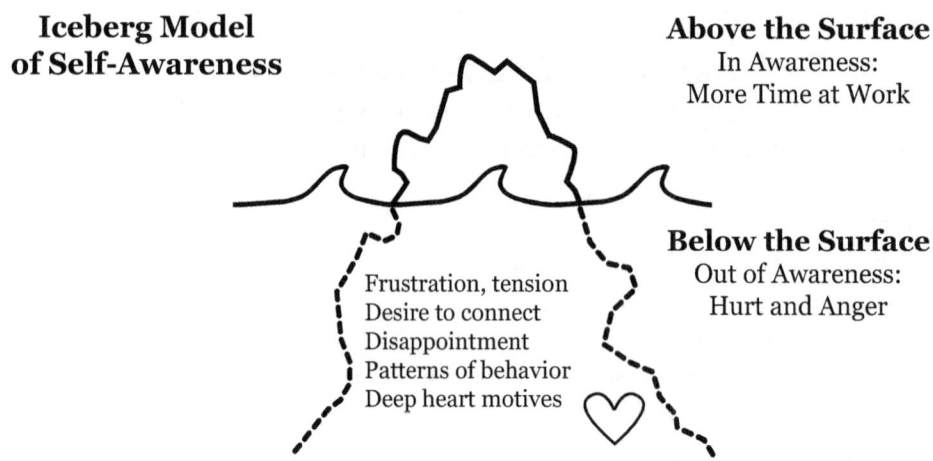

Deep below the surface of observable behaviors are the reasons why Mike chooses denial: hurt, anger, despair, fear, and shame. His anger helps him hide from the betrayal he feels and the rejections he fears.

Motives can be sinful (Matthew 15:19–20a). But a heart ready for intimacy is innocent and open—it means no harm and does not hide from reality.

Achieving Self-Awareness

Beyond what we know about ourselves, what others observe and know about us is another potential source of increasing our self-awareness.

We can achieve greater self-awareness through introspection and receiving feedback from others, including God. Introspection helps us connect what is already within us. Feedback provides new enlightening information based on others' observations or intimate knowledge of us. Our partner is an excellent source of feedback. They represent how others see us and can show us in a loving way how we can grow.

Self-awareness opens up a whole realm of spiritual awareness. As we understand ourselves better, we are better able to understand our creator (Calvin, p. 53). The more self-aware we are, the more we know what we need to change in order to grow. The more we learn from our own growth, the more we can teach others.

For Reflection

1. Another way to look at self-awareness is growing in knowing who you are. God knows you completely. He is the ultimate source to learn more about yourself.
2. Talking about each other's growth is loving and essential to a healthy marriage.
3. You may be inspired to increase self-awareness and growth when you consider that your efforts will reach many generations after you. You can teach others how to teach their students and develop their students into teachers (2 Timothy 2:2).

Next Steps

- How well do you know what is in your heart? Ask God to increase your self-awareness.
- Bring to mind the most intense moments in the past month. What motives were driving your behaviors?
- Read Proverbs 12:12 (ESV). How is your heart like the root?
- Read all of Psalm 139. What does it tell you about you?
- Intimacy ("into me, see") requires you have a self to share. To increase self-awareness, try:
  - Stopping the distractions and busyness around you;
  - Noticing what is going on inside of you; and
  - Sharing your findings.
- Answer these questions to draw out what is in your heart:
  - What thoughts are on your mind right now? What concerns you?
  - How are you feeling right now?
  - Pay attention to your body. What do you notice? What does your body tell you about how you are coping?
  - How are you coping? What are you doing to cope that is only covering up the problem, instead of facing the problem?
  - What are you avoiding? What do you not want to do? What is the best way to proceed?
  - What feelings are associated with what you are avoiding? What would it be like to share them with someone else?
- Take a curious approach to yourself. Answer these questions and then share what you are learning with your partner.
  - What are the reasons you act the way you do?
  - What drives your behaviors?
  - What charges your batteries?
  - How do you feel about yourself?
  - What do you believe God feels about you?
- Review these resources:
  - Movie: *Groundhog Day*
  - Site: en.wikipedia.org/wiki/Johari_window
  - Site: en.wikipedia.org/wiki/Self-deception
- Using your Blueprint Space, fill in your *Johari Window*. For the GOD window, consider asking God to reveal something new about you.

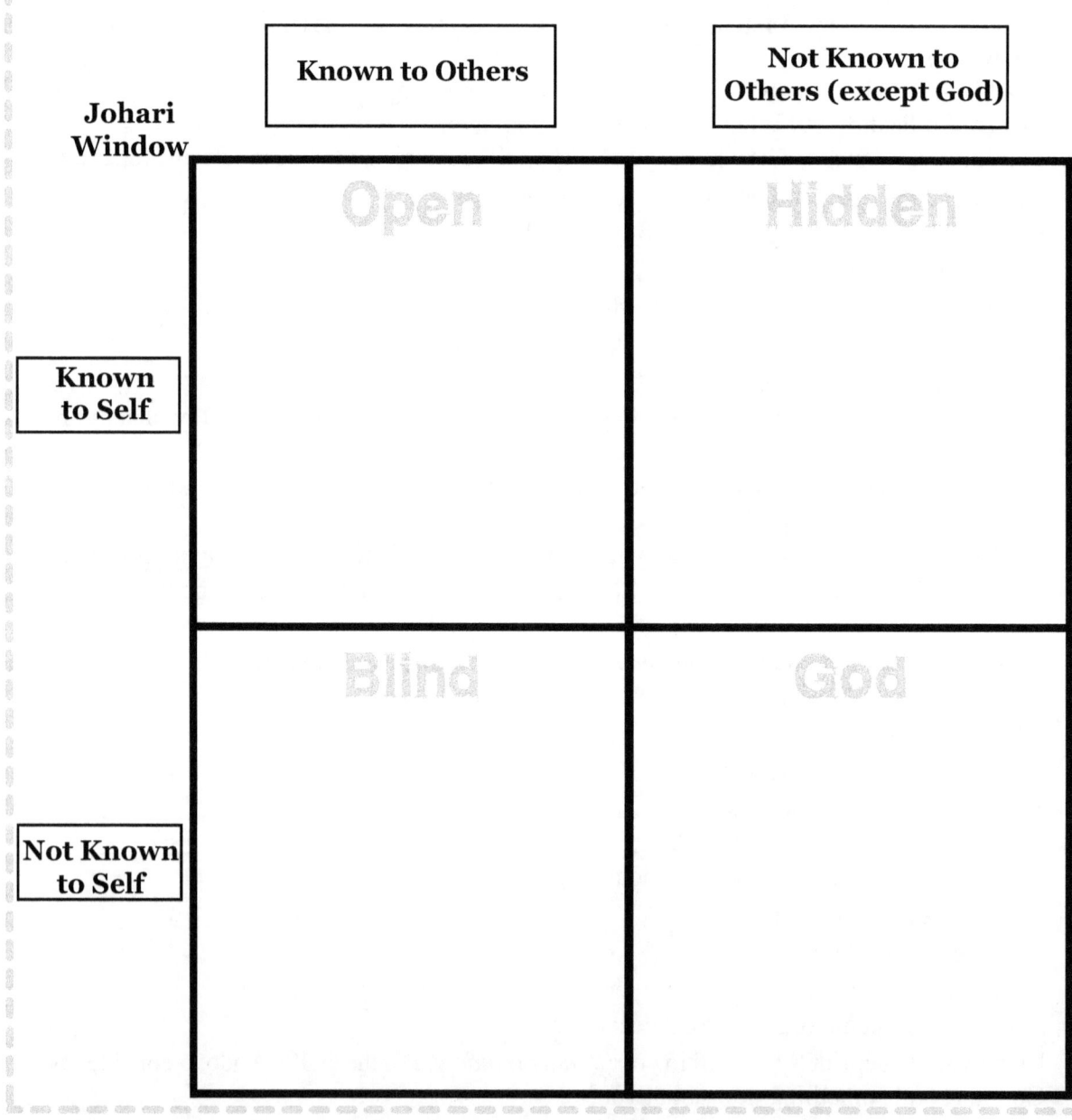

Chapter 10

Become an "I"

Every year Jesus' parents traveled to Jerusalem for the Feast of Passover. When he was twelve years old, they went up as they always did for the Feast.
. . .
The teachers were all quite taken with him, impressed with the sharpness of his answers. But his parents were not impressed; they were upset and hurt.
. . .
So he went back to Nazareth with them, and lived obediently with them. His mother held these things dearly, deep within herself. And Jesus matured, growing up in both body and spirit, blessed by both God and people.
—Luke 2:41–52 (The Message)

Everyone is on a journey of transformation. We are different today than we were yesterday and we will be different tomorrow than we are today. We are caterpillars on a journey to become butterflies. We haven't arrived, but with each passing day we are closer to being who God made us to be.

The Struggle to Become an "I"

Jesus, being human, went through the same developmental process as you, me, and everyone else. Luke 2:41–52 depicts Jesus as mature for his age but with room to grow. We can conclude the developmental growth process involves no sin or shame.

Jesus shares with us the same triumphs and struggles of being human, so much so that He can empathize with our weaknesses (Hebrews 4:15). Of course, Jesus doesn't sin, but this does not diminish his humanness. Because of the fall of Adam and Eve, we live with imperfect conditions. Our natural developmental blueprint doesn't come together as neatly as it did for Jesus.

Eric Erikson, an American developmental psychologist, proposed eight different developmental life struggles, or stages. The stages are not once-for-all achievements, but they begin at a certain point in time and remain with an ongoing tension throughout life (Erikson, pp. 247–274). Each stage has an age range where it first becomes relevant. Good-enough progress of a stage leads to an increased chance of success in following stages. Insufficient progress delays future stages.

Jesus only lived to be about 33, but He clearly passed through all eight stages.	Our good-enough development: Some missed development, but overall, prior stages support later stages.	Our insufficient development: Serious problems at Stage 3 prevent further stages from fully developing. 

41

For each stage, I've included a description of the specific internal conflict to overcome. When possible, I included biblical concepts and references.

1 – Infancy

Internal Conflict: *Trust vs Mistrust* (Birth to 2 years)

Infants develop a sense of trust by bonding with caregivers (usually the mother) who reliably provide them with care and affection. Good-enough progress means being at peace with one's existence and tolerating separation from caregivers. Insufficient progress results in mistrust (separation anxiety or numb detachment).

2 – Early Childhood

Internal Conflict: *Autonomy vs Shame and Doubt* (2–3 years)

Children develop a sense of independence. Good-enough progress leads to confidence and freedom in self-expression. Insufficient progress results in feelings of shame and doubt. These children obsess with the need to control or reject their personal significance.

3 – Preschool

Internal Conflict: *Initiative vs Guilt* (3–5 years)

Children need to assert control over their environment through exploration and play. Here begins an awareness of peers and a sense of competitiveness. Good-enough progress leads to a sense of purpose. Otherwise, children can experience guilt when caregivers communicate too little encouragement or too much disapproval. See Proverbs 22:6; Ephesians 6:4.

4 – School Age

Internal Conflict: *Industry vs Inferiority* (6–11 years)

Children need to engage in new social and academic challenges without losing touch with the relational origins of their first five years. Good-enough progress leads to being productive and a sense of competence while insufficient progress results in feeling inferior. See Matthew 25:14–28.

5 – Adolescence

Internal Conflict: *Identity vs Role Confusion* (12–18 years)

Teens need to develop a sense of personal and sexual identity, including an attraction to the opposite sex. Good-enough progress leads to an ability to stay true to themselves and God's design while insufficient progress leads to role confusion and a weak sense of self. See 1 Timothy 4:12; 2 Timothy 1:6–7.

6 – Young Adulthood

Internal Conflict: *Intimacy vs Isolation* (19–39 years)

Young adults need to form intimate, loving relationships without losing the sense of the self developed in previous stages. Good-enough progress leads to strong relationships while insufficient progress results in loneliness and isolation. See Genesis 2:18, 24; Ecclesiastes 4:9–12.

7 – Middle Adulthood

Internal Conflict: *Generativity vs Stagnation* (40–65 years)

Adults need to work on something larger than themselves such as having children or creating something that will help others. Good-enough progress leads to feelings of satisfaction and accomplishment while insufficient progress results in shallow community involvement. See Psalm 78:4; Psalm 71:17–18; 2 Timothy 2:2; Proverbs 13:22.

8 – Maturity

Internal Conflict: *Integrity vs Despair* (65 to death)

Older adults need to look back on life and feel a sense of fulfillment and also to look forward to the promise of eternal life. Good-enough progress leads to feelings of celebration and anticipation, while insufficient progress results in regret, bitterness, and despair. See Job 12:12; 2 Corinthians 4:16; Psalm 92:12–15; 1 Timothy 6:7; Philippians 1:21.

Delays to Development

Abuse and neglect delay development. Abuse is over-stimulation. Neglect is under-stimulation. They do not fit exclusively into all-or-nothing categories. Everyone has experienced abuse and neglect to some degree.

Abuse is getting what you do not need. Neglect is not getting what you do need.

Over-indulgent care is a mild form of abuse, which keeps a child dependent on the parent. Spoiling a child sends the message, "Don't grow up." Unreliable care is a mild form of neglect that encourages a child to become independent too soon. Parentification, treating a child as if they are a responsible adult, sends the message, "Your needs aren't important."

While different in presentation, abuse and neglect send similar messages to the child such as:
- You are not wanted; you should not exist; your existence is meaningless.
- You are only significant when you are meeting someone else's needs.
- You are not worth the effort; you should not try to be (anything).

Struggles to Take On Before Marriage

Marriage could well be the most challenging, stressful, and enjoyable adventure we will ever attempt. But too many people enter marriage needing significant re-parenting; they are not equipped for a mature opposite-sex relationship. Ideally a person will be well into the Young Adulthood stage before considering marriage. This means marriage has the best opportunity for success when we sufficiently mature in the first six developmental stages.

The first stage alone, when not fully completed, can cause significant marital distress. One of the first truths we need to understand about ourselves is that we are wanted and our needs are met through relationships. If this does not happen in the infant-mother relationship, then the individual may enter marriage with an impaired ability to trust a mate to meet their needs.

Sometimes our mate will be incapable of meeting our needs in the way we want. Instead of seeing the problem in our childhood development, our mate becomes the problem.

The infant who is unable to trust his mother may grow into an adult who is either too unattached or too dependent. This lack of comfort with others sets up never-ending cycles of conflict.

From stages two and three, children gain the ability to say no and make decisions for themselves. The child who faces difficulties in these stages will struggle later in life to set appropriate boundaries. Not correcting this usually results in co-dependency issues. Instead of marrying a peer, we may marry someone we can take care of—or someone who will take care of us. Conflict is challenging for the co-dependent person. Without the ability to communicate, they will eventually feel bitterness and resentment.

From stage four, a person gains a sense of competence. Feelings of inferiority may lead to an imbalance in responsibility and power. Without a sense of being equals, one person in the relationship becomes too dominant while the other grows too submissive.

From stage five, a person gains a strong sense of identity. When incomplete, the marriage may be based on whatever the partner wants instead of the individual's unique gifts and abilities. Conflict often occurs later in life when the person finally figures out who they are, only to have their partner express, "You aren't the person I married."

With healthy development in the first five stages, a problematic sixth stage is unlikely. But problems may exist if a person hasn't neglected social interactions but still feels isolated and different from others. All else being equal, this individual needs to learn socialization skills and find the right people to relate to.

Stages seven and eight will most likely only be relevant to those experiencing multiple marriages, step-families, and those marrying for the first time late in life. With the completion of the previous six stages in a healthy way, the final two stages do not affect the formation of a marital relationship. The couple can work through end-of-life satisfaction difficulties and will be able to manage normal occurrences of depression, conflict, and other struggles.

For Reflection

1. Can you see how each stage builds upon previous stages?
2. Can you see how the first six stages are important to a healthy relationship?
3. Couples get married all the time with problems in multiple stages. This makes marriage more difficult but certainly not impossible. We are all works-in-progress. If you are already married, you can still work through any missed stages.
4. Some needs have gone unmet since childhood. They tend to be more insistent and create more of a crisis than the normal needs of adults. Learn to know the difference.
5. For some people, childhood is a blur. Even if you have difficulty remembering your childhood, your situation is not hopeless. Some trauma occurs before a person can speak. The memory exists but not in conscious awareness. Working through trauma requires trusting your gut feelings about your relationships (including with yourself, your partner, and God).
6. Is this information overwhelming? I understand because of my own experiences with making up for lost time. Though there may be a lot of work to do, God is faithful to walk you through each step so you reach each milestone at just the right time. Resist comparing yourself to others during this process. God's plan for you is specifically for you (John 21:20–23).

Next Steps

- Read through the eight stages and evaluate how well you have completed each stage.
- Would you say you suffered more because of abuse or because of neglect? Rate your levels of each on a continuum from none (0) to total (10).
- Attempt to make links between current marital difficulties and incomplete stages. What do you need to do to resolve these deficiencies? For any significant issues seek personal counseling to repair the abuse or receive what has been missing.
- Do you have related questions about yourself? For example, when you struggle with stage one, Mistrust, you might question, "Am I wanted?" Identify any questions you have from all relevant stages. Chapters 11 through 17 explore topics related to the first six stages.
- Review these resources:
  - Movie: *Butterfly Circus*
  - Movie: *Slumdog Millionaire*
  - Book: *Growing up Again* by Clarke and Dawson
  - Book: *The Beautiful Outlaw* by John Eldredge

Chapter 11

Develop Secure Attachment

*I have set the LORD always before me;
because he is at my right hand, I shall not be shaken.
Therefore my heart is glad, and my whole being rejoices;
my flesh also dwells secure.*
—Psalm 16:8–9

God hard-wired us from birth to bond with others as they care for us. We are designed for this secure attachment bond.

What is Secure Attachment?

Secure attachment is bonding—saying yes to relationship. God made everyone with an attachment system, the part of our brain that allows deep relationships. Being open to our partner's influence allows attachment, which creates new pathways in our brain.

Attachment has to do with how chemicals and pathways in our brain represent our memories and feelings for our partner. The bond we develop with our partner is what allows intense loyalty and commitment. When we are attached securely, no reason exists to end the relationship. However, we can only love our partner as well as we experience God loving (bonding with) us.

We can see from Psalm 16 that David is securely attached to God as evidenced by his:
- High confidence in God;
- Positive experiences of God and his current faith in God; and
- Freeing joy felt throughout his whole being.

Secure attachment is defined as being relaxed:
- During connection;
- While alone; and
- When moving between connection and separation.

Secure attachment begins with experiencing a positive connection in the presence of a caregiver or loved one. Assuming our partner is emotionally healthy, the test of the attachment comes when we separate from our partner. Do we feel equally confident when we are away? If so, we are securely attached. If not, we likely have a negative view of self and/or a negative view of others. When we are separated from our partner:
- If we don't seem to care, we likely have a negative view of others;
- If we feel extremely anxious, we likely have a negative view of ourselves.

The Four Attachment Styles

Dr. Kim Bartholomew, now retired professor, in 1991 categorized attachment into four styles by how we view ourselves (whether positive or negative) and how we view others (whether positive or negative). Understanding all four attachment styles—Disorganized, Preoccupied, Avoidant, and Secure— is the best way to learn secure attachment.

The following diagram presents the four styles as I've applied them to relationships.[2]

```
+ View        ┌──────────────┐           ┌──────────────┐
  Self        │  AVOIDANT    │   [S]     │   SECURE     │       [G]
    ↑         │ Puts Self    │           │ God as Parent,│
    │         │ in place of  │           │ Self as Child;│    [S] [P]
    │         │ God,         │  [G]  [P] │ Partner as Peer,│
    │         │ Devalues     │           │ Self as Adult │
    │         │ Partner      │           │              │
    │         ├──────────────┤           ├──────────────┤
    │         │ DISORGANIZED │           │ PREOCCUPIED  │    [P]
    │         │ Uncomfortable│           │ Puts Partner │
    │         │ with God,    │           │ in place of  │
    │         │ Partner, and │           │ God,         │    [S]   [G]
    │         │ Self         │  [G][S][P]│ Devalues Self│
    │         └──────────────┘           └──────────────┘
    │
  - View ────────────────────────────────→ + View Others
```

Disorganized

"Disorganizeds" have a negative view of self and others. They experienced caregivers as being highly unpredictable—helpful at times and harmful at times. This results in a simultaneous desire to run to them (attach) and run away from them (survive). Disorganizeds:
- Confuse what is safe with what is a threat;
- Try to avoid their feelings because they are usually overwhelming;
- Act like Avoidants by cautiously entering relationships; and
- After attaching act like Preoccupieds by worrying about abandonment and rejection.

To move toward secure attachment, they need to hear the message, "I will protect you and stand up for you. I will repair the relationship when disruptions happen." Improvement comes by small incremental risks to trust others and believe in self.

Preoccupied

"Preoccupieds" have a negative view of self and a positive view of others. They feel exceptionally hungry for closeness and love while experiencing a simultaneous disabling fear of losing it—always wanting, but not having. They experience classic separation anxiety by feeling anxious when contact with others is ending. Preoccupieds desire intimacy more intensely than their partner and therefore expect more than their partner can humanly deliver. Preoccupieds:
- Look away from self and God and toward their partner to find fulfillment;
- Struggle with their feelings becoming overwhelming;
- Fear abandonment and rejection; and
- Seek the approval of their partner, but never seem to get enough reassurance.

To move toward secure attachment, they need to hear the message, "You are loveable. I am not going anywhere. I may leave for a while, but I will return." If their partner fails them, they can become disillusioned with marriage and become Disorganized. If their partner or God proves to be safe, they can learn to value self and become Secure.

Avoidant

"Avoidants" have a positive view of self but a negative view of others. Daniel Siegel describes an Avoidant's life as, "lived without a sense that the past or others contribute to the evolving nature

---

[2] The diagram, categorization, and descriptions of the four styles are adapted from three separate sources: Bartholomew, Clinton, and Heller.

of the self." He is saying an Avoidant lacks awareness that relationships are essential in life. They become this way because they are accustomed to a lack of connection. Avoidants:
- Value self-sufficiency and often feel uncomfortable with intimacy;
- Live in isolation having learned to expect their needs will not be met;
- Tend to feel stressed and need time to adjust when coming into contact with others; and
- Find fulfillment internally, having given up on others.

To move toward secure attachment, they need to hear the message, "I celebrate your existence. What you need is important to me." If they become overly self-reliant and experience failure, they can become discouraged and Disorganized. If they can learn to value and love others, they become Secure.

Secure

"Secures" emerge from childhood with a positive view of self and others. They likely had parents who were present, protective, contingent (attentive and appropriately responsive), available, and respectful of boundaries. We can also learn secure attachment later in life. Secures:
- Find it relatively easy to feel and share their emotions without becoming overwhelmed;
- Empathize well;
- Initiate and receive relational repair attempts; and
- Protect others from outside harm and resist harming others.

What Blocks Secure Attachment?

Several factors prevent secure attachment:
- Valuing independence over marriage or community;
- Choosing technology over direct, personal contact;
- Avoiding connection with God; and
- Living with the effects of abuse or neglect instead of pursuing the care you need.

Unless we've already worked to improve our attachment system, its condition is based entirely on how much nourishing contact we received in childhood. This directly affects our present ability to form intimate relationships.

The blocks to attachment are not always clearly "in our face." For example, the subtle absence of encouragement (neglect) can leave us more confused than a direct verbal attack (abuse). Knowing what we don't know is harder than being aware of what we do know.

Steps to Healthy Attachment

The attachment bond with our partner is the relationship. Without the bond, we lose the sense of having a relationship. We need to know our partner loves us and wants to be with us before communication and conflict-resolution skills will help. A healthy couple:
- Feels a solid sense of "Us" amidst the difficulties of life;
- Depends on each other to be a source of comfort; and
- Repairs hurts so they regain their connection.

When we are attached securely, we enjoy appropriate direct eye contact. When we find kind eyes looking back at us, we are able to receive the love deeply. The courage to be vulnerable creates the opportunity for connection.

No matter how insecure our system, improvement is possible. This involves removing what got in the way, then feeding our attachment system. We can feed our partner's attachment system by using these nourishing bonding skills:

- Attachment gaze: initiating eye-to-eye contact that is kind, smiling;
- Skin-to-skin contact: offering safe, nourishing touch, holding, hugging;
- Love: providing unconditional acceptance and patience;
- Play: engaging in fun and enjoying each other;
- Presence: maintaining undivided attention;
- Soothing voice: speaking in a tone that communicates value and appreciation;
- Persistence: building trust by staying in tune long enough to understand our partner;
- Consistency: behaving predictably without random contrasting behavior;
- Empathy: expressing that we understand how another is feeling; and
- Realistic optimism: being positive, encouraging, and honest.

For Reflection

1. If there is no bond, there is no "Us." Imagine a relationship where the emotional connection has gradually worn away. How can the relationship function?
2. The attachment bond is dyadic (limited to two). This means that the stronger the bond with your partner, the less likely either will seek illegitimate connection outside of marriage.
3. Secure attachment is interactive regulation, which means you and your partner can help regulate each other.
4. Attachment is malleable. It can start badly and improve with support, or it can start well and decline with trauma.
5. When you are not attaching well with your partner, it may be because of your lack of healthy attachment earlier in life.

Next Steps

- ☐ Review the four styles. Which one is most like you?
- ☐ Go on a journey to seek and understand your attachment story. Interview family members and look at old pictures to glean information about the first three years of your life. Document what you have heard about your life and your feelings about what it was like for you to enter the world. Describe the environment in which your life began—the world, cultural, financial, and emotional conditions of both parents' families at the time of your conception. What was going on in the lives of each parent prior to and during your gestational development?
- ☐ How does your ability to attach affect your marriage? How does what you are learning help you understand your present behavior? Your partner's behavior?
- ☐ Pay attention to the patterns in your relationship. How do you and your partner:
  - Connect and play?
  - Fight and argue?
  - Resolve conflict?
  - Repair your attachment bond?
- ☐ Make a goal to improve your attachment system. A book can teach great principles, but only a person can join with you and improve your attachment system. You need both right teaching and positive emotional connection. Good counseling provides both.
- ☐ Review these resources:
  - ☐ Movie: *Curious George*
  - ☐ Book: *God Attachment* by Tim Clinton and Joshua Straub
  - ☐ Book: *The Developing Mind* by Daniel Siegel (for in-depth study)

Chapter 12

Learn Your Limits

Remember this: Whoever sows sparingly will also reap sparingly, and whoever sows generously will also reap generously. Each of you should give what you have decided in your heart to give, not reluctantly or under compulsion, for God loves a cheerful giver. And God is able to bless you abundantly, so that in all things at all times, having all that you need, you will abound in every good work.
—2 Corinthians 9:6–8

God is a God of freedom, but also of order and definition. The more we understand who we are, the more we can filter out what is bad and unhealthy for us while continuing to allow what is good and healthy for us. God wants us to have the freedom to choose, but He also provides truth and accountability. We are responsible for our own actions or inactions; this also means we are not responsible for others' actions or inactions.

The Purpose of Boundaries

Boundaries concern the development of:
1. Identity: the awareness of the limits of who you are; and
2. Self-control: acting according to the freedom God gives you (Galatians 5:1, 13).

Setting smart boundaries means you:
1. Define and communicate who you are to others (according to God's design);
2. Stop tolerating others' harmful or unwanted behaviors (according to God's definition).

That's all. Boundaries serve no other purpose. Healthy boundaries are not any of the following (often sinful) behaviors:

- Setting limits on your partner by telling them what they can and cannot do;
- Punishment or disproportionate consequences for misbehavior;
- A way to fix or change others;
- Self-protective walls that prevent intimacy;
- Justification for selfishness;
- Going on the offensive; and
- A way to avoid growth, giving, responsibility, obedience, and loving others.

True boundaries are always within your control. When you set a limit that is out of your control, it ceases to be a boundary. For example, expressing angrily that your partner stop putting you down is a demand, or maybe a request, but not a boundary. Instead, this is trying to control others—the very thing you are hoping to prevent others from doing to you. While communicating your desires to your partner is helpful, a boundary must focus on and emphasize an action you will take that is within your control.

Boundaries are about you, not the other person. The better you understand yourself, and the more mature you are, the easier boundaries will be. Boundaries are for your improvement and protection. They need to be firm but not punitive. Although boundaries are not selfish, an already selfish person can find a way to use boundaries selfishly. Using boundaries primarily to sway your partner to your position crosses over into manipulation.

Don't bluff with boundaries, but set them in such a way that you can live with all possible outcomes.

God gives us free will. Smart boundaries are a wise use of our free will. In our exercise of free will, we can sin. So it is with boundaries. You have the ability and power to set your boundaries where you want. But just because you can that doesn't mean you should.

Spiderman had to learn, "With great power comes great responsibility" (2002 movie). Jesus said it as, "Everyone to whom much was given, of him much will be required" (Luke 12:48).

Set your boundaries in love in order to achieve a specific goal. Boundaries should be used to invite further relationship, not to shut out relationship. Let your boundaries present the best you, not an ungrateful you.

When you set boundaries, make sure you don't lose grace in the process. The next time you set a boundary, look at where you set it. Reflect on why you chose that particular spot. If your husband is sixty minutes late getting home from work, are you ready to send him to the doghouse or do you simply let him face the natural consequences, such as him having to reheat his own dinner? If your wife fails to vacuum, are you ready to cancel the dinner party, or can you ask how her day went and find out what you can do to help?

Boundaries and Intimacy

Boundaries are needed to have any kind of relationship. However, half the problem in relationships is being comfortable with letting your guard down to allow for a deeper intimacy. Marriage does not work well unless you find a way reduce barriers to closeness without harming each other.

This is exactly what healthy boundaries allow.

If you find you like to use boundaries to avoid closeness, then explore this in counseling. If you are single and need thick boundaries to feel safe, consider staying single until you address this. Reducing barriers allows for the connection needed to experience feelings of closeness and oneness.

For Reflection

1. How well do you know your identity? Boundaries allow closeness without loss of identity.
2. Are you more likely to have boundaries too strict and rigid or too loose and tentative?

3. What are you responsible for? What are you not responsible for?
4. How well do you understand the freedom you have?
5. Limits help define your identity. They also apply to you whether someone else is around or not. A healthy identity includes self-control (see Proverbs 16:32; Proverbs 25:28).
6. How well do you communicate your limits to others?
7. Don't be afraid to explore and experiment with boundaries. To find your limits, you need to push yourself to them and sometimes through them. When you find them, you have a boundary, and life will be easier for everyone involved.
8. Are you allowing yourself to be limited by what others want for you? Have you ever considered whether or not most things you do are an attempt to meet others' expectations? How much of what you do is because of your parents, peers, boss, government, or culture?
9. Be open to hearing how others believe you violate their boundaries. Accepting others' "no" is as important as expressing your "no."

Next Steps

- Make a habit of knowing what you want. Fill in the blank, "What I want is _____." This doesn't mean you should get your way all the time, but at least you will know what you are sacrificing. Jesus knew what He gave up in order to join us on Earth.
- In what ways have you misused boundaries that you can correct now that you know better?
- If you are aware that you are violating others' boundaries, consider how you can change this and make amends.
- Review these resources:
  - Movie: *Spiderman (2002)*
  - Book: *Boundaries* by Henry Cloud
  - Site: cs.cornell.edu/home/kreitz/Christian/Boundaries/all.html
- Use your Blueprint Space to make a list of what you do or tolerate that violates your boundaries. Why do you let these things happen? Develop a plan to correct these violations.

Blueprint Space

Chapter 13

Bring Your Core Longings to Jesus

The LORD is my shepherd; I shall not want.
He makes me lie down in green pastures.
He leads me beside still waters.
—Psalm 23:1–2

Hope deferred makes the heart sick,
but a desire fulfilled is a tree of life.
—Proverbs 13:12

To find the true length of something requires an accurate ruler and an accurate measuring process. When defining yourself, be careful to measure yourself by how radically God loves you. All other measurements will result in a false identity.

Our Longings Make Us Human

God created us with emotional needs also called core longings. We consider them "core" because they are central to our identity. What we long for deep down tells us a lot about who we are. These longings make us human and are part of being made in God's image. However, because of our finiteness, we are dependent (in a healthy way) upon God to meet these longings. If God is our source, then we are "source-needers."

Before the Fall, God's fellowship with Adam and Eve fully met these longings. After the Fall, we lost our perfect connection to God, but we hope for it and we feel our desire for it. Jesus' sacrifice restored our connection so meeting these longings is once again possible. But we are in a state of transition from Earth (imperfect) to Heaven (perfect). We won't experience our longings as fully and permanently met until we reach Heaven.

The pain of unmet longings constantly reminds us that without God we are:
1. Ashamed;
2. Insecure;
3. Lonely;
4. Unfulfilled; and
5. Hopeless.

Our longings drive us back to a relationship with God.

Though others may group them differently, I identify the core longings as:
1. You long for Love ... God accepts you unconditionally.
2. You long for Security ... God protects you.
3. You long for Connection ... God includes you in his family.
4. You long for Significance ... God provides you purpose.
5. You long for Hope ... God guarantees you a better future.

Love
God unconditionally accepts you which means:
- You do not have to perform or change to be loved.
- He will never reject or abandon you.
- You are special, valued, and wanted.
- You can make mistakes (without fear of abandonment).

See Matthew 28:20; Romans 8:38–39; 1 Corinthians 13:4–7; Hebrews 13:5.

Security
God is your shepherd and refuge which means:
- He protects you and provides for you.
- You are safe and secure in His hands.
- You do not need to fear or be anxious.

See Psalm 18; Psalm 23; Matthew 10:29–31.

Connection
God includes you in his family which means:
- You fit with the body of believers.
- He made you to experience intimacy in relationships with Him and others.
- He and others can know and understand you, and you them.
- You are never beyond His reach or awareness.

See Psalm 139; 1 Corinthians 13:12; Luke 15:11–32.

Significance
God has an immediate purpose for you which means:
- There is real work for you to do.
- You are needed and necessary for the body of Christ to function properly.
- You are unique and important.
- No one else can do the work the way you do it.

See Acts 17:26; Ephesians 2:10; 1 Corinthians 12:5–26.

Hope
God has a better future for you which means:
- You are worth the investment of Christ's death.
- You can change and become like Christ.
- He is nurturing and developing your gifts and talents.

See Romans 4:25; Romans 8:29–30; Jeremiah 29:11.

Our Longings are met by God

God can meet all our needs directly or indirectly (Psalm 145:15–19). The younger we are, the more God intends for others, who represent Him, to meet our needs. This dependence is appropriate for a child with their caregiver. However, because parents cannot perfectly reflect God, this creates a perception problem. The distortions created early on can linger an uncomfortably long time. We need to transition to dependence on God because He is the direct source of life.

God is relational and our core longings can only be met in the context of a relationship. In addition to others loving us, He intends for us to have meaningful relationships so that we can learn how to love. When we get it wrong, we can ask for forgiveness and try again.

Have you ever been hungry, smelled good food, but were unable to eat? When others are present but not attentive, this stirs up hunger pangs for connection that are not satisfied. In a dark world with good and evil present, we have to live with the knowledge of something better while feeling the pain of brokenness.

Our longings often go unmet because we do not see God for who He is. Negative experiences cloud our view. When our needs are not met and we are not familiar enough with God, we can form unhealthy relationships with other things and people. We look to them as our god who provides us self-worth.

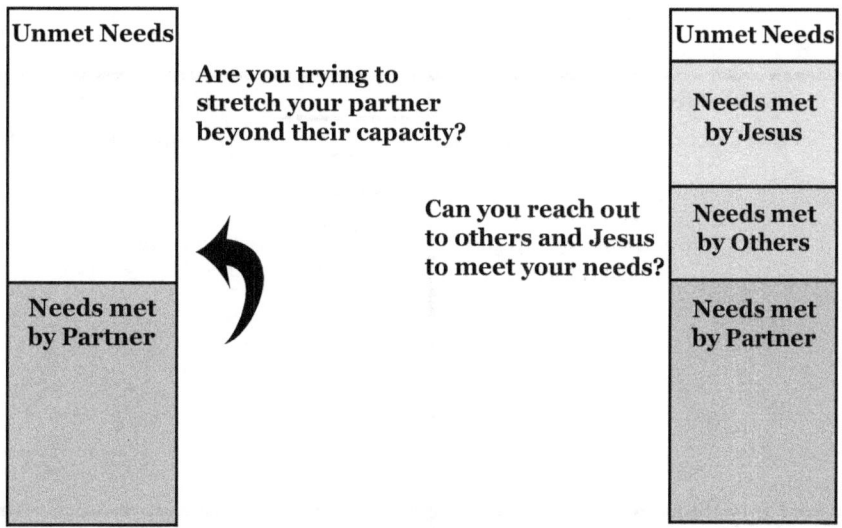

When others don't meet our longings, we might attempt to solve the problem without Jesus by:
- Numbing or ignoring our desires;
- Putting up walls to protect ourselves from further hurt;
- Filling ourselves through people or things; and/or
- Using power or control aggressively to avoid feelings of weakness or helplessness.

Even though other people can meet our needs, we need to recognize God as the source. This prevents us from clinging too tightly to any one person.

For Reflection

1. Everyone has needs—to be alive is to be in need.
2. Was it okay for you to have needs growing up? Could you freely express your needs?
3. Core longings are a blessing, not a curse.
4. If God isn't meeting your longings, or what you think are real needs, maybe He is trying to tell you that you'll be okay. Maybe they are already met, but you haven't registered this.
5. Unmet core longings are not miraculously satisfied on your 18th birthday. No matter how old you are, finding healthy ways to meet your longings is essential.

Next Steps

- Review these resources:
  - Movie: *Simon Birch*
  - Book: *Abba's Child: The Cry of the Heart for Intimate Belonging* by Brennan Manning
  - Site: intouch.org/you/bible-studies/content.aspx?topic=Our_Nurturing_Father_study

☐ Consider how well your core longings are met. For each longing, mark the gauge to represent how full you feel. Then below it, write the reasons you chose that particular level. When you are done, make note of the lowest levels.
- How much do you expect your partner to meet your longings?
- What do you do with your longings when your partner cannot meet them?
- Which longings can only Jesus meet? Only your partner? Only others?
- Bring your unmet needs to Jesus and ask Him to show you how He can meet them.

Blueprint Space

Love
F — Feeling Unconditionally Accepted

E — Feeling Ashamed or Condemned

Security
F — Feeling Safe and Protected

E — Feeling Fearful or Overwhelmed

Connection
F — Feeling Included and Understood

E — Feeling Isolated or Lonely

Significance
F — Feeling Purposeful and Essential

E — Feeling Useless or Worthless

Hope
F — Feeling Optimistic and Encouraged

E — Feeling Doubtful or Despairing

Other
F — Feeling _____

E — Feeling _____

Chapter 14

Believe Lies or Truth

Do not be conformed to this world, but be transformed by the renewal of your mind, that by testing you may discern what is the will of God, what is good and acceptable and perfect. For by the grace given to me I say to everyone among you not to think of himself more highly than he ought to think, but to think with sober judgment, each according to the measure of faith that God has assigned.
—Romans 12:2–3

However threatening our circumstances, we can make them worse through self-condemnation and self-rejection. We have no choice but to look to others to form our identity. Therefore, we must be sure we are looking in the right places. If we look to those who accuse and criticize, we could develop self-hatred. We will believe we are worthless and insignificant. But if we look to God, who calls us Beloved, we will develop a healthy self-love.

Wired for Love

Studies now show that our brains are wired for love. Receiving love from others changes our brains so that we feel good about ourselves and come to expect future interactions to be positive. As Christians we know God intentionally wired us to be able to experience His love. The saying that children are like sponges is truer than we realize. As our parents meet our needs, we learn that life is a safe place. But more importantly, we learn that having needs is perfectly good.

Does God Need Us?

God does not need us for anything *but what He made us for*. He needs us in the sense that we have an intended purpose to fulfill. An important part of that purpose is to be in a relationship with Him.

God is unique and important. You are too. He chose to create you in his image as unique, valuable, purposeful, and significant.

Some things are disposable and some are not. You are not disposable. If you have heard and now believe you are disposable, you believe a lie. Disposable things are intended to be temporary. If you have eternal life, you are no longer temporary. If this were not true, it would mean you are replaceable and therefore not unique in what you can accomplish. You would be common. You would be a numbered product coming off an assembly line. If God found you defective, He would throw you away and get someone else to take your place. You would be insignificant and in direct competition with all the others like you.

But God has a plan and purpose for every one of us (Ephesians 2:10). He calls us to play our positions with all we have. Each of us uniquely bears the image of the God of love and power. Each of us receives His love and power and then reflects it for others to see. We cannot help but glorify God for the beauty of his creation. Some see God's power and love reflected in His children and praise God, but others turn away and refuse to acknowledge Him.

> *Now the Lord is the Spirit, and where the Spirit of the Lord is, there is freedom. And we, who with unveiled faces all reflect the Lord's glory, are being transformed into his likeness with ever-increasing glory, which comes from the Lord, who is the Spirit.*
> —2 Corinthians 3:17–18 (NIV)

Unmet Longings Lead to Distorted Identity

When our core longings are not met, we experience deep pain at the core of our identity. The younger we are when we first experience this trauma, the more deeply our identity is confused.

Don't miss the connection.

Because our experiences easily shape us, we can learn both truth and lies about ourselves. A confused identity means you are deceived into believing lies such as:

- I am worthless;
- I am not wanted;
- I am too needy;
- I don't belong;
- I am insignificant;
- I am a bad person;
- I am unlovable;
- I am hopelessly defective.

Lies cover up our true identity. As a result, we stay out of touch with who we are.

When we believe lies about ourselves, we experience significant pain. Because we don't want to experience pain, we do all we can to eliminate it. When we are not connecting with God to have our core longings met, we will choose some type of personal defensive strategy to manage the pain. These strategies go by other names: dysfunctional behavior, sin, or coping skills.

Typical defenses to emotional pain are:

- Addictions: anything to create alternative sensations to distract from the pain;
- Dissociation: directly disconnecting from the painful experience—like shoving all the bad experiences in a closet and forgetting the closet exists;
- Withdrawal: hiding from others;
- Denial: convincing yourself you have no pain or problems;
- Aggression and control: believing a good offense makes for a good defense;
- Substitution: choosing a superficial or external way to increase self-worth such as perfectionism, achievement, popularity, or money;
- Vengeance: being miserable and making others miserable too.

Coping skills are helpful as long as they do not prevent connecting with God. For example coping with overeating by obsessively exercising may cause more harm than good when it is the only solution implemented. But exercise is helpful and healthy when we also consider the root causes of overeating. The root cause is usually some lie we believe about ourselves.

To correct these deceptions and defenses we must:
1. Repent of our dysfunctional defensive behavior (James 4:1–10).
2. Reconnect with our painful emotions (depression, anxiety, fear, anger, shame).
3. Grieve our losses and lament our pain.
4. Replace lies with truth (know the truth in our heads).
5. Experience the truth (know the truth in our hearts).

Because we learn the lies through real experiences, they are automatically believable. We can override them through even more profound experiences of the truth according to God.

Healing Deep Wounds

Terry Wardle, pastor and seminary professor, suggests these steps to heal deep wounds (Formational Prayer Seminar 2009). I've included a sample prayer for each step.
1. Invite and Acknowledge God's Presence ("Holy Spirit, I welcome you here.")
2. Identify the Wound ("I believe I am not good enough.")
3. Grieve the Loss ("I've believed this lie that I am not good enough for too many years.")
4. Receive the Truth ("Because of your sacrifice Jesus, I now accept how much you delight in me.")
5. Forgive Your Offender ("God, please forgive my partner who taught me to believe that I am not good enough.")
6. Shape a Blessing for Your Offender ("God, bless my partner with positive self-worth.")
7. Identify and Repent of Dysfunctional Behaviors ("I confess I make my situation worse when I turn to alcohol to sooth my pain.")

For Reflection

1. You are not what happened to you. You are what God made you to be.
2. The lies you believe affect you and, by association, your partner. Believing a lie is like carrying unnecessary weight which only slows you down. Also, when you believe lies, your mood is down and your behavior may suffer. You might mistreat your partner and even influence your partner to believe the lie too. And, your partner has their own lies.

Next Steps

- Take a moment to consider if you believe you are disposable. If you believe this lie, ask God to show you the truth—that He created you for a purpose.
- Go on an experiential retreat. For example, go to a park and ask God to show you a symbol of a lie you believe. This could be a rock, a stick, or something else. Be patient. You shouldn't have to force the outcome. Then ask God to show you a symbol of the corresponding truth. Record your findings in your Blueprint Space.
- Experiential therapies work well to heal painful experiences. They go beyond simply having head knowledge of the truth to helping you experience the truth. Consider therapies involving prayer and relaxation techniques, spiritual direction, EMDR (Eye-Movement-Desensitization-Reprocessing, which involves both sides of your brain in your healing), and talk therapy with a focus on expressing feelings in a safe environment.
- Review these resources:
  - Movie: *Ragamuffin*
  - Movie: *A Beautiful Mind*
  - Seminar: *Formational Prayer Seminar* (healingcare.org)

☐ Use your Blueprint Space to write out lies you believe. Which one or two cause you the most trouble? Search the Scriptures for the corresponding "antidote" truth. If you aren't sure where to start, the next chapter lists some specific verses.

Blueprint Space

Chapter 15

Discover Your Unique Identity

For you created my inmost being; you knit me together in my mother's womb. I praise you because I am fearfully and wonderfully made; your works are wonderful, I know that full well. My frame was not hidden from you when I was made in the secret place, when I was woven together in the depths of the earth. Your eyes saw my unformed body; all the days ordained for me were written in your book before one of them came to be.
—Psalm 139:13–16

God in His infinite creativity makes each one of us exquisitely unique. Because, as Christians, we have eternal life, He doesn't need to make duplicates.

Your Identity

We are susceptible to believing lies based on our experiences with others and our circumstances. The way we interpret our experiences reveals what we believe about God. The lies cause us to doubt what God says about us. Our enemy the devil wants nothing more than to spread these lies.

When you understand your unique identity, you are prepared to live your true calling. Marriage is a calling. Spending time learning about yourself is important for your marriage.

Your identity has two parts:
1. Christian Family: your identity in Christ, including core longings.
2. Personal: the combination of your gender, personality, and unique abilities.

Therefore, if anyone is in Christ, he is a new creation. The old has passed away; behold, the new has come.
—2 Corinthians 5:17

As a new creation, you have a new identity which includes:
- A new status as a Child of God (1 John 3:1);
- A new heart sensitive to God (Ezekiel 36:26);
- Spiritual gifts to serve others (Romans 12:5–6; 1 Peter 4:10; 1 Corinthians 12).

Our Christian Family Identity

Every Christian shares the same general identity in Christ because we are all a part of the same family. Family members have certain traits in common with each other that are unique to that family. But we are not exactly alike; we also have specific differences which make each of us profoundly unique.

Who we are in Christ includes both what we have in Christ and how God made us in His image. The Bible contains hundreds of statements describing our identity in Christ. 1 Peter 2:5 designates us as living stones, part of a spiritual house and a royal priesthood, with Jesus Christ as the chief cornerstone.

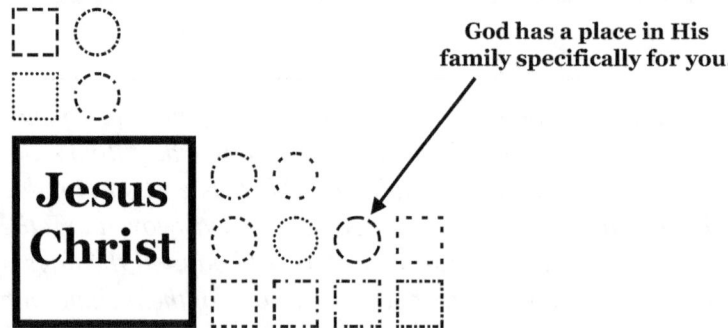

The first verses in Ephesians contain more references to our identity. We are:
- Blessed with every spiritual blessing;
- Chosen before the foundation of the world;
- Holy and blameless;
- Predestined for adoption;
- Redeemed through Christ's blood;
- Forgiven of trespasses;
- Heir to an inheritance; and
- Sealed with the Holy Spirit.

God's identity reveals more of our family identity. In the Bible, each of God's many names reveals an aspect of His identity. The following six particularly also tell us about ourselves.

1) God the All-Powerful One (Elohim)

God has endless power and He created you wonderfully complex. You are not common, redundant, or useless. The word *wonderfully* in Psalm 139 means: to be distinct, be separated, be distinguished, or to make separate, set apart. See Genesis 1:1–3; Psalm 139:14–16; Isaiah 43:1.

God is your master builder and He created you with intention. Therefore, you are not an accident or a mistake. See Hebrews 3:3–4; Ephesians 2:10; 1 Peter 2:5.

2) God as Father (Abba)

Jesus spoke frequently of God as Father. You are God's child, his son or daughter. He lavishes his love upon you. You are wanted; therefore, you are neither rejected nor orphaned. You have a beginning but not an ending. No matter how old you are, you are like a newborn when you consider God's eternal perspective. See Matthew 18:2–4; 2 Corinthians 6:18; John 14:18; 1 John 3:1.

3) God the All-Sufficient One (El Shaddai)

God supplies all you need and encourages your growth and development. You are not forgotten or neglected. His supply is endless; therefore, you can go to God to have any need met. He meets some needs directly and others indirectly through his creation. You are a vessel made for God to fill. This isn't a design flaw, but rather a core aspect of your identity.

God made you to be a strong help to Him, just as He made Eve for Adam. Collectively, all Christians form the body of Christ and are God's chosen bride for Christ. That puts in perspective how much of a strong help you are. Even though you are a strong help, you need to rely on God as your source.

You need God now, and you will continue to need Him in Heaven. The only difference is that in Heaven you will constantly experience God as all-sufficient. You won't know what being without Him is like anymore. See Genesis 17:1; Philippians 4:19; Psalm 103.

4) The Lord My Shepherd (Jehovah-Rohi)

God protects and gently leads us. You are protected and therefore are not defenseless. See Psalm 23:1–3; Isaiah 40:11.

5) God of Compassion/Mercy (El Rachum)

God is merciful and will not abandon or leave us. You are forgiven and therefore are not condemned. See Deuteronomy 4:31; Romans 8:1; Exodus 34:6; Psalm 103.

6) The Lord Who Heals (Jehovah-Rapha)

God heals all our diseases and redeems our life from despair and bitterness. See Exodus 15:25–27; Psalm 103.

Your Personal Identity

You bear the image of God like no one else can. You have your own unique design with your own distinct combination of gifts, abilities, and perspectives. Before God created you, He had a specific purpose in mind for you that cannot be fulfilled by anyone else. You are important and essential for his predetermined plans.

In Psalm 139, the phrase "fearfully and wonderfully made" means to be in awe of being made like no one else. "Your works are wonderful" speaks specifically of David's own formation so we know that God made David distinct and unique.[3] If David is unique, so are we.

For we are his workmanship, created in Christ Jesus for good works, which God prepared beforehand, that we should walk in them.
—Ephesians 2:10

Paul uses the word *workmanship*, meaning "intricate work of art." Imagine the God of the universe standing in front of an easel, before all time, about to create another unique masterpiece—you! You are one of a kind! As one of the living stones, if you were missing, the entire Church would be inadequately formed for God's intended purpose.

Aside from God knowing everything about you, you are the only one who knows what it is like to be you. Your life experience is specific to you. No one else can see life the way you do. You can never be too unique; you can only be more of who God made you to be.

One way to understand who you are is to identify how you fit with others. The many personality and spiritual gift tests available can help with this process.

Your Identity and Marriage

The parable of the talents is about developing and investing gifts. As believers, we have gifts that we invest in others, including our partner, to expand God's work. God wants to give us permanent gifts and wants us to develop them. As we do this, He gives us more, not less. This fits with Him wanting us to desire the greater gifts (Matthew 25:14–30; 1 Corinthians 12:31).

---

[3] biblestudytools.com/lexicons/hebrew/nas/palah.html

Before you can join together with someone to become an "Us," you have to be someone—an "I". Marriage helps you see how you are different from others and helps you learn how to both function as an individual and as a team (as one).

Two unique people becoming one should not reduce the uniqueness of either one. Instead, each should grow over time in appreciating the other's uniqueness. Your marriage has its own identity because it is made of two unique people. No other marriage can express itself the same.

Don't confuse learning how to be you with learning how to be a team. These are two separate tasks. Conflict resolution is easier when there is room for you, your partner, and the one-flesh relationship. While pursuing being one-flesh, you will give up some of what you want but none of who you are.

For Reflection

1. When God makes something, every part is necessary. He designed you just the way He wants you. Suffering results when your identity meets a broken world. This doesn't mean you are defective but quite the contrary! For example, consider a camel's hump.

Do not free a camel of the burden of his hump;
you may be freeing him from being a camel.
—G.K. Chesterton

---

2. God numbers the hairs on your head (Matthew 10:30).
3. God chose the specific place and time you would live (Acts 17:26).
4. No one else in all creation is identical to you. Even identical twins have different fingerprints.[4]
5. When you recognize and appreciate your uniqueness, you no longer have to compete with others. There is so much freedom in this!
6. Don't let your struggle become your identity. You are separate from this world and its evil. This includes your struggles, your job, your boss, and even your partner. In fact, nothing can separate you from Christ (Romans 8:38).

Next Steps

- ☐ How well do you know and understand your unique identity?
- ☐ Take personality and spiritual gifts tests to help you discover your identity.
  - ☐ Personality: personalitypage.com and strengthsfinder.com
  - ☐ Spiritual Gifts: assessme.org
- ☐ Review these resources:
  - ☐ Movie: *The Lion King*
  - ☐ Book: *The Cry Of The Soul* by Allender and Longman
  - ☐ Site: en.wikipedia.org/wiki/Myers-Briggs_Type_Indicator
  - ☐ Site: biblehub.com/commentaries/barnes/psalms/139.htm
  - ☐ Site: hebrew4christians.com/Names_of_G-d/El/el.html

---

[4] todayifoundout.com/index.php/2011/02/identical-twins-dont-have-identical-fingerprints-even-from-birth

Chapter 16

Recognize Your Gender as a Strength

When God created man, he made him in the likeness of God. Male and female he created them, and he blessed them and named them Man when they were created.
—Genesis 5:1–2

Opposites attract. Without differences, there would be no mystery and no spectacular wonder. As much as two people hide who they are to avoid conflict, they drain the relationship of much needed spark and excitement.

Opposites or Complements?

Yes, opposites attract. Yes, men and women are different in every cell of their bodies. Yes, God wired their brains differently. But notice that the word "opposite" contains the word "oppose."

We should not think of the male and female genders as opposites. This leads to the belief that men and women must work against each other. The "battle of the sexes" definitely does not help marriage. Now, I am all for some light-hearted fun and joking. But sometimes I take this too far. At the end of the day, I don't want there to be any hurt feelings between my wife and me.

The popular meaning of "opposites attract" rightfully focuses on "attract"—how God designed the two sexes to be drawn to and complement each other. One of the desired outcomes of marriage is to grow in our ability to fit together.

In Common Where It Counts

Many books have been written on the differences between men and women. While learning to navigate the differences is important, seeing a clear vision of how men and women are perfect for each other is more helpful. Successful couples eventually make this leap in their understanding. They move away from, "My partner is a different species from another planet," towards, "My partner is different, but we are both members of God's family." As Christians, we ultimately have the same goals in life.

The key is our focus. Do we put our focus only on the details of our life or also the bigger picture of what life is about? A successful marriage will balance these two. Are we sowing seeds of discontent by emphasizing the stark differences between men and women? Or can we sow seeds of unity by seeing the value of the differences and focusing on the overall team goals?

If we stop and think about what is important in life, we will see that men and women have more in common than they have in differences. Most of the differences are superficial when compared to the faith we share.

We all come from the same God, and He lives in perfect unity with Jesus and the Holy Spirit, who are both equal with, but different from, God. His design includes the intention that we focus on the things that bring unity.

The Three Stages of Sexual Maturity

The challenge for every married couple is finding satisfaction in appreciating differences while working together instead of becoming hopelessly annoyed by those differences. Finding satisfaction is a three-stage developmental process:

1. Affirm Self and Gender.
2. Appreciate others who have the Same Gender.
3. Appreciate others who have a Different Gender.

The goal of stage one is to become comfortable in our own skin. We all start incapable of meeting our own needs. We rely on our parents to affirm us, including our gender. Eventually we become competent and able to take care of ourselves.

The goal of stage two is to become comfortable with the same gender. Here we learn how to relate to a different other, but this is only moderately difficult because of the shared gender. Same gender friendships are essential in life for both married and single people.

The goal of stage three is to become comfortable with the different gender. Just about the time we've learned how to adequately relate to the same gender, puberty hits! Our hormones equip us to become interested in the other gender. Yet we don't have much of a clue about what it means to be the grown up version of our own gender, let alone the other gender.

A team is most strengthened by adding a person that complements the existing skillset. This is marriage by God's design. God made marriage so that one man along with one woman complete the team. Adding a third member or having a partner of the same gender would be counter-productive.

As we mature sexually, we gradually grow in our ability to achieve unity with diversity. This, after all, is an essential task of marriage. The key is developing appreciation for something beyond ourselves. If we have spent some time around the other gender, the differences are clear. But these differences are neutral.

In the wrong mindset, differences threaten us. When gender differences become a consistent source of conflict, we should evaluate our social life. Maybe we lack enough affirmation of our gender's approach to life. Consequently, we expect our partner to meet our needs for same gender fellowship. However, that's just not possible.

Affirming the same approach as our own is relatively easy. Affirming a foreign approach is easier from a place of security with our own approach.

With an open mind, differences refresh us. Thank God, I am not married to a copy of myself! Instead, I get to be married to someone different from me. How wonderful that God designed the genders to fit together. They present a much clearer image of God together than they do apart.

Men and Women Are Equals

Unity without diversity accomplishes nothing. Unity with diversity strengthens any endeavor. To deny or over-emphasize male-female differences only weakens God's design. Both fuel unhealthy competition rather than cooperation.

Denying the differences destroys diversity and leads to glorifying a small subset of abilities. For example, if being a professional athlete is favored above all other jobs, then we must start believing that everyone is equally equipped to be a professional athlete (no difference exists between me and Peyton Manning). Over-emphasizing the differences also leads to the claim that one particular approach to life is superior. For example, "Women are better than men because they are more compassionate."

The root of the problem is the worship of one particular gender skillset. This throws off the inherent balance in God's design. Solutions other than God's are inferior. Paul addressed this problem in the body of Christ by pointing out God's self-balancing design:

> *But God has so composed the body, giving greater honor to the part that lacked it, that there may be no division in the body, but that the members may have the same care for one another.*
> —1 Corinthians 12:24b–25

Concerning gender, the principle is the same. Each gender has its own strengths and weaknesses. Both are needed and valued. Neither is superior to the other.

Gender Specialization

A gender (male or female) is a specialized version of the divine nature. God intends for us to play a specific role in life. Gender helps describe the role that guides us through life.

Part of a conference I attended focused on the differences between men and women. The leaders asked us to separate by gender then face each other. The men formed a single line while the women bunched together (picture on the left). Granted, the group consisted of more women than men, but the contrast was clear. The men preferred to stand on their own, while the women preferred being

part of a community. In keeping with these instincts, in a threatening environment, the men would likely form a circle around the women (picture on the right). The men could interact with both the environment and the women, while the women would feel safe to interact with the men and complete their work in the context of a community.

We often use these words to describe females:
- Sensitive
- Helping
- Responding
- Strengthening
- Nesting
- Nurturing

We often use these words to describe males:
- Direct
- Powerful
- Initiating
- Pursuing
- Providing
- Protecting

Your "gender strengths" are how well you can fulfill these basic gender roles. Specialization means limitation of the individual for the greater good of the team and those the team serves. Can women be direct and men be sensitive? Of course! But, the point is to get to the essence of who you are so you can live out of your strengths.

God is the one who ultimately knows who you are. We must trust the designer and the design. Learning how to be a team requires a significant investment but with the right team members, accomplishing just about anything is significantly easier and more efficient than going it alone.

For Reflection

1. A biblical gender role is part of your calling.
2. God chose your gender, your parents, your personality—everything about you.
3. You are not a random creation nor a mistake. In love, God designed you with intention.
4. You are the gender that your physical sex indicates. There is no need to doubt this.

Next Steps

- What needs are met by the various roles of men (Father, Brother, Son, Husband) and women (Mother, Sister, Daughter, Wife)? The roles are different and the met needs vary. Review all the roles and identify: 1) what needs they can potentially meet; and 2) how well the needs are met in your life. Are you expecting any one person, such as your partner, to fill too many roles?
- Answer these questions about your gender identity. If you answer "no" to any of these questions, look deeper into your history to find the experiences that could have damaged your gender identity.
  - Your gender is a major clue to how God wants you to spend your life. Are you open to your gender informing your life decisions?
  - Are you at peace with your God-given gender? Can you affirm and accept your gender?
  - Do you feel included by others of the same gender, or do you feel rejected by them?
  - Did your father affirm your gender?
  - Did your mother affirm your gender?
- Review these resources:
  - Movie: *Remember The Titans*
  - Site: marriagebuilders.com/graphic/mbi8120_differences.html

Chapter 17

Play Your Position

The eye cannot say to the hand, "I have no need of you," nor again the head to the feet, "I have no need of you." On the contrary, the parts of the body that seem to be weaker are indispensable, and on those parts of the body that we think less honorable we bestow the greater honor, and our unpresentable parts are treated with greater modesty, which our more presentable parts do not require. But God has so composed the body, giving greater honor to the part that lacked it, that there may be no division in the body, but that the members may have the same care for one another. If one member suffers, all suffer together; if one member is honored, all rejoice together. Now you are the body of Christ and individually members of it.
—1 Corinthians 12:21–27

Achieving Interdependence

Paul makes the point that the parts of the body are different in function but equal in value. As the body of Christ, all believers form a unique interdependent community. Interdependent means each part fully performs its intended function, and all functions are essential to the body. God designed the body optimally to be:

- Interdependent;
- Balanced;
- Efficient; and
- Unified.

Within this environment, everyone is encouraged to reach their full potential. Each person takes on a specialized role according to God's plan. In an interdependent community, members are available as needed to support and celebrate. All members are important and indispensable.

We can say the same for marriage. Ideally, marriage is an interdependent team where both husband and wife are important and indispensable.

Interdependence is the ability to give to others and receive from others in meaningful ways in peer relationships. What we give and receive doesn't have to be identical nor equal in quantity. Fairness means both people feel equally valued, not that they always divide everything 50/50. The stages to reach complete interdependence are:

1. Dependent (D): A young girl learns to be attached. She cannot take care of herself. Physical, cognitive, emotional, and sexual development has yet to occur. She needs to borrow from someone else to perform basic functions.
2. Independent (I): A girl learns to be separate. She can take care of herself but not others. At this stage, she could survive in the world on her own if she had to. She does not yet fully grasp the necessity and pleasure of a mutual give and receive relationship.
3. Limited Interdependent (LI): A young woman learns to be part of something larger than herself. She participates in peer relationships but is not fully able to see life from another person's perspective. Giving tends to be superficial (that is, she gives, but in many cases expects to get). She can give of herself at times, but she usually returns to the default of focusing on herself.
4. Full Interdependent (FI): A woman regularly functions as part of something larger than herself. She grasps the idea of giving sacrificially. She can take on specialized roles and trust others to fulfill their own specialized roles. She can also handle others being appropriately dependent on her. This type of one-way relationship is fulfilling in a different way than a mutual peer relationship.

Interdependence is the goal. Your progress towards interdependence affects your relationship. Your life experiences can slow down or speed up progress. If you have been abused, or you grew up in a particularly dysfunctional home, trusting others can be difficult. Forcing yourself to trust is not the answer. However, learning how to be a team whose members have differing abilities is the goal. Not everyone will reach the same goal in the same amount of time.

> **Dependence, Independence, and Co-Dependence have either too much or too little dependence. In a one-way relationship, one person ends up giving most of the time. In an interdependent relationship, both adults regularly practice their ability to give and receive love, which greatly increases their satisfaction.**

Identifying Being Stuck

If you are stuck at a stage, chances are your real and deepest needs were not and are not being met. Seek what you need to move forward with the understanding that your partner can't meet all of your needs. In the context of a peer relationship:

- Stuck D-stage people lack feeling competent and confident. They usually need more support but also someone who will let them make mistakes so they will grow up. Unhealthy dependence says, "I need you so I can be and feel like a whole person."
- Stuck I-stage people fear that the intimate needs of others will overwhelm them. They usually need patience and positive experiences working as a team. Unhealthy independence says, "I can or would prefer to do it myself. I don't need you to accomplish any greater purpose in life."
- Stuck LI-stage people simply need opportunities to practice being on a team. Marriage is the ultimate practice! Unhealthy interdependence says, "I need you to accomplish a greater purpose, but I don't understand yet what I have to contribute or why I should help you."

A common trap is confusing mutual dependence with interdependence. Have you ever heard that marriage should be 50/50? While this is likely an innocent mistake, the split describes mutual dependence. Two halves make one only in math. Marriage requires two whole people to make one marriage team. Marriage should be 100/100.

Mutual dependence feels like interdependence for a little while. Eventually though, one or both individual's incomplete development surfaces. An unhealthily dependent person will require their partner to be there for them in ways that are not possible. When too much is demanded, the relationship will implode.

For Reflection

1. Your brain is not fully developed until you reach thirty years old.
2. Ideally, a person will at least be in the LI-stage before marriage.
3. The stages overlap, and the exact age of completion of each stage varies. For example, a person might be dependent in some ways but be in a later stage. Or one person might be thirty years old and dependent while another is thirty years old and interdependent.
4. Wherever you are in the process, you can move forward. It's better to be behind and growing than not growing at all.
5. A relationship is strongest and most fulfilling when both husband and wife believe, "I can give to, and receive meaningful love from, my partner."
6. Some needs cannot be met by depending or even interdepending on another human.
7. Marriage functions optimally when both husband and wife reach the interdependent stage. If you get married when one or both are in the D or I stages, it will feel more like parenting (too much dependence) or being roommates (too much independence). You will need to be patient while you both grow up.

Next Steps

- Identify your current stage and any implications this has for your marriage.
- Read 1 Corinthians 12:21–27 again, but this time replace the body parts with husband and wife. For example: The husband cannot say to his wife, "I have no need of you . . ." How does this help you better understand marriage?
- Review these resources:
  - Movie: *Into the Wild*
- Use your Blueprint Space to draw the relevant members of your family in four different portraits. Include extended family and other significant attachments as needed. Let the distance between each member represent how close the members are to each other. Use a star ★ for yourself, squares ☐ for males, circles ○ for females, and triangles △ for other attachments (such as work, exercise, alcohol, etc.). Write the name of the person or object below the shape. Add other relevant details (such as your reasons for closeness or distance).
    - What can you do to move toward the picture you want?
    - Do two more portraits for your family growing up (one as it was and another how you would have wanted it to be).
    - If your partner does the exercise too, compare portraits to find agreements and differences. Discuss differences in perceptions.

Blueprint Space

Way you see it	**Way you want it**
★	★
Way partner sees it	**Way partner wants it**
★	★

Part III – Marital Growth

Chapters 18–20   Defining Marriage

Chapters 21–24   The Stages of Becoming an Us

Chapters 25–28   Communication

Chapters 29–31   Productive Conflict

Chapters 32–37   Conflict Resolution

Chapters 38–45   Betrayal and Restoration

Chapters 46–47   Preventing Divorce

Chapters 48–51   Recovery from Loss

Chapter 52   Making the Journey

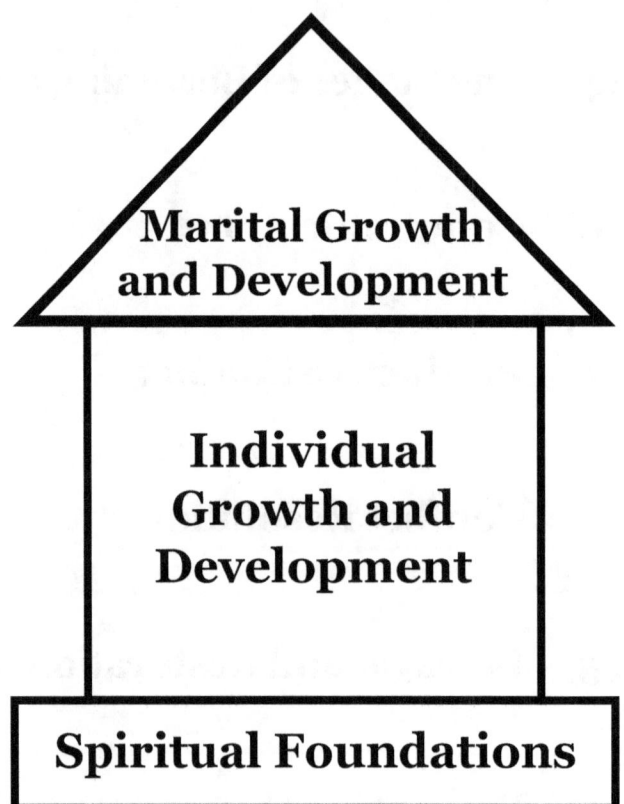

Chapter 18

God Creates Marriage

Then the man said, "This at last is bone of my bones and flesh of my flesh; she shall be called Woman, because she was taken out of Man." For this reason a man will leave his father and mother and be united to his wife, and they will become one flesh.
—Genesis 2:23–24

Coming together is a beginning, staying together is progress, and working together is success.
—Henry Ford

God's Definition of Marriage

Genesis 2:24 contains a succinct and profound description of marriage. The verse includes three essential actions that make an authentic marriage:

1. A man will leave his father and mother;
2. Be united to his wife; and
3. They will become one flesh.

In his book *I Married You,* Walter Trobisch defines marriage as:

1. The Wedding: The public and legal act that announces to the world the formation of a new family unit;
2. Faithfulness: The loving commitment to be faithful companions growing in intimate knowledge of each other; and
3. The Sexual Union: The physical union of husband and wife that represents their faithfulness.

However, this doesn't give the impression that marriage is a dynamic and cyclical process.

In Genesis 1:28 God exhorts Adam and Eve to be fruitful, multiply, and to fill, subdue, and have dominion over the earth. Bearing fruit and multiplying ensures theirs will not be the last marriage. Adam and Eve's children eventually form their own families. This fourth step brings the process full circle:

1. Leave past affiliations;
2. Protect growing intimacy;
3. Join together as one to produce fruit; and
4. Multiply and release offspring into the world.

Based on these four steps (and some thoughts from previous chapters), I propose the following as a working definition of marriage:

> **God joining together a man and a woman, loyal to each other for life, who each contribute distinct but equally important abilities towards the completion of a fruitful mission greater than can be accomplished apart.**

God's Marriage Maintenance Plan

I have another garden analogy to help you remember the four steps of marriage. To maintain a healthy garden you: Weed, Wall, Seed, and Feed.

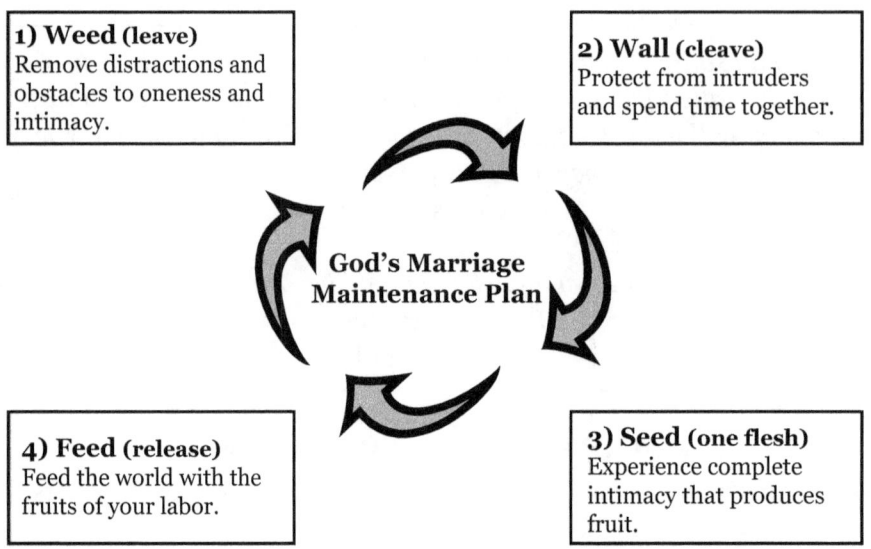

Step 1: Weed (leave)

Planting a garden requires clearing the land of all the rocks and weeds. Similarly, we must clear out everything that chokes out what we are trying to grow in our marriage. Some of these weeds will be our own weaknesses while other weeds may be the weaknesses of those seeking to destroy our marriage. Unfortunately, weeds will find their way back into the garden after we plant the seeds we want, so we need to be vigilant.

> **When you weed, you prepare for a strategic joining with your partner by leaving behind all that will interfere.**

Leaving is a transitional process of separating physically, intellectually, and emotionally from one's family of origin. This involves a shift in perspective and in priority from your family of origin to your new family. Leaving does not mean abandoning, but it does mean you become first and foremost loyal to your mate. There can be no marriage without leaving.

Step 2: Wall (cleave)

After investing effort to weed, the natural next step is putting a fence around the garden to keep out unwanted visitors that would steal the seeds or eat the fruit. A marriage, like a garden, is worth protecting because it can provide so many benefits.

All marriages need a boundary between the couple and the rest of the world. This boundary serves two purposes:

1. Keeping out intruders or anything that interferes with intimacy. This could be other people but could also be things like addictions, work, or other interests.
2. Cocooning the couple together to keep intimacy alive.

Chapter 18 - God Creates Marriage

A husband and wife can cleave to each other only to the degree that they leave past competitive affiliations.

Husband and wife engage each other by moving toward each other; they cleave to each other (and no others). In the companionship aspect of marriage, the couple spends time growing together in intellectual and emotional intimacy. The couple works at developing their purpose for being together and understanding what strengths and weaknesses each brings to the team.

Husband and wife completely share not only their bodies and their material possessions but also their joy and suffering. They live together as one unit and experience life alongside each other. Though they remain two distinct persons, they are one in body, soul, and spirit.

Step 3: Seed (becoming one flesh)

Genesis 2:25 goes on to qualify that the one-flesh relationship involves no barriers or shame. But the Fall introduced shame, so if intimacy appears to be limited, verifying the garden is free of weeds is always a good idea.

A fully effective one-flesh marriage requires both male and female contributing in a way that bears fruit. Becoming one flesh represents the culmination of husband and wife cleaving to each other.

The degree to which husband and wife succeed in leaving and cleaving is the degree to which they experience the benefits of being one flesh.

Seeding involves joining together to create something new from the two. This can be children or perhaps a ministry made possible by the marriage. What "children" do you want to have?

In a garden, you plant seeds and anticipate growth. You water and care for the "children" that are dependent on you. You see the maturation of your efforts.

Step 4: Feed (release)

Fruits are not meant to remain with harvesters. What the two of you have created is ultimately God's; therefore, it must be set free to have a life of its own. Young adults must leave the nest so that they can form their own families and continue the cycle.

Feeding is letting go of mature fruits permanently, so that the seeds from the fruit will be planted elsewhere.

Instead of investing directly into your children, the time has come to completely relinquish control of your children. Both celebration and grieving are necessary to release your offspring to fulfill their own mission in life.

Parents release their offspring as arrows to go beyond where they are to a place they cannot go. God has His plans and is always doing something new. This "pushing out of the nest" allows children to "enter a new promised land" even while you remain behind.

For Reflection

1. What aspects of marriage are represented in Genesis 2:24? Which aspects, if any, are not mentioned? How well does Genesis 2:24 describe (or at least summarize) all areas of potential marital discord?
2. With a significant enough purpose and mission, a husband and wife will be sufficiently motivated to work through obstacles to see the fruit of their labor.

3. None of the four steps is optional. We need to revisit them perpetually to keep a growing and intimate marriage.
4. Your marriage will be only as strong as the weakest step.
5. Don't isolate yourself from your partner. You need to feel you are in this together. Don't be self-sufficient. Share life together.

Next Steps

- ☐ What interferes with your marital intimacy the most? Consider influences both external and internal to your marriage.
- ☐ Are you spending sufficient time together to develop closeness and safety?
- ☐ How is your sexual intimacy? Be willing to work hard to keep this in your marriage. Likely, you will need to revisit leaving and cleaving to make this happen.
- ☐ Review these resources:
   - ☐ Movie: *The Joy Luck Club*
   - ☐ Book: *I Married You* by Walter Trobisch
- ☐ Using your Blueprint Space:
   - ☐ Write out **your** definition of marriage.
   - ☐ Brainstorm ideas for your marriage plan using Purpose, Project, and Process.
   - ☐ **Purpose:** You have your specific reasons for being married, but God had a purpose in mind when He created marriage (See Ephesians 5:25–32; Genesis 1:28). Purpose provides direction in choosing a project.
   - ☐ **Project:** The project is a joint effort that accomplishes work for God's kingdom. What mission and goals do you have? How important are they to you? What kind of seeds are you going to plant? The way you go about completing a project makes a difference.
   - ☐ **Process:** With a project and a reason for doing it, how do husband and wife go about reaching their goals (See Genesis 2:24)?

Blueprint Space

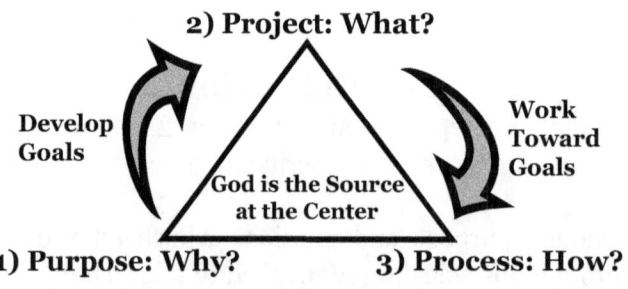

Chapter 19

Living Your Gender Identity

*So God created man in his own image, in the image of God he created him;
Male and female he created them.*
—Genesis 1:27

*The woman was made of a rib out of the side of Adam; not made out of his
head to rule over him, nor out of his feet to be trampled upon by him, but
out of his side to be equal with him, under his arm to be protected, and near
his heart to be beloved.*
—Matthew Henry

Different and Equal

God designed men and women with significant differences and equal value. Because of their design differences, one gender will be more efficient in some activities than in others. But more importantly, our gender provides God-given clues as to how to live.

Other views attempt to minimize or eliminate the differences between men and women. Egalitarians downplay gender roles and believe men and women should work together without hierarchy. That may work well in many cases, but it disregards biblical teaching. To avoid the risk of falling into the rut of male dominance, egalitarians remove hierarchy and authority from the home. Such thinking waters down God's intention for marriage. This model of marriage no longer reflects the image of God.

Likewise, any belief that considers women as less than men also fails to meet biblical standards. Jesus valued women as much as He valued men. He treated them the same as men at times, but differently at other times. He did not include any women in the twelve disciples. However, He broke significant cultural norms while relating to women. Jesus allowed women to travel with Him and they helped support Him financially. He taught, corrected, and healed women (Luke 8; Luke 10:38–42; Luke 13:10–17). He heeded His mother's direction (John 2:1–12), and He saw that she was cared for after His death (John 19:26–27). Jesus clearly valued women, or He would not have bothered to interact with and minister to them.

Marriage is Hierarchical

The Bible inseparably links marriage with relating to God in Ephesians 5:24–25:

*Now as the church submits to Christ, so also wives should submit in
everything to their husbands. Husbands love your wives, as Christ loved the
church and gave himself up for her.*

Because hierarchy exists between God and us, hierarchy exists in marriage. While most people will acknowledge this truth in theory, our culture's pressure to be politically correct often causes us to act another way.

God designed marriage to include hierarchy; marriage would be chaotic without it. But He also balanced the hierarchy with love. This eliminates any advantage and preserves equality between men and women.

By choosing marriage, we are choosing to live with hierarchy. Those who don't like this structure and marry anyway upset the balance between hierarchy and love. Marriage won't function as God intends because if one gender becomes more than God intended, the other becomes less.

Jesus makes understanding His truth easier through parables that utilize real-life examples. Likewise, God uses our real-life experience of a male-female relationship to help us better understand our relationship with Him.

When lived correctly, hierarchy in marriage becomes a model of our relationship to Christ. Rather than creating an advantage for one gender (usually considered to be males), the model requires the man to be trustworthy for his woman (just like God is faithful to us) and the woman to trust her man (just like us putting our faith in God). Without this need to trust, marriage loses some of its distinctiveness.

As husband and wife participate in this model, they learn hands-on about God. Tinkering with the model results in bad theology. If we declare no hierarchy exists between husband and wife, we are simultaneously declaring no hierarchy exists between God and man. Therefore, a Biblical marriage is inseparably hierarchical.

Gender is an Essential Part of Identity

Gender is a permanent part of our identity, not a temporary role we play as actors on a stage. It is no different from other personality traits that shape our life experiences and decisions.

Actions based on gender roles come from God's design, not random impulses. However, rigid gender roles such as, "only women should change diapers" or "only men should mow the lawn" are misguided opinions at worst and a matter of preference at best.

We can make life decisions by considering these criteria in the order presented:
1. What is God leading us to do? Is our choice based on the truth of the Bible? We have freedom when the Spirit leads us.
2. Does our choice glorify God by reflecting the relationship between Christ and the Church?
3. Which option makes best use of each person's gifts and abilities?

In Paul's letter to Titus, he instructs men and women differently.

Older men are to be sober-minded, dignified, self-controlled, sound in faith, in love, and in steadfastness. Older women likewise are to be reverent in behavior, not slanderers or slaves to much wine. They are to teach what is good, and so train the young women to love their husbands and children, to be self-controlled, pure, working at home, kind, and submissive to their own husbands, that the word of God may not be reviled. Likewise, urge the younger men to be self-controlled.
—Titus 2:2–6

A woman can work outside the home, but a woman's first priority should always be her husband and children. When a woman has fulfilled these responsibilities, she is free to focus upon the

Lord's work outside the home. This might be why Paul warns us that marriage takes some of our focus off pleasing the Lord (1 Corinthians 7:32–35).

Complementarianism is Optimal

Wayne Grudem, theologian and seminary professor, defines five different categories for the evaluation of beliefs about gender. Moving left from the middle, men are increasingly devalued. Moving right from the middle, women are increasingly devalued.

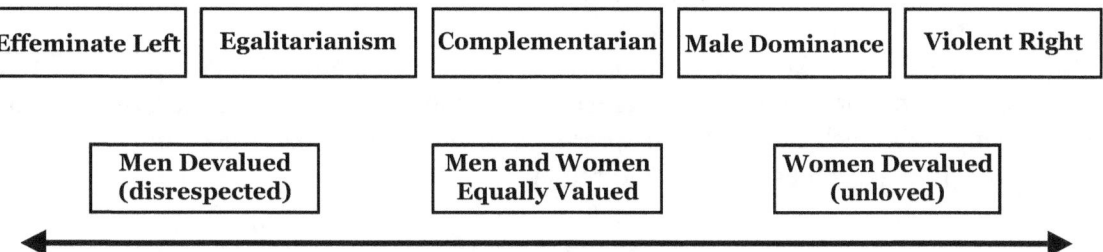

The following definitions are adapted from *Biblical Foundations for Manhood and Womanhood* (pp. 62–63).

- **Effeminate Left:** Every effort is made to eliminate all differences between men and women. No differences between God and creation.
- **Egalitarianism:** Authority and hierarchy are removed in male and female relationships. Responsibilities are assigned only by ability and gifting, not by gender-roles. Women compete with men to prove they do not need them. Women emphasize mutual submission, but this often ends up as the wife ruling over her passive husband. No hierarchy or authority exists within the Trinity.
- **Complementarian:** Men and women recognize each other as equal and different. Husband and wife have equal value, different roles. The husband is to exhibit loving headship. The wife is to exhibit joyful submission. The Trinity is recognized as having hierarchy. The Father, Son, and Holy Spirit have equal value, but different roles.
- **Male Dominance:** Men take advantage of the differences between men and women. Men exploit women for their own pleasure. Men compete with women to show women as inferior. The husband is a harsh, selfish dictator and his wife is a weak slave and doormat. The Son and Holy Spirit are not considered to be fully God.
- **Violent Right:** Men have all the power and are superior to women. Only one God-person exists; the Trinity does not exist.

Complementarianism is balanced and biblical. Notice that egalitarianism appears to be the over-correcting reaction to male dominance. While this is understandable given the past era of male dominance, egalitarianism falls short of God's ideal.

Complementarianism follows God's design and matches biblical teaching about the Trinity. Complementarians are comfortable with gender differences and an interdependent team approach. The saying, "Do not throw the baby out with the bathwater!" applies here. When someone misuses a screwdriver as a hammer, we do not throw away the screwdriver and buy two hammers.

Learning to take advantage of differing gifts and abilities can be hard work. But we can find great beauty in how God made men and women different.

For Reflection

1. To move in the direction that little difference exists between male and female is to say we don't need one of the genders.
2. The members of the Trinity do not swap identities or roles; neither should men and women.
3. God does not want us to compete with Him. He wants us on His team. Likewise, men and women are not supposed to compete against one another.
4. Headship does not mean the wife is inferior. Keep in mind that Christ submitted to the Father.
5. God created Eve to complete Adam not to compete with him. This has little to do with gender ability—it has to do with God's plan.
6. When compared to a six-inch paintbrush, a two-inch paintbrush appears to be inferior. However, no superiority or inferiority exists between the two sizes of brushes. If we try to paint a wall with a two-inch brush, it will wear us out. If we try to paint the trim with a six-inch brush, we will make a mess and have to redo it.

Next Steps

- What you believe has a lot to do with how your parents raised you and your other life experiences. If men dominated women, women might take a defensive stance to prove that "women can do anything men can do." A relationship then becomes more of a competition to see who can do everything the best. If women dominated men, men may continue in passivity to avoid unpleasant conflict.
- Are you being true to your gender identity? Do you have any internal conflict over embracing your identity? Are you sure you understand your identity correctly—as a gift and not a hardship?
- Review these resources:
  - Movie: *Cinderella Man*
  - Movie: *You've Got Mail*
  - Book: *Biblical Foundations for Manhood and Womanhood* edited by Wayne Grudem

Chapter 20

Headship and Submission

The head of every man is Christ, the head of a wife is her husband, and the head of Christ is God.
—1 Corinthians 11:3

Wives, submit to your husbands, as is fitting in the Lord. Husbands, love your wives, and do not be harsh with them.
—Colossians 3:18–19

Submission does not give a husband a license to annex decision-making territory from his wife. A wife is only submitting when she is doing so by her own free will. Headship does not give a wife a license to abandon responsibility. A husband exhibiting true headship encourages and considers all his wife has to offer. The Bible says that Sarah considered Abraham her master, but it doesn't say that Abraham treated her as a slave.

God is the Highest Authority

God is over all and reports to no one. He is both the first and the final authority. Nothing else exists that can rank above or beside Him. We have one God, creator of all, who has full authority to set his direction for all of life. He is the head.

Any being, organization, or government with two (or more) heads is ultimately doomed to eternal gridlock because it's impossible to go in multiple directions at the same time.

Besides, a two-headed creature is not natural.

Fortunately, Scripture gives us an organized chain of command. Paul describes God's hierarchy in 1 Corinthians 11:3.

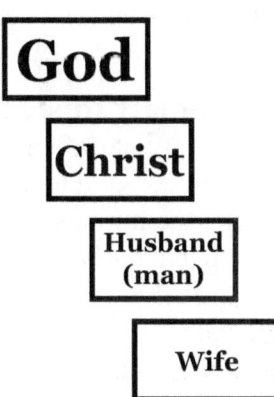

The Bible is clear that humility is required of men and women alike (Philippians 2:3–4). Both genders need an attitude of humility because both equally depend on and submit to Christ. Also,

God designed men and women so that each gender significantly benefits the other. Men need and are blessed by women, and women need and are blessed by men.

For a husband, the challenge is to be confident and trustworthy without being selfish. For a wife, the challenge is submitting and trusting without presuming she knows where Christ is leading better than her husband.

God's Plan for Gender

Headship and submission are God-ordained. He commands men and women to fulfill these roles, but He does not command for the sake of commanding. He is reminding us of who He is and His design.

Headship and submission are essential to God's plan for his creation. They enable order and unity, and He hardwired them into gender:

- Order is significant in God's design. He created Adam first, then He created Eve. This represents that God existed before man.
- Part of God's identity is unity. God, Jesus, and the Holy Spirit live with perfect unity. God wants this for us too. He uniquely equipped man and woman to model the relationship between Christ and his bride, the Church (Ephesians 5:25–32).
- God created us with gender to influence every aspect of our lives, and our gender strongly shapes our reality. We can try to get around this, but not without a heavy dose of denial. God wants us to cooperate with his design rather than make up our own ideas.

A person's gifts and abilities include gender. Nothing feels better to a husband than when his wife respects and submits to him. Nothing feels better to a wife than when her husband loves her and serves her best interests. Husbands and wives are to offer these blessings to each other freely and unconditionally. Neither should withhold love or any other benefit of the relationship when a partner fails to do his or her part.

Fulfilling these roles cannot be demanded or forced. The husband's role is not to make his wife submit; obeying God is her responsibility. A husband telling a wife to submit because the Bible says so is not appropriate. The wife's role is not to coerce her husband into leading; obeying God is his responsibility. A wife telling her husband what to do all the time is not appropriate.

The headship and submission responsibilities should not be used to gain an advantage through selfish behavior. For example, a husband should not claim headship and favor his ideas over his wife's ideas. One responsibility of headship is integrating all ideas when possible. Likewise, a wife should not claim submission and remain silent when she believes her husband is about to make a big mistake.

Biblical Authority for Husbands

Responsible headship requires a man to initiate often and to sometimes override his wife's wishes or sacrifice his desires. A spirit of humility and love should always accompany his actions. To be successful in this God-ordained role, the husband should be a lifelong learner of what the Bible teaches about being a godly man. When a husband is growing spiritually, he stays ahead of the game and will usually make wise decisions.

A godly wife appreciates a husband who:

- Initiates a direction by sharing his thoughts and convictions;
- Is patiently firm when the situation warrants;
- Is loving and understanding;
- Stays present in the relationship;

- Invests time to keep in touch with how she is doing;
- Protects her by looking out for her best interests;
- Has enough confidence that he doesn't dominate her nor let her rule him;
- Doesn't use his authority to his advantage;
- Doesn't make demands for obedience-without-question;
- Doesn't become passive, leaving her to make most decisions; and
- Doesn't speak down to her or treat her harshly, damaging her self-worth.

> *Likewise, husbands, live with your wives in an understanding way, showing honor to the woman as the weaker vessel, since they are heirs with you of the grace of life, so that your prayers may not be hindered.*
> —1 Peter 3:7

A husband who can live out these principles has an excellent grasp of his gender role. Hopefully, a husband can enjoy his wife at all times, but his role will sometimes require taking a firm stance.

A husband is responsible before God for his family, but he is not "above the law." A husband should never ask his wife to participate in something which will cause significant emotional distress. Doing so isn't loving her according to 1 Peter 3:7. A wife, who attempts to please her husband by complying anyway, compromises her personal integrity. A husband must sacrifice his desires when a wife reaches this level of distress.

A husband is obligated to acquire whatever Christ-like attributes he desires in his wife. Even though he doesn't behave perfectly, responsible headship includes confronting poor behaviors in both himself and his wife.

Biblical Submission for Wives

Submission requires a wife to trust in God's established chain of command which ranks her beneath her husband. Since the chain of command also shows that a wife ultimately reports to Christ, she is never obligated to submit to her husband for anything that violates biblical teaching.

Submission does not mean silently giving up personal choices since submission cannot exist without the freedom to choose to submit. If that freedom is nonexistent, the wife isn't submitting, but merely obeying demands.

God gives us free choice in many matters. However, when sin is not involved, God requires a wife to submit to her husband's direction.

God does not intend for a wife to go along with anything that would result in physical, emotional, or spiritual harm to her or others. Harm includes significant emotional distress. A wife is not required to participate in anything that violates her sense of personal integrity (her boundaries).

However, if the matter is reasonable, she is responsible for pursuing healing in hopes she can eventually submit comfortably.

A godly husband will appreciate a wife who:
- Respects him;
- Supports and strengthens his potential;
- Voices respectfully and directly her opinions, concerns, and convictions;
- Is flexible and accommodating when possible;
- Accepts his strengths along with his weaknesses;

- Is attentive to his needs as much or more than her other responsibilities, including children;
- Doesn't compete with him in a way that devalues him;
- Doesn't operate independently by doing what she wants regardless of his wishes;
- Doesn't enable her husband to be a passive puppet;
- Doesn't obstruct progress of his positive decisions and desires.

A wife who can live out these principles has an excellent grasp of her gender role. Hopefully a wife will be able to focus on the more fun aspects of her role, such as supporting and strengthening her husband's potential. But sometimes her role will require confrontation.

A wife can learn how to choose her battles by saving confrontation for what matters most—her stronger spiritual convictions. She can be secure enough with God to allow her husband to make mistakes while he is learning to be responsible for his family. But she shouldn't step aside in silence if she is convinced he is making a poor decision. She should go on record before her husband and God.

A wife may consider her husband's ideas as undesirable, but she is to submit to them provided they are not immoral. However, a wife must bring her honest feelings and concerns to her husband. She must fully communicate and give him the opportunity to understand her concerns. The more significant the issue, the more time she needs for fruitful discussion.

Rarely, if ever, should both partners move forward with a decision without agreement. Disagreement in significant matters indicates a lack of unity and that a blunder could be on the horizon. Anything that is seriously distressing is significant. A wife that remains concerned or confused about a decision should continue to talk about the issue. She should always have a voice with her husband, unlike children who may be told "no more discussion."

But when a wife has made her convictions known to her husband in a matter in which they disagree, and she is sure he understands her position, then the responsibility of the outcome is 100% with her husband. She can rest securely knowing that ultimately she is resting in God.

If submission remains confusing, a wife can always focus on doing what is best for her husband. Most of the time this means following his leading. But even Abigail directly disobeyed her husband Nabal (1 Samuel 25). She did this because David and his men planned to slaughter Nabal and his entire household. Proverbs 31:12 says that a noble wife, "does him good, and not harm, all the days of her life."

Shared Rule

God asked both Adam and Eve to subdue and have dominion (Genesis 1:26–28). Husband and wife are co-rulers in their marriage. God intends for them to function as a team.

Teammates confer with one another. A husband is wise to consider the opinions and wisdom of his team. Strong leadership desires, invites, and accepts input from everyone: God, his wife, peers, and even children. If this was not true, then the family would only be as strong as the one leader instead of as strong as the whole family or whole community.

Husband and wife need to work together to reach agreement. The majority of the time, they should be able to reach a mutually satisfying agreement without needing overt sacrifice or submission. But when necessary, sacrifice and submission preserve unity.

Headship and submission work best with two developmentally mature adults. When either husband or wife has some significant growing up to do, this requires more endurance of their partner. To preserve unity, we need to lower expectations while remembering our responsibility to God. A husband should sacrifice when his wife is not mature enough to follow him properly. Likewise, a wife should submit when her husband is not mature enough to lead her properly.

We should make decisions based on spiritual conviction, not only on personal preference. Sometimes we need to stand our ground patiently, and sometimes we need to sacrifice or submit then move on.

Both husband and wife are works in progress learning how to make headship and submission work. Both partners need grace when they make mistakes. Headship and submission work best when both invest in developing a strong relational bond and are able to say, "I know you well enough to comfortably trust you."

Putting this all together, you can live well with your partner by:
- Knowing God's design and order;
- Knowing your partner well;
- Being yourself and having fun;
- Trusting God is ultimately in control; and
- Returning to the basics of your gender responsibilities when something isn't working.

For Reflection

1. Headship does not mean the husband is perfect.
2. Even though responsible, the man is not always right.
3. Submission does not mean the wife is unintelligent.
4. God does not hold the woman responsible for her husband's poor decision but does hold her responsible for her submission.
5. A wife should speak up if she has valuable input but ultimately allow her husband to make and be responsible for the decision (or mistake).
6. If you are a single female, avoid men who cannot admit when they have made a mistake.
7. If you are a single male, avoid women who challenge you on every point.
8. Husbands don't make all the decisions, but they are responsible for all the decisions.
9. Wives make intelligent decisions and can be excellent managers (Proverbs 31).
10. The submissive woman enhances her husband's life instead of competing with him.
11. Children will instinctively base their behaviors on how dad and mom treat each other. A wife that wants her children to follow her direction is wise to model submission to their father. A husband that wants his children to respect him and his wife is wise to model loving interaction with their mother.

Next Steps

- ☐ Husbands, have you identified any ways you have misused your authority? Ask God to reveal any ways you fall short. Commit to changing, and go to your wife to make amends.
- ☐ Wives, have you identified any ways you have not been appropriately submissive? Read 1 Peter 3:1–6. Ask God to reveal any ways you fall short. Commit to changing, and go to your husband to make amends.
- ☐ Headship and submission are hard to do well. If you've also identified wounds in your heart that hinder your relationship, make a commitment to find healing.
- ☐ Review these resources:
  - ☐ Movie: *Evan Almighty*
  - ☐ Book: *Boundaries in Marriage* by Henry Cloud
  - ☐ Audio: *Let the Men be Men and Let the Women be Women* by Chris Mueller (found on sermonaudio.com)

☐ Use your Blueprint Space to draw both a simplistic and a sophisticated representation of marriage. For example, how does an umbrella represent marriage?

Blueprint Space

Chapter 21

On Becoming an "Us"

For everything there is a season, and a time for every matter under heaven: a time to be born, and a time to die; a time to plant, and a time to pluck up what is planted; a time to kill, and a time to heal; a time to break down, and a time to build up; a time to weep, and a time to laugh; a time to mourn, and a time to dance.
—Ecclesiastes 3:1–4

An excellent marriage does not just happen automatically. It happens when a couple stays the course of intentional hard work.
Marriage is an achievement.

How Relationships Develop

Relationships develop in stages similar to individuals. Our brain changes as we influence our partner and they influence us. Take a moment to consider how much you spend your life interacting with or thinking about your partner. All those experiences are stored in our brains!

Most everything stored is ultimately about ourselves, but most of what we know about ourselves is through relating to God and others. While every couple is different, every thriving marriage will progress through five developmental stages:

1. Blinded on the Rocks: 18 to 34 years old.
2. Disillusioned on the Path: 20 to 44 years old.
3. Distracted among the Thorns: 30 to 59 years old.
4. Fruitful in the Good Soil: 40 to 69+ years old.
5. Regrouping during Winter: 50+ years old.

Different stages require different types of growth from us. Because we can't predict the future, flexibility is important. It allows us to adjust to the climate of each new stage.

Notice the overlap in the age ranges. The stages map to specific periods of life, but they also cycle more quickly whenever new or novel challenges upset the normal flow of marriage. A couple can graduate to later stages but occasionally return to earlier stages. For example, a Good Soil couple in their fifties could return to the Path when an adult child moves back home.

Hopefully, the couple can handle difficult situations with more grace than when they were first married. But a chance exists that any trials will uncover weaknesses which return them to an earlier stage.

A person's emotional age is an average of their developmental progress. Developmentally, a ten-year-old doesn't complete all tasks from prior years on his birthday. Sometimes a ten-year-old acts like he is five. Since growth does not occur on a rigid schedule, we complete some tasks sooner than average and some later.

Similarly, some couples remain stuck in a stage for their entire marriage. For example, I've counseled couples stuck in stage two, Disillusioned, who have been fighting for thirty years.

All relationships have changing needs over time. Our expectations for a two-year-old are less than that of a twenty-year-old. Likewise, a less-developed couple will not be capable of functioning as well as a more-developed one. They are much more susceptible to turning against each other. Therefore, they must invest significant energy weathering the pressure needed to develop a solid "Us" identity.

The Stages of Developing "Us"

Tuckman's developmental stages for groups can be adjusted to apply to marriage—a team or group of two people. The seasons of God's natural design (spring, summer, fall, winter) fit the same stages.

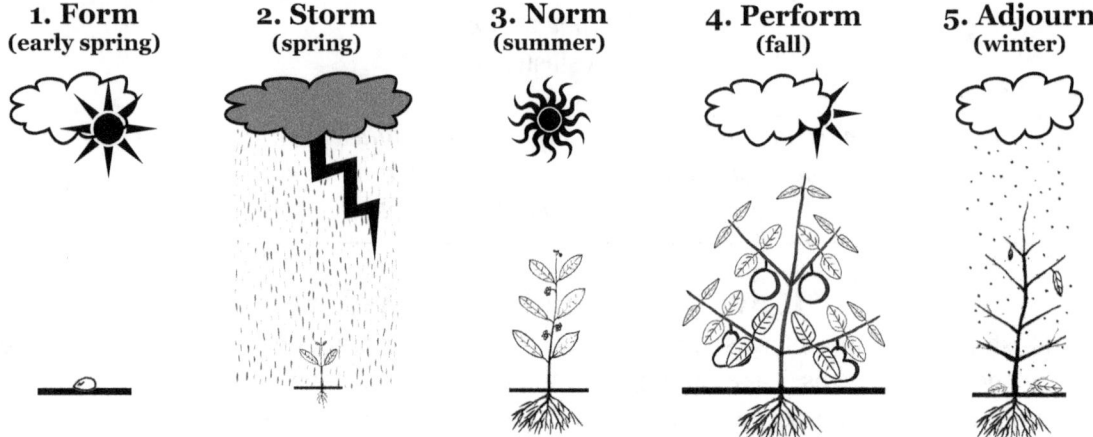

1. Forming on the Rocks – Early Spring

Early spring is a time to find suitable ground, cultivate it, and then plant what we want to grow.

This season of dating and courtship is the ideal time to experience each other, examine and test character, and evaluate whether or not God is calling you together for the rest of your lives. Success means developing a hunger for more than a superficial relationship.

When we start a relationship, we act cautiously, put our best foot forward, and usually hide our significant vulnerabilities. By default, relationships start out looking like the Rocks type—seeking the benefits of the relationship before putting much work into it. We are overly dependent upon an easy-going relationship to be at peace. This is by design, but a relationship needs roots in order to survive life's challenges.

No matter how well character is tested, the relationship starts fresh with the wedding. Dating, courtship, and premarital counseling provide knowledge but cannot provide the wisdom that comes from experience. After we've been married awhile, we have experiences to guide us for the future.

2. Storming on the Path – Spring

Spring is a time of rapid growth. Compare a newly planted seed (early spring) with a full-grown plant capable of flowering (summer). A lot must happen for a seed to become a flowering plant. A seed must take root, drink in nutrients, build a plant above ground, and produce flowers.

Spring is the time to establish the marriage, which can be challenging. A couple must go from being strangers to marriage, to achieving a basic competency in marriage. They must develop all kinds of intimacy with each other to be able to produce future fruit.

This stage is not called Storm by coincidence. Marriage has a way of bringing out each person's true self. They cannot accomplish tremendous growth while remaining isolated from the Storm. Success means developing the skills to resolve conflict rather than becoming consumed by it.

Husband and wife are blind to their own faults and focused on the other's faults. They become disillusioned by realizing their partner is not who they imagined before marriage. A feeling of desperation permeates the relationship because they have everything to lose. Moods tend to be at all-time lows.

The couple's hearts are much harder than they were at the beginning. They most resemble the Path type—fighting to form each other into their ideal mate. "I will fix my mate into the person I thought he or she would be," is currently the best solution to the crisis. To survive, they must address the crisis as efficiently as possible.

3. Norming among the Thorns – Summer

The chaos and frantic pace of spring ends with the long days of summer—scorching temperatures and cloudless skies with an occasional thunderstorm. If plants have not developed a sufficient root system, they will wither and die in the heat.

The relationship becomes sustainable when the couple is able to integrate the lessons learned from the Storm into their everyday lives. The relationship's growth is now steady rather than intense. This time of established routine allows for an important transition. The focus shifts from building intimacy to developing fruit because of the intimacy. Success means finding a balance between togetherness and separateness rather than settling for an increasingly distant relationship.

If husband and wife did not learn how to embrace conflict positively during the Storm, then the summer peace might be an attempt to avoid conflict. The Thorns represent a false victory. During the Storm, they failed at trying to change each other and lost hope in the relationship. Divorce is not an option, so they must find a way to make the best of the situation. Fearing further disappointment, they disengage from each other to focus on their own interests. Improving themselves remains out of the question as does risking intimacy. So the discouraging and selfish sentiment, "It's not worth the effort," rules their minds. They settle for distance by distraction.

4. Performing in the Good Soil – Fall

Fall is a joyous time as the couple harvests the fruits of their labor. Fall is also a time of peak performance where fruit can be multiplied many times over. Surviving spring and summer rewards the couple with delicious fruit. They have endured both unstable and stable times to finally experience tangible evidence of maturation. Success means reaping rewards without being selfish or becoming complacent.

Moods are at all-time highs. When you reach this stage, savor these moments. Save the memories to uplift others and yourselves at a less optimal time. In addition to enjoying your time of blessing, make use of the lessons learned and the wisdom you've gained.

Husband and wife juggle both individual and couple interests. Satisfaction replaces the anxious desperation of the Path and the numbing distance of the Thorns. They are able to experience gratitude for the positives and function as a productive team without harshness or indifference. They are ready to work but not desperately dependent on making the marriage work. The danger, if one exists, might be enjoying the relationship so much they neglect the outward fruitful mission.

5. Adjourn – Winter

Winter is a time of rest, renewal, and regrouping. Plants and seeds return to the ground. Husband and wife can pause and reflect on how far they have come and equip themselves for what is ahead.

Husband and wife continue to be positively focused on each other like in the Good Soil. The only exception would be if either experience a loss. Then, they could become stuck in their grief and neglect each other. Success means being prepared for next season rather than decaying into irrelevance. Preparations should be for the couple and for leaving behind a legacy.

There may be aspects of the relationship that can no longer be—not in this life anyway. Grieving these, if done right, strengthens the couple and prepares them to face future seasons. Health, career, and children all change while the relationship remains constant. Winter provides the opportunity to let go and embrace a new path, which will be a new season in this life or the next.

Surviving the Stages

We have our whole life to grow, but fully engaging in the present moment makes all the difference. We survive the stages and thrive by focusing our efforts on:
- Knowing and accepting where we are in our development;
- Catching up where we are behind (before marriage if possible);
- Embracing the unique purpose of each stage;
- Understanding the relationship between present difficulty and past wounding; and
- Seeking healing at the root of our wounding.

Focusing on one's own maturity benefits both partners. In moderation, spending time away from each other to recharge is healthy too. But pursuing an independent, "single" lifestyle robs marriage of its lifeblood. Every couple will find a different way to balance life successfully. However, we should not deceive ourselves into thinking marriage can survive with the leftovers.

For Reflection

1. Each season of marriage has a unique role is forging a strong relationship. You need to identify and embrace each season to make marriage last.
2. Marriage is a dynamic relationship. Because we change and grow over the years, we might be married to a "different" person during the different seasons of life. A successful marriage, then, means we adapt to the changing environment. We learn how to fall in love with the same person multiple times.
3. You need a "heads up" and goals for each stage so you do not become lost, overwhelmed, or stuck too long in any stage. Accomplish the detailed goals of each stage without lingering longer than necessary. Otherwise, you may lose sight of the bigger picture.
4. Below is a simple graph of morale across the stages. Find and label each stage.

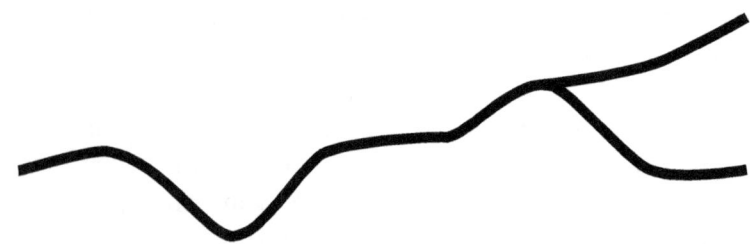

Next Steps

☐ What season are you currently in? How long have you been there? Are you stuck?
☐ Review these resources:
  ☐ Movie: *The Four Seasons*
  ☐ Book: *The Divorce Remedy* by Michele Weiner Davis

Chapter 22

The Storming "Us"

Everyone who comes to me and hears my words and does them, I will show you what he is like: he is like a man building a house, who dug deep and laid the foundation on the rock. And when a flood arose, the stream broke against that house and could not shake it, because it had been well built. But the one who hears and does not do them is like a man who built a house on the ground without a foundation. When the stream broke against it, immediately it fell, and the ruin of that house was great.
—Luke 6:47–49

Count it all joy, my brothers, when you meet trials of various kinds, for you know that the testing of your faith produces steadfastness. And let steadfastness have its full effect, that you may be perfect and complete, lacking in nothing.
—James 1:2–4

A bruised reed he will not break, and a faintly burning wick he will not quench; he will faithfully bring forth justice.
—Isaiah 42:3

What doesn't crush our spirit makes us stronger. Struggle and suffering will deepen our faith and connection to God, if we let it.

Why the Storm is Necessary

Surviving marriage requires navigating all the stages, especially the most difficult one: Storm. Storming is essential because it builds endurance. Attempting to avoid or skip this phase in any way means choosing to be an "I" instead of an "Us." Developing the "Us" requires:
- Investing time (and everything else you have too);
- Committing to complete honesty with no secrets;
- Valuing the idea of "Us" (married) over "I" (single);
- Realizing "Us" won't happen without effort and cost;
- Pursuing a win-win resolution as part of every decision.

Newlyweds who struggle the most begin marriage with four storm-causing liabilities:
1. Immaturity: needing to complete growth to be marriage-ready (the couple's baggage, emotional wounding, and brokenness).
2. Inexperience: lacking marital skills and intimate knowledge of each other.
3. Independence: familiar with thinking like an "I-ingrained" single.
4. Indecisiveness: aimlessly wandering from a lack of a defined mission.

We might take note that this list in some way or another describes all newlyweds.

During the honeymoon and the following months, a couple faces numerous adjustments and decisions. The primary goal of this stage is surviving; a close second is finding stability. Imagine this: after a pastor pronounces a couple husband and wife, we drop them into a forest in the middle of nowhere. If they immediately plan for their rescue, they will starve before help arrives. If they focus only on finding their next meal every day, they may never have enough time to think about how to get themselves rescued.

Since they might be there for a while, setting up camp is critical to their survival. They can focus on being rescued after they establish a way to last more than a day. Either way they must decide who will do what to keep them going until help arrives.

The Storm is not the problem; it is a necessary step towards becoming an "Us." The Storm transforms the couple. Before this stage, husband and wife are babes in the wood. They have their identity as husband and wife on paper but not much else. The couple needs the Storm because they don't know how to survive a Storm. What does not kill the couple makes them stronger.

Establishing Your Marriage

Spring is an essential season of marriage where we work hard on the relationship to clear the ground and establish plants in anticipation of a good harvest. But we must move on to summer (maturation), otherwise we will never get to autumn (and experience the fruit of our investment) and winter (where we can genuinely look back with satisfaction on our labor).

Spring is a time of transition not unlike childbirth. A dormant seed transforms into a living, growing plant. The necessity of rapid growth results in stress and pressure. By the end of the Storm, the couple has numerous shared life experiences.

A plant makes efficient use of spring to prepare for summer. A wise couple does too.

Challenges we face may not mean something is wrong with us, but instead, God provides them for us to grow through and become stronger. This is the only way to experience joy amidst trial. Just because life doesn't seem to be working doesn't mean it isn't. What's above the ground might not look like much, but below the ground, a root system is being established.

Establish[5] has three meanings that are particularly relevant to marriage:
1. To begin or create (something that is meant to last for a long time);
2. To cause (someone or something) to be widely known and accepted;
3. To put (someone or something) in a position, role, etc., that will last for a long time.

Often as early as the honeymoon, a couple's attempt to be closer automatically reveals areas of weakness:
1. Are they too guarded with "I" (too independent)? This prevents "Us" from developing because the two remain two.
2. Are they too careless with "I" (too dependent)? This prevents "Us" from developing because becoming one unified team requires two individuals.

Skipping the Storm holds a couple back from deeper, more intimate bonding and leaves them weak. Facing the Storm means finding answers to essential questions, such as:
- Given "Who am I?" and "Who are you?" then "What do we stand for?" and "How are we going to do this together?"
- Which direction should we take? How do we take all of who we are as individuals and move in the same direction?
- Can I be me and still be valued in this relationship?
- Who's in control? Can I trust my partner?
- How should we approach problems?

---

[5] learnersdictionary.com/definition/establish

- What is the right way (God's way) to do this?
- Where is our brokenness getting us stuck?
- What are our goals, priorities, and mission?
- Who is going to assume what roles to accomplish the goals?

These questions are not completely resolved during this stage, but they move from the back to the front of the couple's minds. They establish a new order to the relationship. Even with a lifetime together, a couple will not completely master being a team. Instead, they can ask themselves, "Are we growing better every year?"

Husband and wife during the Storming stage:
- Start to communicate their feelings but are often misunderstood;
- View themselves as (and act like) individuals rather than part of a team;
- Express dissatisfaction;
- Resist seeking and following God's input;
- Learn by trial and error;
- Experience low morale; and
- Struggle for order.

To succeed, the couple must:
- Allow time for the united partnership to develop;
- Tolerate a time of relative chaos while the relationship is forming; and
- Not leave each other behind as an isolated "I."

The transition to becoming a couple requires great transformation that involves leaving behind the familiar and entering the unknown. We must plant the seed (the "I") so it can grow into something else (the "Us").

> *Truly, truly, I say to you, unless a grain of wheat falls into the earth and dies, it remains alone; but if it dies, it bears much fruit.*
> —John 12:24

For Reflection

1. Faith is exactly what we need as God establishes us in our relationship with Him and our partner (Genesis 12:1–5).
2. Antonyms for mission are "hobby" or "recreation." Without entering and passing the Storm, your marriage is like a hobby. There may be superficial enjoyment but no fruit or legacy.
3. The relationship needs vulnerability and endurance.
4. Husband and wife achieve the majority of this stage's work during their first years together, but there is always room to improve. The patterns of this stage will recycle hundreds of times during the life of the marriage.
5. The Storm provides the opportunity for you to find your bearings (setting a new course as a married person) and your boundaries (what needs doing and who is responsible for what):
   - Know your partner's basic preferences;
   - Realize what you have gotten yourself into;
   - Know how to fight fairly or productively;
   - Know what your partner is like under pressure;
   - Find a working balance between closeness and separation; and
   - Establish a working routine for marriage.

Next Steps

- ☐ Consider a game where you and your partner each start with $5k and you each have $10k in debt. You can pay down your own debt or your partner's. To play, write down your choice before disclosing your decision. If you both choose to pay down your own debt, you will both owe $5k. If one of you pays the other's debt and the other pays their own debt, a $2k transfer fee applies, so the one will owe $12k and the other, nothing. If you both pay the other's debt, your debt is reduced by an additional $2k and you will both owe $4k. Play several rounds before discussing a strategy, then discuss a strategy and play again. For each round, start over with $5k each and $10k debt each. How does (or could) this exercise illustrate the Storm?
- ☐ Review the resources:
  - ☐ Movie: *Miracle*
  - ☐ Music: *Broken Together* by Casting Crowns
- ☐ Design a symbol that represents you in all your uniqueness. Have your partner do the same. Then work together to come up with one word that symbolizes the focal point of your marriage. Draw one picture that represents your marriage. Develop a motto (short phrase) that represents your marriage's purpose, aim, style, and mission.

Blueprint Space

Chapter 23

The Norming "Us"

The LORD is the everlasting God, the Creator of the ends of the earth. He does not faint or grow weary; his understanding is unsearchable. He gives power to the faint, and to him who has no might he increases strength. Even youths shall faint and be weary, and young men shall fall exhausted; but they who wait for the LORD shall renew their strength; they shall mount up with wings like eagles; they shall run and not be weary; they shall walk and not faint.
—Isaiah 40:28b–31

May the God of endurance and encouragement grant you to live in such harmony with one another, in accord with Christ Jesus, that together you may with one voice glorify the God and Father of our Lord Jesus Christ.
—Romans 15:5–6

A hobby is different from a personal mission. Jesus didn't live on Earth as a hobby. He came for a purpose and accomplished all God sent Him to do. A hobby is relaxed experimentation, similar to Sabbath. We should spend more time on mission than hobby. A person on a mission leaves no room for failure or giving up, only commitment, persistence and resolve.

What Is Normal?

Norming is an opportunity to recover passionate enjoyment. The Storm leaves us feeling defeated and needing to solidify the relationship. God provides summer so we can pause and figure out what happened during the Storm. Summer is the stepping-stone between the difficulty of the Storm and the joy of the Harvest. Without determination to overcome discouragement, couples drift further apart until they are virtually strangers.

Are you tired with weariness? Is this not what you signed up for? Be comforted. God never runs out of energy. His understanding is beyond us, but we are totally within His grasp. No matter your life situation, God will not abandon you during your journey! As you wait on (put your hope in) God, your inexhaustible source, He will revive and strengthen you.

Putting your hope in God by faith is renewing in itself.
God has not forsaken you! He is Faithful!

To successfully find normal, we can pursue these eight steps:

1) Grieve Individual Losses

Some things we wanted at the beginning of the relationship are no longer possible. We need to open our hands and let God have them. If they are part of God's plan, He will give them back to us when the time is right. For now, we grieve what cannot be and take time to heal from any discouragement uncovered by the Storm.

2) Keep the Household Running

Summer is a time to make the most of what we have. When coming off a setback, staying motivated to complete the endless list of household chores and work tasks is challenging. But being task-oriented for a while provides an opportunity to rest from the intensity of the Storm. Following an established routine most of the time helps to conserve energy. We are better off when we find a rhythm between the rest we need and the busyness of life.

However, we need to be careful. Summer can be long and hot. We can lose heart Norming as easily as Storming. Complacency can set in. Many couples hide in the routine and busyness—slowly drifting apart. The dryness of routines can sap the strength forged while facing the Storm.

3) Plan Fun Adventures

A lack of fun interaction can lull a marriage to its death. To avoid drifting, we can be intentional. Planning just-for-the-fun-of-it adventures is enough to keep us engaged with our partners. We can choose simple and low-key activities to avoid unnecessary conflict. We don't want to make the activities so intense we end up back in the Storm. We need to learn to communicate our feelings without serious conflict.

4) Empty Ourselves

Having tried all our own ways to make marriage work, we have no choice but to surrender. Our flesh tends to engage in wishful thinking. The dryness of the desert has a way of emptying us of our fleshly efforts that bear no fruit. This must happen so that we develop a passion for teaming together as an "Us."

We can use the time to maintain our gardens and pull the weeds that caused trouble. After all, we don't want to let the weeds grow so big they create another crisis.

One goal of Norming is to find contentment. Realizing we have nothing to lose quiets our fears and brings peace. We'll be okay even if nothing much changes anytime soon. Contentment recognizes what we have is good enough for now. All we need is enough to survive this day and to make it to the next day.

5) Learn from the Storm

We also need improvement, even if slow, over a lifetime. This kind of growth takes a lifetime, but the effort is worth the reward. As we find contentment with today, we can consider investing in what will move us to where we need to be tomorrow.

After the Storm, we know what works and what doesn't work. We should take advantage of this as nothing we experience is wasted. God makes use of our experiences, good and bad alike. By stepping back from the chaos of the Storm, we can plan to endure for the long haul.

6) Wait for God

We don't have to rush into discussing difficult topics. When we seek God, He moves us forward when the time is right. The relationship will grow steadily and surely when we take the needed time to work out serious disagreements. By waiting upon the Lord, we experience increased morale. He renews our energy so we can leave behind what has been and look forward to what will be.

7) Dare to Hope Again

We can take risks, and our partner will still be with us. Marriage might not be everything we wanted, but by no means has anyone ever exhausted its potential. We can dream with our partner about all that is possible. Each step brings us closer to the goal: a stable and fruitful marriage. This kind of marriage matters to:

- Us and our partner;
- God;
- Our children; and
- The community around our marriage.

8) Build from a Renewed Vision

Having waited on God, we are ready to move forward with our goals. This time around, we have enough experience to choose more realistic but still positive and stretching goals. We don't have to start from scratch. Perhaps with God's help we can even salvage the original vision.

Marriage is better when we implement it God's way—resulting in 100 times the investment. God gives us this priceless, unique building opportunity. He provides the materials and the design, and He does the heavy lifting. All we have to do is decide to participate.

For Reflection

1. Without a clear vision and a desire to see a vision become a reality, rebuilding will be difficult, if not impossible. What is your vision?
2. The opposite of love is not hate; love and hate share the same degree of passion. The opposite of love is indifference.
3. The first few verses of Psalm 40 keep hope alive. Return to them when you feel discouraged.

I waited patiently for the LORD; he inclined to me and heard my cry. He drew me up from the pit of destruction, out of the miry bog, and set my feet upon a rock, making my steps secure. He put a new song in my mouth, a song of praise to our God. Many will see and fear, and put their trust in the LORD.
—Psalm 40:1–3

Next Steps

- Be intentional about refreshing your understanding of why you are staying together. Know the answer to: "Why is the struggle worth staying married?" You won't drift as long as you act on this knowledge.
- Answer these questions about your garden:
  - What weeds do you need to pull?
  - What structure do you need to put in place to keep your garden maintained?
  - What adventures have you been on as a couple?
  - How long has it been since you enjoyed life's adventures together? If it's been awhile, plan something now.
- What do you need to commit to in order to move your relationship to the Perform stage?
- Review these resources:
  - Movie: *Shadowlands*
- Use your Blueprint Space to plan your future. Ask the tough questions. Write about what you want to be doing in one, three, five, and ten years.
- If any of these topics are difficult to discuss, be sure to complete following chapters on communication and conflict resolution.

Blueprint Space

Chapter 24

The Performing and Adjourning "Us"

---

*Other seeds fell on good soil and produced grain
some a hundredfold, some sixty, some thirty.*
—Matthew 13:8

*Love is patient and kind; love does not envy or boast;
it is not arrogant or rude. It does not insist on its own way;
it is not irritable or resentful; it does not rejoice at wrongdoing,
but rejoices with the truth. Love bears all things,
believes all things, hopes all things, endures all things.*
—1 Corinthians 13:4–7

*There is no losing with God,
only learning how to do it better next time.*

Harvest Time

To be mature enough to bear fruit, a couple works hard and endures many ups-and-downs. But celebrating their accomplishments and victories is an essential step in the growth process. God wants us to enjoy the fruits of our labor. We need to find ways to remember the victories because hard times will likely visit us again.

---

*I perceived that there is nothing better for them than to be joyful and to do
good as long as they live; also that everyone should eat and drink and take
pleasure in all his toil—this is God's gift to man.*
—Ecclesiastes 3:12–13

Fruitful Teamwork

God sees a husband and wife's fruitfulness according to how well they love each other and how well their love reaches outside the marriage. A loving couple bears, believes, hopes, and endures. No couple will perform like the perfect team, but we need a clear picture to guide our efforts. In practical terms, the Performing husband and wife:

- Work proactively to benefit each other;
- No longer need to be "fair" about everything—their growing love and history together tolerates imbalance;
- Communicate their feelings with openness and trust;
- Experience increasingly positive moods and morale;
- Recognize the mission is more important than petty details;
- Embrace responsible ownership of their roles;
- Function efficiently as an interdependent team—better than as individuals;

- Balance task completion (working in the relationship) with process communication (working on the relationship).

The Secret to Abundant Fruit

To establish our marriage, we should focus inwardly for the first few years. This builds a foundation for strong growth and fruitfulness in later years. Attempting to produce fruit for others too soon could weaken the foundation. Besides, our children will benefit as much or more than we will from the fruit of a thriving marriage. They will feed off it. However, if we invest all our energy into our kids, they will lack a strong model to copy when they are adults. Everyone is better off when we prioritize our lives from the inside out.

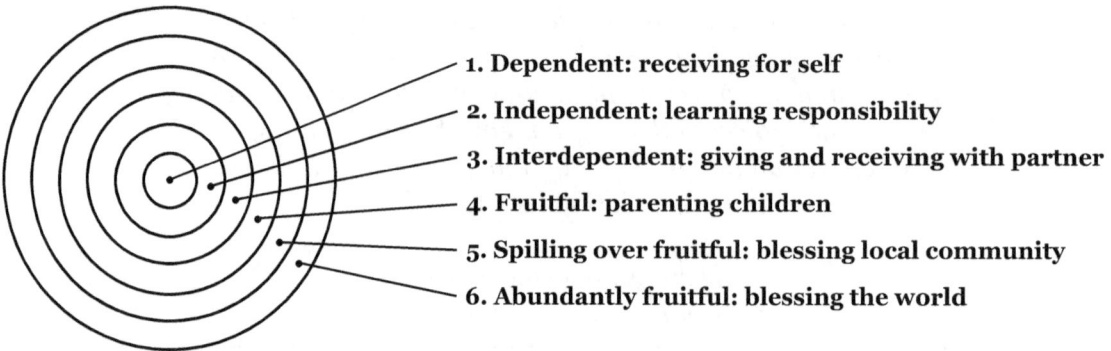

1. Dependent: receiving for self
2. Independent: learning responsibility
3. Interdependent: giving and receiving with partner
4. Fruitful: parenting children
5. Spilling over fruitful: blessing local community
6. Abundantly fruitful: blessing the world

Getting to the finish line at all costs is not the goal. In fact, skipping steps short-circuits the whole process. Completing each step in turn is not selfish but ensures abundant fruit. God's plan really is a long-range plan that requires patient endurance at each stage.

To succeed, we need to be fully present in the season of life at hand. God's design for marriage gives us the assurance we need to embrace the work He has for us.

*Let your work be shown to your servants,
and your glorious power to their children.
Let the favor of the Lord our God be upon us,
and establish the work of our hands upon us;
yes, establish the work of our hands!*
—Psalm 90:16–17

Whether we work hard in our hometowns or share the gospel in the remotest parts of the world, we shouldn't neglect our families. What a tragedy it is if we consistently neglect our own families while meeting the needs of strangers! We should only expand our territory as we can manage the territory we already have. As God provides for and blesses us, we can give more. From the abundance of a life well-lived, there is an overflow that leaves a legacy.

Winter

The stillness of winter begs for taking the time to pause and reflect. We know that rest is part of life—God rested on the seventh day. We would be foolish not to rest and listen to God. What does He have in store for us in the coming year?

De-reflection[6] is letting go of our normal level of intensity and letting life be. For example, after trying to make a difficult decision without success, de-reflect by watching a movie or going bowling with friends. This provides an opportunity to relax with one another and to see our past performance from new perspectives.

Grieve and Grow

The Winter season is also a time to process loss. We experience sadness and grief over what will never be and acknowledge and accept permanent changes. For example:
- Death of a partner, child, or parent;
- Health issues; infertility;
- Job loss;
- Empty nest; and
- Other life transitions.

If our partner passes before we do, we grieve, but we shouldn't give up on life. In the movie *Up*, Carl learns that when the journey together is over, a new journey can begin.

Multiply the Mission

We shouldn't stop growing when we reach fruitfulness. Mastering the stages includes staying hungry for more growth. God has more for us in the right season.

But what if we evaluate our lives and find ourselves lacking? Then we can savor what worked and learn from our mistakes.

If we've made it to the Performing stage and have seen fruit, is a false victory possible? Maybe. But, this does not mean we've failed. We are never losers. Even when we don't win, we learn how to do it better next time.

Attitudes that stall future growth include:
- We're happy—no need to talk about those difficult topics.
- We're good at loving each other—no need to bother with others.
- We've arrived at the finish line—no further growth is needed.

Remember that God's design for marriage is for us to subdue and dominate. We have a mission to focus our efforts. God wants us to keep expanding our spheres of influence as He provides for us. Our current plans might be well suited for the coming seasons, or a greater transformation may be necessary. We might end up going in a completely new direction which we couldn't possibly have planned because we had no idea where we'd be at this time in our lives.

Leave a Legacy

Whether on a small scale or a large scale, God would have us live in a way to leave behind a legacy for future generations. This can be raising children, focusing on grandchildren, developing a ministry that serves people, or making any other positive lasting changes.

We will not hide them from their children,
but tell to the coming generation
the glorious deeds of the LORD, *and his might,*
and the wonders that he has done.
—Psalm 78:4

---

[6] medical-dictionary.thefreedictionary.com/dereflection

For Reflection

1. What is the best way to celebrate your accomplishments?
2. What kind of person do you want to be? Can you be the person who loves unconditionally?

Next Steps

- [ ] The five stages might cycle around every year, ten years, or even twenty years depending on the difficulty of what you are trying to accomplish and how much energy you have to focus on growth. A pattern exists to the stages and cycles. Learn to recognize which stage you are in, so you can adjust your expectations. When you are in a difficult season that is dragging on, see your progress in the bigger picture so you can remain positive. Look to the stages as a map so you don't become lost in the midst of the trials and busyness of life.
- [ ] Answer these questions to evaluate and plan for your marriage's next season:
  - What should you a) start doing, b) continue doing, c) stop doing?
  - What is one thing your partner would change about you (if they could)?
  - What is one thing you would change about your partner (if you could)?
  - What is one thing you want to change about yourself?
  - What is one thing God wants from you?
  - What is one thing you wish your partner understood about you?
- [ ] Review these resources:
  - [ ] Movie: *Up*
  - [ ] Movie: *The Story of Us*
- [ ] Use your Blueprint Space to review your vows. Consider renewing your vows. What changes, if any, would you make to them? Share your vows with your partner.

Blueprint Space

Chapter 25

Your Past Affects Conflict Resolution

Know this, my beloved brothers: let every person be quick to hear, slow to speak, slow to anger; for the anger of man does not produce the righteousness of God.
—James 1:19–20

Our past can only have power over our present when we ignore or discount it. Unprocessed, it has the power to influence every aspect of our present moment and therefore limit our future. No matter how long ago we experienced neglect or abuse, it shapes who we are today unless we override it with a new, more powerful experience.

Your Past and Your Conflicts

We can better manage conflict by understanding the driving motives behind our behaviors. Two husbands with different motives could say the same words each to his own wife. And each wife, based on her life experiences, could interpret those words in different ways. One husband could speak from a good spirit, yet his wife can still interpret his words negatively. The other husband could speak with a bad spirit, and yet his wife interprets it positively. For example, both husbands could say, "Would you like me to help with the dishes?" One wife, believing her husband wants to help, responds, "Sure. Thanks for helping!" Another wife, believing her husband is suggesting he can do it better, responds, "No thanks! I can handle washing the dishes."

How is this possible?

Despite how extreme it may sound, this type of miscommunication happens all the time. The key to understanding *why* has to do with how our brains store our experiences. We have two main types of memories:

1. Implicit memories are beyond our conscious awareness and are more emotion-based. We experience implicit memories subjectively, with little or no distance between ourselves and the memory. Often, we can experience the effects of the memory without actually remembering what happened. We relive the experience as if we had hopped into a time machine and travelled back to the experience. Concerning self, implicit memories are, "how I feel about myself."

2. Explicit memories are easily recalled and are more fact-based. We experience them objectively, with some emotional distance between ourselves and the memory. We recall them as historical, autobiographical events. Concerning self, explicit memories are, "how I think about myself."

Explicit and Implicit memory observations:
- There are more memories below the surface than above;
- The memories below the surface continue to influence behaviors and decisions;
- To the degree significant unprocessed memories exists below, we fly blindly;
- As we become more aware of what is below, we become whole and integrated.

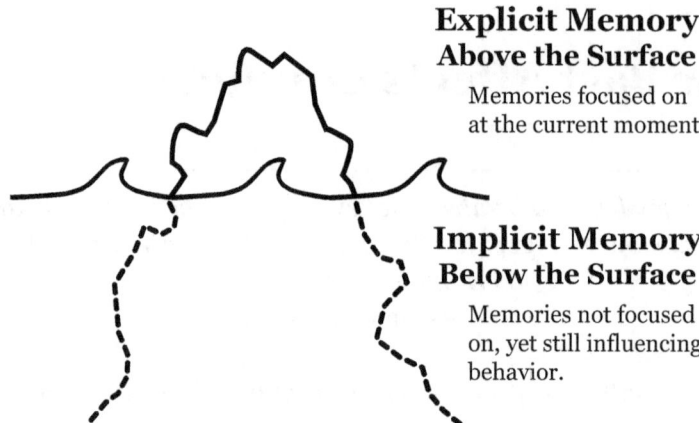

Past hurtful experiences will affect us until we work to heal them. A good goal to reduce conflict involves an ongoing plan to explore below the surface and make the unknown known. Here is an example that details how painful events are stored in the brain and what must happen to heal them.

- Eight-year-old Mary is verbally attacked by her dad for not playing well at her soccer tryout. The brain stores traumatic events as raw sensory data in the brain. The stored data might be feeling scared, having a headache or stomachache, smelling her dad's coffee breath, and sweating from the hot sun on her face. The memory stays in this form until Mary is ready to process it.
- Mary's mom is aware of the situation but fears being yelled at herself so she doesn't comfort her daughter. When a caregiver is available to help process the experience, emotional situations normally are resolved as they happen. But overwhelming experiences without any support must be frozen in time and saved for a later day.
- Mary disconnects from her heart, perhaps while still believing the truth, "God loves me," in her head. But she isn't aware of her core longing to feel accepted even though it drives her behaviors.
- Her dad's verbal attacks fester and feed her the lie, "I am not good enough," even after she forgets the incident by putting it out of her conscious awareness. Believing the lie, Mary doesn't perform well in other areas of her life.
- When Mary is sixteen, she tries out for high school basketball, but feels anxious and sick to her stomach when she smells the male coach's coffee breath. Having forgotten what happened when she was eight, Mary is confused as to why she doesn't feel well. She doesn't make the team.
- To heal her wounding, Mary must revisit the pain in her implicit memory with another person so she can be comforted. As she was hurt in the context of a relationship, so she needs a relationship to help her metabolize her pain.
- After Mary tells her mom about not feeling well at the basketball tryouts, her mom helps her remember what happened eight years earlier during the soccer tryouts. Her mom's compassion helps Mary process both experiences and let go of some of the "I am not good enough" lie.
- Processing the trauma transforms how the brain stores her experience. The implicit memory becomes an explicit memory and is stored in the brain differently—in a logical, organized story format.

- Mary will know she is healed when she no longer becomes triggered in the present and can tell her full story about trying out for sports. When she tries out for soccer, she feels more confident, and makes the team.

Amygdala Gender Differences

The part of the brain called the amygdala is the emotional learning center. It processes sensory input, sorting experiences by their significance. Terrifying, life-threatening experiences rank the highest. The amygdala aids other parts of the brain in organizing memories. It prioritizes our memories, storing more intense experiences in more detail, so we have sufficient information to heal when we are ready.

The amygdala promotes the organization of implicit memories by evaluating sensory input to determine if a threat exists. During a perceived threat, it can tell the body to react before the rest of the brain can analyze the data to determine if the threat is real. The hippocampus, another part of the brain near the amygdala, organizes explicit memories (short- and long-term memories that we can actively recall from conscious awareness).

Males and females are wired to use the amygdala differently:
- Males have larger amygdalae;
- Females tend to retain stronger memories from emotional events;
- The right amygdala is linked to taking action; when processing fear, males use the right amygdala more than the left;
- The left amygdala is linked to recall and thinking through details; when processing fear, females use the left amygdala more than the right;

These differences might explain why women are more likely to either shut down ("freeze") or want to talk through and make sense of a tense and difficult conversation while men either become violent ("fight") or withdraw ("flight") from a perceived threat.

The Problem is Not the Problem

During a conflict, we are only aware of our explicit memories. Even though we are not aware of our implicit memories, they nonetheless contribute to our behaviors and responses. Any reaction not from an explicit memory must come from an implicit memory. This adds many unknown variables to any emotional experience, such as conflict with a partner.

Our brains are made up of associated networks. Our memories are stored in a generalized way, and therefore, they can be triggered by similar experiences. Mary didn't remember having a bad experience with soccer as a child, but she became uneasy trying out for basketball and didn't understand why. Similar experiences are linked together so that if she experiences something similar ("smelling coffee at basketball tryouts"), nearby networks ("dad's coffee breath") might activate ("I feel uneasy"). This is called a generalization, which may be why we speak in exaggerated language at times. Without her mom to help her remember, Mary might have settled somewhere in her heart, "I hate playing sports," or, "all older men are mean."

In the future, when Mary's husband yells at her for breaking the lawn mower, she is primed to over-react because of her prior similar experiences. She would be especially vulnerable if she didn't have a healing experience with her mom when she was sixteen.

Understanding how the brain works, can you see how two people might have a difficult time managing their reactions during a heated conflict? Most of the time, the problem is more about implicit memories than present circumstances! The problem is what each has learned about themselves and others through previous experiences. Because many of those experiences are not in conscious awareness, many couples do not understand what they are fighting about.

For Reflection

1. The past is alive until fully processed and healed. We won't be fully healed in this life, but we can make significant improvements. No matter how old the memory, it can be healed.
2. If you don't like the iceberg analogy, consider you are walking late at night. All you have is a flashlight. Whatever you can see with the flashlight represents your conscious thought. Everything else is "out of sight, out of mind."
3. Memories need to be reinterpreted with the understanding of the truth we know today. Consider revisiting significant memories every five-to-ten years to see how your perception of them has changed.
4. Does conflict from unfairness ("everything must be fair") come from a selfish partner or from unresolved childhood issues of never feeling like things could go your way?
5. We are most hurt when we receive a message that we are deficient or lacking in some way. We need encouragement (positive reinforcement), but we end up discouraged (because of negative reinforcement).
6. How vulnerable are we to believing the wrong things about ourselves? Don't we all battle every day with putting off what is false and putting on what is true? Any healthy conflict should not lose sight of this. Say what is encouraging for building others up. Speak the truth, but only in love.
7. Because of childhood abuse and neglect, we can choose independence as our primary mode of living. We might dismiss our natural God-given desires to be close and affectionate, and to make purposeful life decisions from our heart, the center of our being. We tune out the spiritual life. Despite all this, we wonder why life seems meaningless and drab. We say we cannot remember our childhood. But maybe we rationalize that the past is irrelevant so we don't have to face the pain. In truth, the past and others are a rich source of meaning that we cannot ignore.

Next Steps

- ☐ Do you ever feel a strong sense of rejection, negativity, or depression when you have a legitimate heart's desire and your partner either does not want to cooperate or cannot cooperate with meeting your needs? Review earlier chapters on core longings and lies. Identify any lies you are believing during conflict about meeting your needs.
- ☐ Think through a recent, difficult conflict with your partner. Identify at least one prior experience that made the conflict even worse.
- ☐ Create a map of your memories related to your reaction to conflict. Record the narrative of what happened, the sensory experiences, and the associating links between memories.
- ☐ Leaving is an emotional process. Just because you have physically left your parents' home, doesn't mean you've left completely. You could be hundreds of miles away, but still be inappropriately attached to your parents. Or you could be living around the corner and be healthily separated. Weeding is removing obstacles to intimacy. Anything that prevents one-flesh intimacy is a weed. For example, remaining overly attached to parents can prevent intimacy. Other life events can result in us choosing to insulate ourselves against genuine intimacy. What weeds are growing in your marriage?
- ☐ Review these resources:
  - ☐ Movie: *Good Will Hunting*
  - ☐ Book: *The Developing Mind* by Daniel Siegel (for in-depth study)
  - ☐ Site: en.wikipedia.org/wiki/Amygdala
  - ☐ Site: en.wikipedia.org/wiki/Implicit_memory

Chapter 26

Intentional Communication

Do not lie to one another, seeing that you have put off the old self with its practices and have put on the new self, which is being renewed in knowledge after the image of its creator.
—Colossians 3:9–10

And the man and his wife were both naked and were not ashamed.
—Genesis 2:25

The worst way to communicate is to say nothing or do nothing to confirm others understand you. The best communication is intentional, honest, intimate, affirming, and confirming.

Revealing our Truest Self

Speaking is as easy as opening our mouth. Communication requires intentional thought to reach mutual understanding. Successful communication is not super-complicated, but it does require significant effort. This chapter identifies and explains communication's essential components.

The goal of communication is understanding. But understanding does not guarantee agreement. Actually, understanding highlights both agreements and differences. Differences can be bonding, repulsing, or sometimes both! Abraham received a message from God to sacrifice Isaac. He understood clearly what God wanted. The message repulsed him, but because of his previous positive experiences with God, he trusted Him and received the message anyway (Genesis 22).

To communicate clearly, we must know and reveal ourselves. I've divided communication into nine levels from revealing to concealing:

Level	What is Shared	
4	Hopes and Dreams	Increasingly **Revealing**
3	Feelings	Complete and Truest Self:
2	Opinions	Transparent, Vulnerable, and
1	Facts	Intimate
0	Cliches	
-1	Omissions	
-2	Lies	Increasingly **Concealing**
-3	Deceptions	Complete and Truest Self:
-4	Only what serves Self-Purpose	Hidden, Guarded, and Distant

To the degree couples miscommunicate, they miss each other's meaning and are no longer building the relationship. In the worst case, they introduce harmful words that not only block communication but multiply emotional harm. An innocent miscommunication can turn into a full conflict because of our core longing to be understood.

Four communication goals bring order to otherwise chaotic discussions: Intimacy, Integrity, Clarity, and Agreement. Each goal has its own efficient "language" that focuses communication efforts. Like any language, familiarity and practice increases skill.

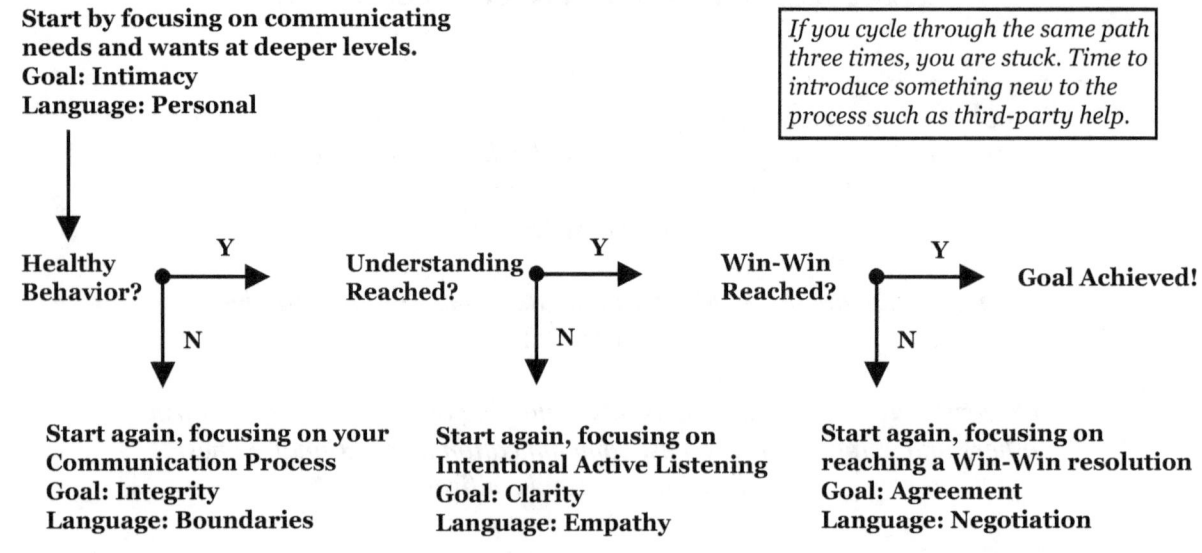

Goal: Intimacy; Language: Personal

We communicate to reveal more about ourselves—specifically, our opinions, feelings, needs, and desires. Ideally, our goal is to share fully all that we are, our most complete and truest self, with our partner. The language style to use is the most personal we have. We can use romantic pet names like "honey" or "babe." We can say, "I love you. I need you. I am glad you are in my life. I am so happy you are here by my side."

Deep personal language is like a secret code. Only the couple can possibly know the real meaning because of their experiences together. Developing this language strengthens the couple's unique bond.

Intimacy is increased to the degree we are fully present in body, mind, and spirit. The most intimate communication involves touching body, mind, and spirit. To be intimate requires transparency. Disclosing your truest self means sharing your dreams, plans, secret sins, weaknesses, and vulnerabilities.

Intimacy has a positive side and a negative side. But in reality, the negative can become a positive when the message is communicated openly. Honesty increases closeness even when the message is bad news. "I am falling out of love" is as important as "I love you." Both are positive when the heart behind the message is pro-marriage. Both statements fight for marriage.

Deception is a form of avoidance. When we avoid problems and conflict, we avoid closeness. We shouldn't see our partner as someone we might hurt or offend. We can respect them by giving them the opportunity to handle what we have to say. "My partner will be angry if I say that. We are better off if I keep my mouth shut." This is only rationalizing wrong thoughts and behaviors. We can let our goal be to push for the crossover point in marriage where we will only gain by deeply sharing our innermost thoughts with our partner. We can speak up now instead of waiting until after we sin and are caught.

Communication only makes sense when it adds value. If we've addressed our concerns and our partner is not hearing us, then we need to use discernment to determine how often we should revisit the issue.

Goal: Integrity; Language: Boundaries

When unhealthy behaviors show up during conversations, we need to shift away from the subject of our communication (the content) towards how we are communicating (the process). Before we can make progress with our concern, we need to make progress with our communication skills. The new focus becomes improving the communication process. The language style utilizes cause and effect by setting clear boundaries. For example, "If you can't keep your voice down, I am going to leave the house for a while."

In analyzing communication, we look for goodness and assertiveness. How loving and encouraging are we versus being hateful and bitter versus being indifferent and cold? How assertive are we versus being aggressive versus being passive? The purpose is to step back and restore order to the conversation to prevent further harm.

In the best case, we can pro-actively plan an important conversation. The plan should include the "pre-talk": how we are going to introduce our topic. We say what we are going to do before we do it. We talk about what we want to talk about, before we talk about it. We own the responsibility by gaining our partner's permission to speak freely. For example, "I'm feeling angry. Is now a good time to talk about how I'm feeling?" This sets expectations at levels that increase the chance for success.

Goal: Clarity; Language: Empathy

When frustration escalates, husband and wife need to focus more specifically on understanding each other. The language style to use is active and empathic listening. For the moment, solving the problem is second to understanding each other. If necessary, they can further slow things down by having one person focus on sharing while the other focuses on listening. The speaker should speak as succinctly as possible. The listener can encourage the speaker to move into deeper, more revealing communication. Both work together to eliminate assumptions and gain insight.

Goal: Agreement; Language: Negotiation

The goal of negotiation is reaching agreement with one another. This is more difficult when husband and wife lack intimacy, integrity, and clarity. For negotiation to be successful, we must strongly desire unity and respect each other's preferences. An agreement will not last if either one feels the terms are imbalanced.

Brainstorming is the first step of negotiation. For example, "What if we vacationed in Florida instead of California?" Negotiation will also be easier to the degree husband and wife have the same spiritual worldview. No husband and wife share the exact same values and priorities. However, life is easier when the big picture items match.

Blocks to Communication

Miscommunication is a normal part of life. But chronic miscommunication is concerning because it leads to chronic unresolved conflict which leads to distance, relationship breakdown, and dissolution. All the things that make people unique and special are the very things that can lead to miscommunication. We can boil down communication problems into differences in Nature, Nurture, and Needs.

Nature and Nurture

Differences in gender and personality may result in frustration when trying to understand each other. Likewise, differences in experiences can make communication difficult.

"Let's get a pet dog." Imagine what this conversation might look like when one person has had mostly positive experiences with dogs, but the other has had mostly negative experiences. Consider the conversation both before and after the couple realizes their experiences are different.

We interpret words by the vividness of prior experiences. Our native language is the sum of our experiences and the identity God wires into us. Experiences and identity determine current needs. Therefore, to avoid miscommunication, we must:
- Be aware of our experiences and identity.
- Be aware of our partner's experiences and identity.

Intimacy suffers when we don't reveal our true identity. Shame is a distortion in our identity that we agree with deep within ourselves. It greatly muddies the waters of communication.

> **God made us unique for good purposes, but our enemy twists all that is good for evil purposes. Evil can press us into shame by influencing us to believe we are uniquely and hopelessly different. Evil tries to tell us, "You are not uniquely capable of valuable contribution. You are a freak of nature: worthless, pointless, and useless for anything good." When we feel shame, we feel it to the depth of who we are, and this distorts our ability to communicate meaningfully.**

We need to develop the patience and desire to both know and be known. Without understanding who we are or who our partner is, appreciation is impossible. Miscommunication is an opportunity to discover and accept more of who we really are.

Needs

Problems surrounding our needs further confuse communication:
- Personal dysfunctions (sins) while trying to meet core longings, including passive conflict avoidance and aggressive conflict pursuit;
- Not knowing what we want or why we want it;
- Not differentiating between needs and wants;
- Not desiring the same levels of intimate communication.

Also, technology can allow communication when it would otherwise be impossible. But technology can also reduce intimacy when it would otherwise be possible. When we use technology, are we avoiding more intimate contact for any conscious or unconscious reasons? Anything less than fully present face-to-face relating means some aspect of communication is missing. When using technology, think about what is missing or what could be hidden.
- Video Chat: cannot touch or smell;
- Phone: cannot see, touch or smell;
- Chatting, texting, writing letters or email: cannot hear, see, touch, or smell.

For Reflection

1. When you are honest, you are always vulnerable to rejection. But love is not a shelter from the truth. It empowers us to face the truth.
2. Communication is more than an exchange of information; it transforms both the speaker and listener. The more we are present with each other, the more we influence each other. Presence means we are open to allowing another's words and actions to change us. Real communication

involves two vulnerable people ready to influence and be influenced, to impact and be impacted.
3. Conflict could result from misunderstanding or misperception. Therefore, fifty percent of conflict resolution is sorting fact from fiction, perception from reality.
4. Will what you have to say improve upon the silence?
5. Frustration with communication happens all the time because we want to be understood implicitly (without effort). Not being "gotten" isn't much fun. Being understood is a core longing for all of us.
6. Communication is an iterative process. To communicate effectively, you first have to know what you really want. If you don't understand yourself, how will it be easy for others to understand you? However, often the only way to get better at knowing what we want is to practice talking about it.

Next Steps

- ☐ For each statement below, answer these two questions. Do you agree or disagree? How does it play out in your relationship?
    - You cannot love without knowing who you are trying to love.
    - The closer two people appear to be, the greater the room for miscommunication.
    - I am only responsible for what I say, not for what you understand.
- ☐ Consider how each of these statements could lead to miscommunication. Add a pre-talk sentence to introduce the topic.
    - _____ I'm ready for a vacation.
    - _____ Let's decorate the house.
    - _____ Would you like some help?
    - _____ Why are you late?
    - _____ Let's go out for dinner.
    - _____ I'm going to bed early.
    - _____ You never initiate sexual intimacy.
    - _____ You spend too much money on frivolous things.
- ☐ Eliminate secrets between you and your partner. Identify the oldest truth your partner doesn't know about you. Remove the barrier to intimacy. Tell your partner.
    - How does it benefit you to keep secrets?
    - Who is the real you that you are afraid to reveal?
- ☐ Review these resources:
    - ☐ Movie: *The Horse Whisperer*
    - ☐ Book: *Why Am I Afraid To Tell You Who I Am?* by John Powell
    - ☐ Book: *Love and Respect* by Emerson Eggerichs
    - ☐ Book: *Fighting for Your Marriage* by Scott Stanley
    - ☐ Book: *Released from Shame* by Sandra Wilson
    - ☐ Book: *Shame & Grace* by Lewis Smedes

☐ Use your Blueprint Space to plan a pre-talk with your partner.

Blueprint Space

Chapter 27

The Four Languages of Love

Husbands, love your wives, and do not be harsh with them.
—Colossians 3:19

And so train the young women to love their husbands and children.
—Titus 2:4a

Let my beloved come to his garden, and eat its choicest fruits.
—Song of Solomon 4:16b

God intends for us to love with a complete love. When attended to, love and romance grow as we progress through the stages of life. Time and effort allow love to reach its passionate potential. If your love grows stale and you feel distant from each other, something is not going well; your relationship needs renewed attention to become an amazing experience.

Stepping into Love

We need four types of love for complete love in marriage. C.S. Lewis calls these *agape*, *philia*, *storge*, and *eros*. They correspond easily to four different expressions of our being: Spiritual, Thinking, Emotional, and Physical (STEP). We reach the deepest intimacy when we develop all four expressions in the right order.

Spiritual—Agape

The first STEP is discovering your, and your partner's, spiritual worldview. Spiritual love, the supernatural *agape* love that can only come from God, is the foundation for a successful marriage. Initially, appearance attracts most people to each other. But understanding each other's spiritual worldview is essential before sharing other loves. *Agape* love is an unconditional commitment to your partner and ultimately to God.

If you happen to be single, learn your potential partner's character and belief system before progressing too far in a relationship. Character and worldview provide a framework of safety for the other loves to flourish and are essential in establishing a godly marriage.

In Colossians 3:19, the word for love is *agapate*. Paul is instructing men to unconditionally love their wives. Men typically find it easier to like their wives than to love them. A man appreciates his wife's inner beauty more easily than he can sacrifice his desires for her benefit.

Thinking—Philia

The second STEP is developing a friendship by sharing and learning intimate details about each other. We need to share our thoughts to gain understanding of our partner. In Titus 2:4, the word for love is *philandrous*. Paul is instructing women to like their husbands. Women typically love well but might struggle to like their husbands. A woman naturally sacrifices her needs to take care of her husband and children, but she finds it harder to genuinely like her husband's crudeness. Husbands tend to like their wives but struggle to express the liking in words.

Emotional—Storge

The third STEP is sharing affection with each other. As we move closer together, our "liking" of each other produces a natural affection and emotional attachment. Being emotionally demonstrative and vulnerable with someone is not possible without first knowing something about them (STEP Two) nor is it prudent without knowing their spiritual maturity (STEP One).

Physical—Eros

The fourth STEP is sharing all we have physically with our partner. After sharing everything spiritually, intellectually, and emotionally, the natural next step is being as physically close as possible. This is the most personal, intimate connection and the only STEP God reserves exclusively for marriage. We maximize its potential to the degree we love with the first three STEPs.

Preparing a Banquet

Moving toward complete love requires an openness to embracing all four loves. God intends for a couple to build and maintain their relationship by walking the STEPs. A couple needs to walk the STEPs at the beginning of their relationship as well as throughout their relationship. Revisiting the STEPs allows the couple to focus on new aspects they missed during previous walks.

We can compare full love to a banquet:
1. Spiritual unconditional commitment is best represented by the table service. You cannot eat a plate or a cup, but they provide easy delivery of the food. An unconditional commitment protects the other more vulnerable loves.
2. Thinking about and knowing one another is best represented by the main meal—the "meat and potatoes." The main meal provides a primary source of energy.
Companionship is the day-to-day relationship that holds everything else together.
3. Emotional affection is best represented by the side dishes of various dairies, grains, vegetables, and seasonings. They provide essential flavor and nutrients to sustain our bodies. Affection involves the more personal and endearing aspects of a relationship.
4. Physical intimacy is best represented by dessert (fruits and sweets). Dessert is intensely pleasurable and therefore addicting. Sexual intimacy provides the ultimate personal touch for our enjoyment. We become addicted (bonded) to our partner in a good way.

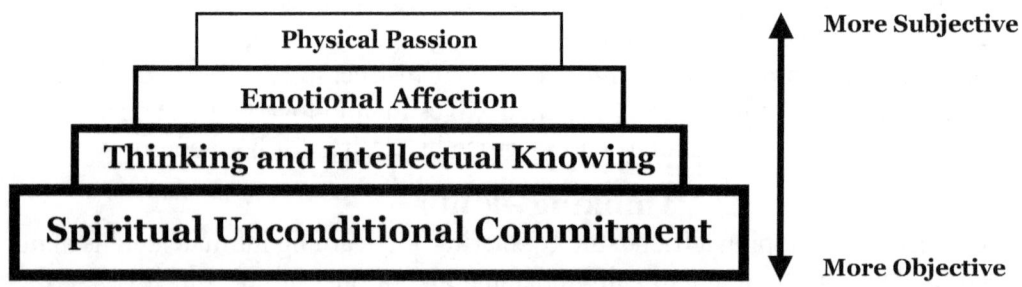

We can still eat without the table service, but doing so is messy and the clean-up is harder. And while a diet of sweets is possible, we would eventually become sick without the main and side dishes. The same is true in marriage. The commitment supports the knowing and affection, and they in turn support the sexual pleasure.

A passion-only relationship (without knowing or commitment) is based solely on biological urges, and therefore isn't much different than a one-night stand. This is having sex for the sake of having sex. The relationship doesn't exist.

An affectionate, passionate, and knowing relationship (without commitment) is an attempt to experience a relationship but with an escape pod standing by. The couple's fears hold them back from completely trusting each other and experiencing a deeper intimacy. The nagging worry, "Is he going to leave me?" never goes away.

A commitment-only relationship (without knowing, affection, or passion) is a paper marriage. The marriage is impersonal by the couple's design for purposes other than God's design.

A committed, knowing, and affectionate relationship (without passion) is a strong friendship. This also might describe positive family relationships.

None of these compare to a fully committed, knowing, affectionate, and passionate marriage. Combining all four loves increases:

- Unity: a couple's mature love results in frequently moving in the same direction with the same goals.
- Safety: a couple rests securely because of their common belief and value systems.
- Depth: each of the four loves enhances the other three; the more loves a couple practices, the stronger the bond.
- Exclusivity: a couple knows God brought them together; they appreciate the other's unique personhood and, therefore, they need no other romantic partner.

For Reflection

1. Marriage involves the discipline of sharing, which updates your partner's internal picture of you. In a strong relationship, you make time to share new information and personal changes. Exchanging information levels the playing field, moves you into sync with each other, and builds a sense of togetherness. This allows you to speak from the same context.
2. Consider how each of the four loves is like a language. What can you say?
3. You can use each language for good or for ill.
4. Busyness can cause sex to become a task to complete rather than a dessert you share after a full meal.

Next Steps

- How are you using these love languages to communicate with your partner? What are you saying or not saying? What do you need to say?
- How have others spoken these languages to you? What has been the net effect on you?
- Which languages are the easiest for you? Why might that be?
- Which languages are the hardest for you? Why might that be?
- Review these resources:
  - Movie: *Beauty and the Beast (Disney)*
  - Movie: *Shadowlands*
  - Book: *The Four Loves* by C.S. Lewis
  - Book: *The Book of Romance* by Tommy Nelson
- Use your Blueprint Space to prepare a full meal for your partner.

Blueprint Space

Chapter 28

Healthy Sexual Intimacy

The husband should fulfill his marital duty to his wife, and likewise the wife to her husband. The wife's body does not belong to her alone but also to her husband. In the same way, the husband's body does not belong to him alone but also to his wife. Do not deprive each other except by mutual consent and for a time, so that you may devote yourselves to prayer. Then come together again so that Satan will not tempt you because of your lack of self-control.
—1 Corinthians 7:3–5 (NIV)

Men and women follow unique paths of sexual arousal to reach climax. Their different physical experiences highlight their different gender roles. A husband is usually ready more quickly, but he must manage his excitement by being patient and firm enough to allow his wife to be able to participate fully in the experience. A wife trusts her husband by offering her whole self, spirit, soul, and body, without knowing how she is going to respond. She must enter into the experience by faith.

Sex is Bonding

God designed masculinity and femininity to attract each other. Removing your gender distinctiveness would be a serious mistake. To the degree you succeed in becoming similar, you drain the relationship of its natural sexual energy. Instead, look for the ways that differences strengthen your passionate bond.

Men generally have stronger sex drives. But either way, God calls a man to be proactive in loving his wife in all the ways of love. A man attracts a woman by initiating and protecting but also by being firm and patient. God calls a woman to be one with her husband, joining with and respecting him. A woman attracts a man by being available, open, vulnerable, and responsive.

Sex is experiential. Positive sex builds implicit memories by positively reinforcing our internal picture of our partner. Good sex creates a desire for more sex. More than just a few hormones regulate our sex drives. Testosterone and estrogen are the top two familiar hormones, but oxytocin is becoming more common in discussions. Oxytocin is one hormone that increases bonding and facilitates commitment. Touching, empathy, and orgasm all increase the level of Oxytocin. Following are some of its many benefits:

- Assists with attraction, touch, attachment, and trust;
- Produces a feeling of closeness;
- Provides calming and soothing;
- Allows feeling the desire to love unconditionally;
- Reduces the effects of the stress hormone cortisol; and
- Naturally decreases depression and anxiety.

Sex is Essential

Marriage without sex ceases to be marriage. The exception would be for medical reasons which make sex unhealthy or impossible. But even in these situations, more medical solutions exist today than they did twenty years ago. When the lack of desire is hormonal, hormone replacement therapy is an option to consider. God also permits a short time of separation to focus on prayer. But a desire for a sexless marriage is an indication of a serious problem.

Couples avoid sex for physical reasons but also for emotional reasons such as shame from past abuse, awkwardness, and emotional distance. Passive participation in sex is different from active participation. Those who approach sex passively tend to feel more used while those who approach sex actively, even with a lower libido, tend to feel better about themselves. When libido is different, finding a way to meet in the middle is better than giving up altogether.

Regular and enjoyable sex should be a goal for every couple. As with any marital goal, communication and feedback are critical to moving toward fulfillment. To reach this goal, talking about your sexual relationship is required.

Realize that a more frequent sex life has all kinds of relational and health benefits. Do not deprive each other of God's gift. The benefits of a regular and frequent sex life go beyond immediate physical pleasure. In the safety of marriage, sex provides:

- A stronger bond;
- Improved health;
- Reduced stress; and
- Longer life.

With these significant benefits to sex, why withhold sex from each other?

Sometimes women have a stronger libido than men. For them, the rejection is double because the man is supposed to be the one with the stronger desire. These women usually feel something has to be wrong with them. They are pained with, "Why doesn't my husband initiate with me?" Even though this is probably more awkward for both husband and wife, the same principles apply regardless of which one wants sex more often. Find a way to maximize your time together.

Sex is Communication

Sex is a way to communicate using your body—a language which husband and wife must learn. Speaking without knowing or believing the meaning of the "words" is possible, but not nearly as effective. During sexual intimacy, what are you saying to your partner with your body?

Wives, by being women, have the power to communicate, "I affirm, accept, admire, believe in, and receive you. I offer my beauty to you." Husbands, by being men, have the power to communicate, "I love and accept you. I care for you and will protect you. I offer my strength to you."

Full body communication allows full immersion into lovemaking. It involves all of our senses and more: touch, taste, smell, sight, and sound (words and pleasing noises). Find what pleases your partner and try to offer it. But keep in mind that moods change. Sex is as dynamic as we are. What worked well during one union might not the next. This keeps lovemaking new and exciting.

A wife needs tenderness and positive communication. This helps calm her so she feels safe. A wife desires and needs full access to her husband, which includes her husband's heart. A husband will do well to find the words to describe how he feels about his wife.

A husband desires and needs full access to his wife, which includes his wife's body. A wife will do well to practice the art and discipline of freeing her body for her husband's delight.

Sex is Diagnostic

Sex is an integral part of marriage. God does not intend for it to be isolated from the rest of the relationship. Sex reveals what is going on in a marriage. When sex is not going well, why is that? Maybe one or both people are harboring bitterness, hurt, or anger.

Unresolved hurt can get in the way of sexual intimacy. Making sure both consciences are clear before initiating sex is an excellent idea. If you don't, you might still have decent sex, but you will miss a deeper connection with each other. If you are upset about something, bring it up during a neutral time, not when your partner asks for intimacy. Anger, resentment, and unforgiveness shut down desire. When these dark emotions surface during lovemaking, most of the time the healthiest choice is to suspend the immediacy of sexual pleasure and focus on resolving the conflict. After the conflict is resolved, return to your sexual intimacy.

Be sure you are enjoying **each other** and not only the physically pleasing sensations. The best sex is supported by liking and loving. A husband may be enthusiastically agreeable to sex under most circumstances, but sex is considerably less enjoyable when his wife is not passionately engaged. The same applies to a woman who is initiating sex.

Both the husband and his wife need to be aware the husband is not with his wife just for sex. A husband may be blinded by his strong sex drive and unable to comprehend why his wife is not as interested in physical pleasure. However, if he goes out of his way to be kind and helpful, his wife will remember this when he initiates intimacy.

You must communicate about everything, including all aspects of your sexual life.

Sex is Loving

Remember that sex is first and foremost an act of love. When there are disagreements about sex and all else fails, choose the way of love. Love does not insist on its own way (1 Corinthians 13:5). If there is an aspect of sex that is uncomfortable (physically or emotionally) or repulsive to your partner, you must act in love and not force the matter. However, confronting your partner gently but purposefully when they fall short of marriage essentials is loving. When our heart's motive is a better marriage, we should confront our partner when they refuse sex for no good reason.

We can divide sexual activities into three classes:

1. Red Light activities should never be considered: watching pornography, anal sex, anything that inflicts pain, forcing sex, sex with other people, inviting other people into your marriage bed, etc. Don't do these kind of things! Keep your marriage bed pure (Hebrews 13:4).
2. Yellow Light activities require two enthusiastic votes: oral sex, unfamiliar positions or locations, etc. Be playful and experiment with them, but drop the matter if your partner provides a reasonable explanation and permanently vetoes them. But you must have some path to a fulfilling sex life. If you block one path, be sure to keep at least two others open.
3. Green Light activities should be pursued to their fullest. This is basically unashamed, frequent, full-access, full-contact sexual intimacy. When you or your partner experiences discomfort here, talk about it, agree to keep trying, and seek professional help to address the roadblocks to a healthy intimate life.

For Reflection

1. The sexual union between male and female has potential that is not present in any other relationship. Physically, this is conception and the raising of children. But the sexual union points to something deeper. God made men and women with enough space for each other. This special fitting together is only possible between male and female. Male and female bear fruit in a unique way. This increases the value of marriage.
2. How has your sexual communication been? Mostly positive or negative? Non-existent?
3. Since sex is a language, refusing sex is like giving your partner the "silent treatment."
4. Don't use sex as a bargaining chip: "If you do things the right way (my way), you will earn the right to have sex with me."
5. Be aware of sex becoming a chore or becoming isolated from the other kinds of intimacy.

Next Steps

- Invite your partner to communicate about your sex life. Discuss questions like:
  - How are you enjoying or not enjoying our sex life?
  - Could anything increase your interest in sex?
  - Why haven't we been having sex very much anymore?
  - How engaged is your heart during lovemaking?
- Many reasons exist for low libido. Get some help if any of the following keep you from pursuing sexual intimacy.
  - Past or present guilt from sinful sexual behaviors;
  - Past trauma in the form of abuse or neglect;
  - Extremely strict views of sex (usually learned from parents); or
  - Poor partner communication and boundaries.
- Keep your sexual intimacy sacred. Keep your marriage bed from becoming tainted by discouraging comments. Try using a room other than your bedroom to resolve intense conflicts.
- As you anticipate being sexually intimate, be aware of who your partner is. Recognize your partner by seeing them through God's eyes. Find ways to express how awesome and wonderfully made they are.
- There are many great detailed books on sexual intimacy. Try out a few and see which one fits with your approach to sexual intimacy.
- Review these resources:
  - Book: *Sheet Music* by Dr. Kevin Leman
  - Book: *Intended for Pleasure* by Ed Wheat
  - Book: *A Celebration of Sex* by Douglas E. Rosenau
  - Book: *Love and War* by John and Stasi Eldredge
  - Article: *Beyond Chemistry* by James K. Childerston found in *Christian Counseling Today*

Chapter 29

Productive Conflict

You desire and do not have, so you murder. You covet and cannot obtain, so you fight and quarrel. You do not have, because you do not ask.
—James 4:2

*Better is open rebuke than hidden love.
Faithful are the wounds of a friend;
profuse are the kisses of an enemy.*
—Proverbs 27:5–6

*Conflict is normal, healthy, and necessary.
But a sick heart can turn any conflict into an all-out war.*

Causes of Conflict

God intentionally created us to have needs that only other people can meet. Therefore, we are dependent on others for our quality of life. Because we set individual goals to meet our own needs, conflict results when two people assert mutually exclusive goals.

Unhealthy conflict is a tug-of-war to make others meet our needs. When we marry someone, we wed their unmet emotional needs. But we cannot possibly meet all of those needs, especially when we marry a person who is in serious pain.

Whomever we marry, the situation is not hopeless. As adults we are responsible for seeing that our needs are met, even if we need outside help to do so. Though it may feel impossible, even a deeply hurt person can reach a point of stability and contentment.

We have three options to move beyond unhealthy conflict:
1. Re-examine our pool of "need-meeters." God doesn't intend for us to depend exclusively on any one person for our needs.
2. Realize our seemingly urgent need is really a would-be-nice want or an unhealthy desire. We won't explode if the day goes by without getting what we want. Contentment may be the answer.
3. Resolve the conflict in a way that respects each other's goals. Some conflict is resolved by acceptance and other conflict by resolution.

Finding the Rhythm of Marriage

A healthy marriage has a rhythm similar to healthy breathing: deep and relaxed, in and out. In a relationship, the rhythm is engaged and disengaged: moving together and moving apart. As breathing helps our bodies adjust to stress and other circumstances, marriage breathing helps the couple adjust to each other. The adjustment brings the couple into further oneness. The pattern looks like this:
1. **Engage** all-in and see what happens. Keep moving closer as long as serious problems do not surface.

2. **Disengage** when the relationship appears to be moving in reverse. Failure to stop counter-productive behaviors only makes the situation worse. Slow down. Shift into an easier, light-hearted style of relating. Make needed corrections, then try moving forward.
3. **Engage** again when you are feeling better. Go deeper. Focus on performing well with your strengths.
4. **Disengage** to evaluate progress. Even when the relationship is going well, take a break to evaluate direction and growth.

Repeat by starting at step 1 again.

When conflict is out of control, implementing two transitions helps move us toward healthy conflict. The first transition moves from unhealthy engagement to healthy disengagement. The second moves from healthy disengagement to healthy engagement.

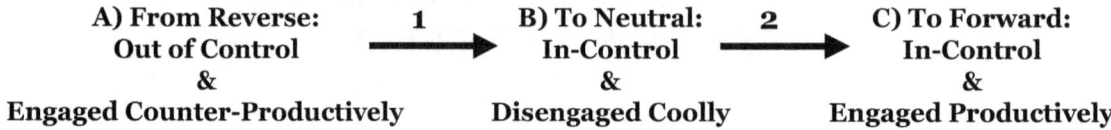

The middle step is necessary because when we are fully engaged in a disorganized way, we are out of touch with where we end and our partner begins. By first disengaging, we regain a deeper awareness of who we are, or we have an opportunity to develop our awareness anew. Disengaging retrains us to be responsible for our desires and lets our partner be responsible for their desires. This associated internal dialogue sounds like this:

- A: "What I want must happen yesterday. Even if you were to do what I want now, it already feels too late. I am in emotional pain, and you are the cause. You could have prevented this if you had only…"
- B: "Actually, I am okay today. You haven't changed into who I want you to be, and I don't have everything I want, but, I feel good about who I am."
- C: "I can pursue a better relationship with you now and in the future. I can wait as long as it takes. I can communicate my needs and hear your needs."

Otherwise we stay destructively engaged because we feel threatened when our deepest needs go unmet. Giving up on meeting our needs is not a logical option.

We need to risk moving towards our partner. But having our needs met is not guaranteed. Finding and negotiating these limits is exactly what relating is about—this is developing intimacy.

Unhealthy conflict is caused by insisting on getting what others cannot or will not do for us. When we aggressively pursue what we want, we remain stuck at A. When we passively disengage from the relationship, abandoning it, we remain stuck at B. Either way we must come to terms with two truths:

- We cannot control whether other people will meet our needs (don't stay stuck at A).
- We need other people to meet our needs (don't stay stuck at B).

The tension caused by these truths, if followed to their logical conclusion, will result in a healthy brokenness. A healthy brokenness recognizes we are utterly dependent on those outside of ourselves, and ultimately, we are dependent on God. The best response to this is patient trust.

Patient trust means acknowledging our dependence on God while at the same time recognizing that He does not owe us anything. This is a position of true humility that allows us to stay faithful to our partner. Instead of giving up on them, we believe they will eventually soften, grow up, and be able to meet our needs.

Freedom in Marriage

We all need freedom in order to grow. The opposite of freedom is control. Instead of managing our partner, we offer freedom. Freedom works the same way as God's grace. We are not supposed to continue in sin so that grace abounds all the more. If we need grace we have it, but we shouldn't use it to continue in wrongdoing. Likewise, we shouldn't abuse freedom in our marriage.

God gives us total freedom to leave and come back to Him when we are ready (Luke 15:11). Even though freedom doesn't have an immediate return on investment, our partner needs the same freedom that God gives us. We can offer freedom because we are not responsible for our mate's wrong decisions.

Trusting our partner doesn't mean being permissive or becoming a doormat. When we are too permissive, we are at least partially responsible for another's actions. If we know our partner is heading in the wrong direction and we do not speak up, we have not shown love. But speaking the truth in love doesn't mean we exist to catch all the mistakes of others. We are free, too.

If we are fearful and seek to control our partner, we increase the chances of weak, unproductive behavior (A & B). But this won't happen if, by faith, we offer loving concern and freedom (C).

For Reflection

1. When all you have is a hammer, every problematic symptom looks like a nail. When all you can see is your partner, everything looks like their fault. This implies that when one is right the other is wrong. What is the third option? Many issues are not black and white. Both of you can be right from your own perspectives. You each have unique needs. Just because one person is in need that doesn't mean the other person is to blame. But even if not to blame, you can participate in meeting the needs.
2. Neither conflict nor our partner is the enemy. The "enemy" is our belief that we must have a solution now and that solution must come from our partner.
3. I want my partner to comfort me. But I just hurt her, and so I cannot receive her comfort. She might feel that way about me too. I just hurt her, so how can she come to me for comfort?
4. Conflict is about the deepest need for validation. We want to know we are valuable, important, needed, and wanted.
5. A fight can be supremely intimate. You learn your partner's limits and vulnerable spots. You learn your blind spots. In a bad fight, you use this information against your partner, escalating the conflict (becoming further entrenched at A). You can feel alive because some form of connection exists. At least when you are wrestling with each other, or wrestling with God, you are in a relationship.
6. Avoid trying to resolve conflict when you are HALTSB (Hungry, Angry, Lonely, Tired, Stressed, or Bored).

Next Steps

☐ How does conflict help you? How does it help you know yourself better?
☐ Identify where you spend most of your time (A, B, or C), then take action to move towards healthier conflict.
☐ Apply fair fighting rules to your conflicts. If necessary, develop your own specific rules.
  - No degrading language, name-calling, or yelling to intimidate. If your behavior is not helpful to your partner, then find another way to communicate your point.
  - No use of force. No throwing or breaking things. No person should be harmed, intimidated, or threatened.

- No discouraging or manipulating talk. No talk of divorce or suicide as an empty threat to get your way. If you really intend to pursue divorce or suicide, you should speak up with your valid reasons why. If you are simply discouraged, speak your feelings in a non-threatening way. Don't respond to empty threats.
- No mind-reading. Speak about what you want rather than making assumptions about what your partner is thinking. And, don't assume your partner knows what you are thinking.
- No dominating the conversation. Take turns listening and speaking. Alternate frequently enough to hear both sides, but allow enough time for your partner to communicate deeply from the heart.
- No unnecessary avoidance. If you can both resolve the problem now, don't wait. If the problem is big enough to fester and cause more problems later, don't ignore it. However taxing, stay with it until it is resolved. Taking breaks and allowing a conflict to span multiple days is okay so long as you don't allow distractions to bury the issue prematurely.
- No unnecessary restrictions. If you sense a rule is preventing forward progress, let your partner know you want to experiment by temporarily suspending a rule. If you need to use "blame language" or "talk about the past," go ahead! But only do so if your motive is to reconcile and you are also willing to accept responsibility for your hurt feelings. Your partner may have hurt you, but only you can choose to forgive and heal.

☐ Review these resources:
☐ Movie: *Fireproof*
☐ Book: *The Love Dare* by Alex Kendrick

Blueprint Space

Chapter 30

Two are Better than One

Two are better than one, because they have a good reward for their toil. For if they fall, one will lift up his fellow. But woe to him who is alone when he falls and has not another to lift him up! Again, if two lie together, they keep warm, but how can one keep warm alone? And though a man might prevail against one who is alone, two will withstand him—a threefold cord is not quickly broken.
—Ecclesiastes 4:9–12

But the Lord is faithful. He will establish you and guard you against the evil one.
—2 Thessalonians 3:3

When husband and wife understand that they are on the same team, and act like it, one winning and the other losing is impossible. Both win or both lose. If you find yourself losing, maybe you've lost sight of what makes a great team.

Who Has Your Back?

A marriage is a team of two people—three, including God. What happens to one member also happens to, or directly affects, the other. If Bob and Karen hike together and Karen twists her ankle, Bob doesn't leave her behind to fend for herself. He carries both packs, slows down, or goes for help. Similarly, being married means our fates are bound together.

In marriage, husband and wife are one. They are on the same side. One winning and one losing is not possible. Both of them win or both of them lose. For example, in financial matters, both of them win the lottery, go bankrupt, or find contentment living within their means.

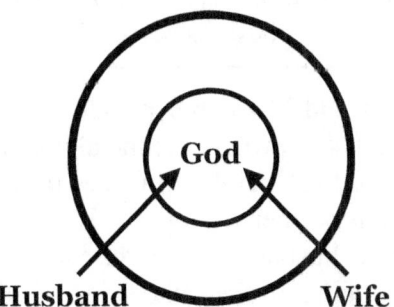

As husband and wife move closer to God, our immovable target and example of love, they automatically become closer to each other. The closer they are, the more they guard each other's back and keep each other warm. They cover each other's vulnerabilities, blocking out those who seek their destruction. Christ is for us and not against us. Nothing can separate us from His love (Romans 8:31–39). We need to experience the same fierce loyalty in our marriage.

Two are better than one as long as they act like they are one. An adversary is an opponent: one who opposes or attacks. Our partner is not our adversary. If our partner hurts us, we shouldn't retaliate, but instead work on building the cord of three strands. Husband, wife, and God, on the same side, form the cord of three not quickly broken.

How Your Partner Becomes the Enemy

How does someone on our team become our adversary? How would our partner ever appear to be our enemy? We have an adversary working against us who tries to make us appear as enemies and keeps us believing we are enemies.

What if Bob appears to be Karen's enemy by acting like the enemy? He may block her from her goals or refuse to help her reach her goals. In this situation, most people feel betrayed or left for dead. Our real enemy uses this against us, subtly convincing us to split apart into separate teams. The problem has the potential to become an all-out war when, from our own perspective, our partner crosses over from deficient partner to hated opponent.

When our partner blocks us from realizing our heart's desire, we may question how this person, who is supposed to be for us, could be any more against us. Instead of showing support, they are in the way. Rigid. Unmovable. Though they hold the key to our relief, or so we think, they refuse to use it. Our frustration may turn into a desire to retaliate. Or we might choose the seemingly kinder approach. Go around! Avoid them altogether! Pretend they don't exist.

Sow an Action, Reap a Habit

Patterns of conflict resolution will eventually shape our characterization of our partner. This characterization becomes our approach to our partner. If we see our partner negatively, they quickly become like an enemy. A simple matter can become ongoing guerilla warfare.

Once we frame our partner as our enemy, and we believe it, all is lost. Tearing apart our partner is the same as attacking our own flesh. The husband's and wife's fates are bound together, but their attitudes are not. Either one can choose to believe a different reality—based on truth.

Finally, be strong in the Lord and in the strength of his might. Put on the whole armor of God, that you may be able to stand against the schemes of the devil. For we do not wrestle against flesh and blood, but against the rulers, against the authorities, against the cosmic powers over this present darkness, against the spiritual forces of evil in the heavenly places.
—Ephesians 6:10–12

Our struggle is not against flesh and blood but powers of darkness. Whether our partner's negative actions are intentional or not, somewhere behind all that is a spiritual battle. Our partner's mistreatment of us is the result of their flesh being influenced by spiritually dark forces. Our enemy intends to keep us divided against our partner.

When oneness is broken between husband and wife, can you see how vulnerable they are? When a marriage loses the sense of being on the same side, it will not last very long. Fortunately, one person realizing the reality of oneness is enough. One person refusing to retaliate and remaining open to reconciliation is often enough to reverse bitter conflict.

For Reflection

1. Teamwork sounds so obvious, so perfect. Then why is it so hard to achieve? Fear is likely involved one way or another:
   - Fear of the unknown.
   - Fear of never being truly understood.
   - Fear of never having our longings validated.
2. It takes two to make a marriage a success and only one to make it a failure.—Herbert Samuel
   When is this true and when not true?
3. If you hurt your partner, you damage your interest and make life worse for you. Retaliation only escalates the struggle. Pain doesn't erase pain. Don't join the enemy in the destruction of your partner.

Next Steps

- ☐ How do you characterize your partner? How do you speak of your partner to others? How positive? How negative? In what ways do you need to forgive or accept your partner?
- ☐ Review several of your conflicts. Identify root causes for the conflict. Here is a partial list of possibilities:
  - The Husband or The Wife
  - Stress
  - Sickness
  - Hormones
  - Loss (of a child, job, etc.)
  - Lack of needs being met growing up
  - Trauma
  - Spiritual Attack
- ☐ How many of your conflicts involve feeling as if your partner is your enemy? Pay attention to the pattern so you can recognize it in the future.
- ☐ Ask God to help you see your partner as your partner, not your enemy. Pray for discernment so you can see with spiritual eyes. Look for evidence they are only misguided or under a strong influence to guard their own vulnerabilities. Use this truth to reinterpret your interactions. Think: Since we are actually on the same side, this must mean . . .
- ☐ Review these resources:
  - ☐ Movie: *Marriage Retreat*
  - ☐ Book: *DNA of Relationships* by Gary Smalley
  - ☐ Book: *Love and War* by John and Stasi Eldridge
  - ☐ Next: how to resolve conflicts and wounds to restore oneness
- ☐ Use your Blueprint Space to draw a picture of your oneness.

Blueprint Space

Chapter 31

Healthy Expectations

"And when you pray, do not heap up empty phrases as the Gentiles do, for they think that they will be heard for their many words. Do not be like them, for your Father knows what you need before you ask him."
—Matthew 6:7–8

*God made us for Heaven, but we must live a while on Earth.
Accept and grieve the difference while accepting God's comfort.
Then adjust your expectations accordingly.*

Understanding Expectations

An expectation is an anticipation that something will happen or be a certain way[7]. Whenever we expect something, we take on the risk of being disappointed. The Latin derivative of expectation means essentially "to wait."[8] Three popular meanings are relevant to our expectations of our partner:

1. A hope, belief, and faith in God's promises.
2. A desire or want for something to happen.
3. An anticipation for something that should be happening.

Expectations are not the Problem

Desires, whether innocent or evil, lead to expectations. Evil desires result in some harm to self or others. Examples include: lust, envy, and jealousy. These desires need to be dropped, not negotiated. However, they are associated with legitimate desires. For example, when we struggle with jealousy, we might really be feeling insignificant when we want to feel important.

Expecting a legitimate desire to be met is a good thing!

Our innocent desires (see chapter 13 on core longings) might be realistic or unrealistic. And we might express our expectations with either positive or negative attitudes. Even a healthy desire can become an unrealistic expectation by reasoning:

1. I have an innocent desire.
2. The desire has gone unmet (usually for a long time).
3. I have a sense of desperation (the thought of it not being met is unbearable).
4. My partner is available (so I expect them to meet the desire).
5. I rely too much on my partner (I expectantly see them as someone they are not).
6. I have a need, therefore my partner must be able to meet it.

This line of reasoning is only possible when our heart sees people the wrong way. Our heart attitudes make our expectations realistic or unrealistic.

---

[7] yourdictionary.com/expectation
[8] vocabulary.com/dictionary/expectation

Maintaining Good Attitudes

Healthy expectations have a reasonable probability of fulfillment. When we have a good attitude, we recognize and accept that they might not be fulfilled. In fact, God wants us to be a cheerful giver, free to choose how much we want to give (2 Corinthians 9:7). At the same time, God wants us to be hopefully expectant about all that is good (Ephesians 3:16–20; Hebrews 11:1). We can apply God's promises to ourselves and to our partner. Reasonable expectations:
- Begin as a desire for something good;
- Are either encouraged or commanded in the Bible or are not offensive to our partner in areas of freedom (grey areas not specifically mentioned in the Bible);
- Are capable of being met by our partner; and
- Are persistently held convictions or boundaries but we should not force them on our partner. We can drop them if we want, but we don't have to.

Therefore, good attitudes:
- Recognize the limits of our partner by not pushing them to the breaking point;
- Encourage and challenge others to grow.

Managing Bad Attitudes

When our partner does not meet our expectations, conflict can result. The conflict can be a minor disappointment or a major disruption that threatens the marriage. Expectations also create problems when they are unrealistic or demanded.

Consider Brittany who has expectations for her husband Chris. To resolve a conflict, Brittany needs to recognize that Chris:
- Is not her source (God is);
- Is not ultimately responsible for her unmet childhood needs;
- Might not have the capacity to meet her expectations;
- Might not be able to meet her expectations in the timeframe she wants; and
- Does not owe her anything.

Despite this, there are at least two areas in marriage where having strong expectations are reasonable:
1. Sexual intimacy needs cannot be legitimately met outside the marriage. We can expect our partner to fulfill their marital responsibilities (1 Corinthians 7).
2. God has expectations for our behaviors. We can hope for loving behavior and enforce our boundaries on sinful behavior.

However, even with these areas, one partner cannot control what the other does. Brittany might have legitimate needs that Chris cannot meet. Or he might not want to meet them. He might even sin. However he behaves, she can survive his limitations and continue to love him unconditionally. Lowering expectations might be appropriate when any of the following occur:
- A change in health or work circumstances;
- A major life transition (getting married, job loss, having a newborn, elderly parents are sick);
- A traumatic event such as miscarriage, loss of child, death in the family, car accident; or
- An honest change of heart.

Given all the limitations, is Brittany better off to not expect anything from Chris? Her expectations might be healthy, but bad attitudes such as these are a warning sign that they're not:
- She feels entitled to demand her expectations be met. She might even say, "It's my right that you fulfill my desire."

- She wants what she wants when she wants it.
- She is unwilling to consider other people besides her husband who can legitimately meet some of her needs.

Testing Expectations

Our partner cannot solve every problem for us or be everything to us. A relationship is like a bridge. The bridge is only as strong as the maturity of the husband, the wife, and the relationship between them. The relationship bears the weight of the couple's expectations. Marriages collapse all the time under this weight because of carelessness.

To experience relating to each other, we must attempt to drive our expectations over the bridge. Both husband and wife need to take turns driving and bearing the expectations. When Brittany drives, this tests the strength of the relationship in several important ways[9]:

- Her attitude and reasonableness of her expectations for Chris; and
- Chris' attitude and his ability to meet the expectations.

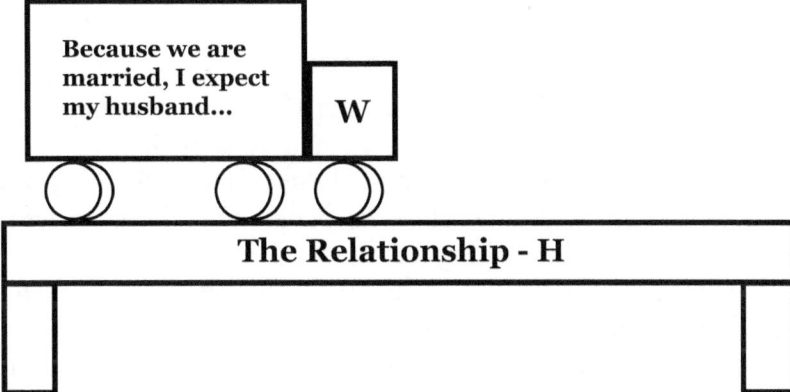

The outcome of the test can play out in four ways:
1. Success: Brittany has realistic expectations and makes it across.
2. Recognition: Brittany recognizes her unrealistic expectations and backs off the bridge. She may try another way, another time, or she may negotiate with Chris.
3. Lost Potential: Brittany has realistic expectations, but is fearful of driving across the bridge. The couple will not experience the joy of knowing the full potential of their relationship.
4. Stress Fractures: Brittany does not recognize, or recognizes too late, her unrealistic expectations. In a worst-case scenario, she realizes the damage and stays on the bridge anyway. An attitude such as, "My needs are more important than your emotional health," violates the sense of oneness between them.

Notice that while Brittany (W) is driving her expectations, Chris (H) appears to bear the weight on his own. In reality, Brittany is testing how well she loves Chris and knows what he can handle. This is a test of their oneness. Driving heavy, unrealistic expectations only emphasizes, "We aren't in this together." Testing the weight limits is productive when done in the right spirit, as in: "Oh, I can see that is too much for you. Let me try that a different way." But testing is disastrous with an attitude like: "You need to bear this weight, or I am leaving you."

---

[9] the test remains equally valid when the roles in the example are swapped

A Place of Encouragement

Marriage has limits, but is also meant to be a place of profound encouragement. Expectations have value because they encourage healthy growth. They communicate, "I believe in you." Love pushes us just enough but not too hard that we give up and not too easy that we don't try. With practice, we learn to find the balance.

For Reflection

1. What makes expectations reasonable?
2. Be prepared to deal with the fact that there are no guarantees that others will meet your expectations.
3. Realize the difference between being single and being married and the process of transitioning from one to the other. You cannot expect to continue to act as if you are single when you are married. Being married changes (almost) everything. Life is about adjusting and stabilizing.
4. Learn to relate to others for who they are at the present moment, not who you want them to be.
5. Get what you can from others, then get the rest from God.

Next Steps

- ☐ Read 2 Corinthians 9:6–8. How does it change your view of expectations?
- ☐ Read Matthew 6:7–13. How can you pray when you need something?
- ☐ Unfulfilled, unhealthy expectations are often the basis of the initial disillusionment or Storm after the honeymoon. Do you have any active disappointments from earlier in your marriage?
- ☐ Drop the demanding attitude when asking for what you need.
- ☐ Read Luke 18:1–8. Do not give up when your needs go unmet. Continue to ask your partner for what you need. Ask with patient persistence.
- ☐ What do you need most right now with respect to your goals? Do you need more grace or more encouragement to press forward?
- ☐ What do you and your partner want from each other? Who is responsible for what? What is at stake? What is threatened? Who is responsible for filling your buckets?
- ☐ Review these resources:
  - ☐ Movie: *The Thing About My Folks*
  - ☐ DVD: *iMarriage* by Andy Stanley

Chapter 32

From Conflict to Harmony

For am I now seeking the approval of man, or of God? Or am I trying to please man? If I were still trying to please man, I would not be a servant of Christ.
—Galatians 1:10

For by the grace given to me I say to everyone among you not to think of himself more highly than he ought to think, but to think with sober judgment, each according to the measure of faith that God has assigned.
—Romans 12:3

*To make an apt answer is a joy to a man,
and a word in season, how good it is!*
—Proverbs 15:23

A word fitly spoken is like apples of gold in a setting of silver.
—Proverbs 25:11

Without a struggle there can be no progress.
—Frederick Douglass

Be Assertive

How do you approach conflict? Do you tend to avoid it? Do you pursue it aggressively? How does your partner pursue it? With two people, seven main patterns are possible:

1. **Chase:** One pursues aggressively; one avoids.

2. **Fight:** Both pursue aggressively.

3. **Dominate:** One pursues aggressively, one gives in passively.

4. **Isolate:** Both avoid.

5. **Block:** One responds assertively, one pursues aggressively.

6. **Wait:** One waits assertively, one avoids.

7. **Resolve:** Both pursue assertively (firmly and flexibly).

Of the seven possibilities, the first six are anger- or fear-based and therefore dysfunctional. The aggressive pursuing partner is looking to the other person as a means to an end. The avoidant partner looks at their self as less than or not good enough so they hide. Both styles of relating fail to accept the reality of their limits and potential. But the final option, pursuing assertively, allows for the possibility of achieving the greatest potential.

The following information helps clarify the three approaches[10]:

	Passive	**Assertive**	**Aggressive**
During Conflict	Avoids (lose-win)	Pursues resolution (win-win)	Over-pursues (win-lose)
Dependency	Dependent, codependent, compliant	Independent, interdependent, confident	Counter-dependent, controlling
Self-Worth	"I don't count"	"I count me and I count you"	"I don't count you"
Choice	Allows others to choose for self	Chooses for self; lets others make their own decisions	Chooses for self and for others
Power	Relinquishes power, feels powerless	Seeks healthy balance of power and humility	Always seeking more power
Verbal Style	Rambling statements, qualifiers and fillers	Clear and concise statements	Interrupting and often unverified statements
General Posture	Moving away, hiding	Moving toward, connecting	Moving against, destroying
Outcome	Does not achieve desired goals	Might achieve desired goals	Achieves desired goals by hurting others

Moving from Passivity to Assertion

Passive people think of themselves as less than God intended them to be. By giving up their basic right to assert their identity, they place themselves at a severe disadvantage. While God does not want us to be prideful, He does want us to think of ourselves "according to the measure of faith that God has assigned." The following "rights" help move us to a place of confidence and humility:

1. I can ask for what I want.
2. I do not have to be perfect; I can accept responsibility for my mistakes.
3. I can express all of my feelings.
4. I can be my unique self.
5. I can have my own personal space and time.
6. I can change my mind; I can change and grow.
7. I can say no to what is harmful and yes to what is good for me.
8. I can have a support system.

With these rights, we need to be careful not to become too independent. If we wait until we feel like doing something, we may miss good times, and we will starve our relationship of needed togetherness. If we engage our partner when they are ready and go where they want to go, much of the time we will become interested too. Or if we are capable of participating with a positive spirit, we will witness our partner's enjoyment. No small achievement!

---

[10] Some parts adapted from *Your Perfect Right* by Alberti and Emmons.

Life is short. Experimenting and learning is not being passive. Create some exciting memories!

Moving from Aggression to Assertion

Anger-inducing beliefs[11] fuel aggressive over-reaction:
1. I must be treated fairly and considerately;
2. People who act unfairly, deceitfully, or inconsiderately deserve to be condemned;
3. Not getting what I want is intolerable;
4. I cannot be happy unless I am treated how I want to be treated;
5. Other people are worthless unless they are of benefit to me.

The opposite beliefs help reduce anger:
1. I prefer to be treated fairly and considerately, but if not, I'll be just fine.
2. People who act unfairly, deceitfully, or inconsiderately should not be condemned, but they might deserve to be penalized;
3. Not getting what I want is unpleasant and frustrating, but I'll find another way;
4. I can be happy no matter how I'm treated;
5. I can learn to accept people for who they are, not who I want them to be.

Anger is not bad when it helps us become motivated to make life better. However, we are not supposed to make life better at the expense of others. Our anger's strength can initiate positive direction and change. As long as aggressive people learn to respect others' limitations, they will have more potential to change the world through positive influence and confrontation.

Being King and Queen

Marriage is a transformational process. To have a healthy marriage, we cannot afford the luxury of remaining in our passivity or our aggressiveness. With a commitment to be healthy, all that we need is another person to practice being assertive.

Marriages start out with two individuals who know much more about being single than being a couple. If we stay with a single mindset, we focus on the ways we've always done life alone. Marriage is that process by which we rid ourselves of a selfish mindset. Though entering marriage as selfish is normal, and finding out how selfish we really are is normal, staying selfish is a choice. With time we can mature.

If we are too passive or aggressive, we are likely focused on keeping our old mindset. This is a shame because relating doesn't have to be that way. Being assertive means stepping fully into who God made us to be. In a marriage this means fully stepping away from past affiliations. We need to be able to look objectively at who we've become. When our partner does this at the same time, we have enough space to develop a completely new way of doing life together.

Marriage is a chance to start over. Graduating from a "single" to a "married" mindset is like graduating from "Prince and Princess" to "King and Queen." We need to accept that a fundamental change has taken place. We have complete freedom to set up our kingdom however we want (within God's moral limits). This doesn't mean we have to throw out what we've known to be good unless it will not fit within the new relationship.

We can determine the values, rules, structure, roles, and activities that work for our new family. We shouldn't let outside influences (usually parents) rule our relationship. Recall that being assertive includes the interests of both husband and wife and, therefore, balances power and humility. Being assertive allows us to shift from focusing on what we want, to what we can create together as rulers of our new kingdom.

---

[11] Some parts adapted from *The RET Resource Book for Practitioners* by Wolfe & Bernard

While making the shift, we need to keep in mind that God is the one who provides our coronation ceremony. Marriage has a purpose beyond setting up a kingdom to meet only the needs of the king and queen. A healthy kingdom is capable of supporting its own economy. Likewise, a healthy marriage develops the capacity to support children and other missions. The governing values of the marriage should be co-authored by husband, wife, and God (the principles in the Bible).

For Reflection

1. Where there are extremes there are fears of being invalidated, rejected, or found unwanted or useless.
2. A healthy relationship will balance individual and relational pursuits. Neglect either one too much and both will suffer. Couples need the same balance between marriage and parenting pursuits. Children benefit significantly, even though indirectly, from their parent's healthy marriage.
3. Marital success requires belief in the idea of marriage. You must know and believe in what you need to do.

Next Steps

☐ TheFreeDictionary.com defines *priority* as a "precedence, especially established by order of importance or urgency." What do you value before all else? What is most important in your life? Write out a prioritized list of your ideal values. Here are some categories to get you started: Partner, Self, Hobbies, God, Children, Parents, The Needy, Money, Career, Siblings, and Security. Next, examine your life. Based on your efforts, write another list by ordering your actual values.

- Have you discovered any ways in which your actual values (day-to-day reality) are in tension with the way you want to live (your ideals)?
- What would your life be like if you lived closer to your ideal values?
- What is keeping you from living according to your values?
- What can you do to remove these obstacles?
- What changes will be necessary to live closer to your ideal values?

☐ Becoming one requires merging two ways of doing life into one way. As single adults we start with what our parents taught us about how to do life. Hopefully, we make some of our own choices rather than blindly doing everything the same way. As times and technology change, we are smart to embrace better ways of living. Likewise, your partner has figured out ways to make life work that might be an improvement over your ways. Come together to find the strongest path forward in your marriage by writing all your rules, beliefs, and preferences onto strips of paper. Throw them into a bag. Forgetting whose is whose, draw one strip at a time and decide together whether you want to keep it, modify it, or throw it out of your marriage.

☐ Review these resources:
  ☐ Movie: *Gladiator*
  ☐ Book: *From Bondage to Bonding* by Nancy Groom

Chapter 33

Optimal Decision Making

Do nothing from selfish ambition or conceit, but in humility count others more significant than yourselves. Let each of you look not only to his own interests, but also to the interests of others.
—Philippians 2:3–4

We need both wisdom and perseverance to resolve the problems of life. If you are not realizing the results you want, be sure you are allowing enough time. Even Einstein admitted to needing to persevere to find solutions.

Five Options for Conflict Resolution

Conflict isn't always caused by overt sinful behavior or poor communication. Often its primary cause is a couple's inability to make a mutually satisfactory decision. In such cases, an established win-win model provides five options for resolving conflict. Typically, the more time a couple has available for deliberating, the closer they will come to finding an optimal solution.

H. Norman Wright, author and counselor, and Ralph Kilmann, author and CEO of Kilmann Diagnostics, include the same five options in their models, but label them differently:

You-Your Partner	H. Norman Wright	Ralph Kilmann
1) Win-Lose	Win	Competing
2) Lose-Win	Yield	Accommodating
3) Lose-Lose (or no decision)	Withdraw	Avoiding
4) Equally Win and Lose	Compromise	Compromising
5) Win-Win	Resolve	Collaborating

The five points in this diagram represent the five options:

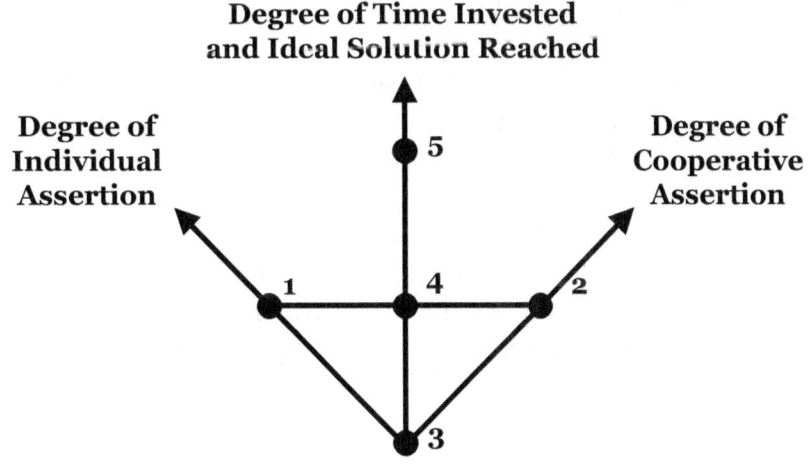

When used correctly, the model provides a clear roadmap for finding the optimal solution under a variety of circumstances. We can use it for:
- Improving upon the default 50/50 compromise where both parties end up equally satisfied and dissatisfied.
- Encouraging the negotiation of a win-win solution instead of one or both parties feeling as if they've unnecessarily abandoned their interests.
- Highlighting the positive use of the more imbalanced options (win-lose, lose-win, and lose-lose).

When to Choose Each Option

While some styles are usually superior to others, all styles have their place and time. The following describes the optimal use of each option.[12]

1. Competing: Pursue your interest regardless of your partner's opinion.
   Use when:
   - A decision is especially important to you, and your partner will take advantage of you unless you stand up for your desires.
   - You must make a decision quickly, and no action will create a bigger problem.
   - You are ready to be responsible for any consequences of your actions.
   - You know you are right (but be careful with this one; don't use it just to get your way).
   - You're thinking, "I am qualified to make this decision."

2. Accommodating: Pursue your partner's interest regardless of your opinions.
   Use when:
   - You know the issue is more important to your partner than it is to you.
   - You don't have a strong opinion, or other issues are more important to you.
   - You believe sacrificing your desires in the current situation is the best way to love your partner.
   - Your partner is qualified to make the decision and your input is unnecessary.
   - You know you are wrong.
   - You're thinking, "You're right. We've done it my way the last five times."

3. Avoiding: Pursue nothing or something else altogether.
   Use when:
   - Other issues are a higher priority.
   - Neither of you urgently depend on this decision.
   - You need more time to gather information.
   - Discussion has become unproductive, and you need time away from the problem.
   - You're thinking, "Why are we spending time on this when we could be . . ."

4. Compromise: Pursue a 50/50 split down the middle.
   Use when:
   - You need a fair solution relatively quickly.
   - You and your partner are strongly committed to mutually exclusive goals.
   - You're thinking, "I'm sure there is a better way to do this, but we need to make a decision now. We can rest easy knowing neither of us is being cheated."

---

[12] Adapted from Thomas-Kilmann.

5. Collaborating: Pursue an optimal win-win solution.
   Use when:
   - You have the time to find the better-than-average solution.
   - Both your and your partner's feelings are vulnerable to a careless solution.
   - You need a solution that meets all, or close to all, of both your goals.
   - You're thinking, "Splitting everything in half doesn't make sense, and besides, we have time to find a better way to do this."

Putting it Together

A false dichotomy is a situation where there appears to be only two (usually opposite) solutions to a problem. However, in reality, nearly everything is negotiable. Usually many more than two options exist. To insist no other options exist than the ones already presented is to deny the hope of resolving the conflict. Believing that, "The only way to prevent me from losing is to make me win by making you lose," is tempting early on in a conflict.

The optimal resolution to conflict is usually found somewhere along the middle line as a perfect balance between individual and relational concern (options 3, 4, and 5). The middle axis equally represents both parties' interests. When both are interested in a fair solution, the limiting factor in producing an optimal result is the amount of time invested in finding a solution.

Other choices result in a lose-win outcome at best. These scenarios block a clean resolution:
- Both choose 1: conflict is never resolved, or conflict is resolved by going separate ways;
- Both choose 2: conflict is never resolved because neither has a strong enough opinion;
- One chooses 1, one chooses 2: classic lose-win scenario;
- One chooses 3: classic avoidance, but understand that no decision is, in itself, a decision.

God's Principles and the Five Options

God's principles are essential in choosing one of the five options. The goal of individual assertion is to preserve individual interest when the issue is more important than the relationship. For example, God would always have us obey His principles above our partner's desires.

The goal of cooperative assertion is to preserve the relationship when the relationship is more important than the issue. For example, God wants us to count others as worthy of serving.

Sometimes we know the right way to proceed without having to think very hard. At other times, we need to give considerable thought to discover the best way to proceed. A good first step is to determine if a clear right or wrong is in play. Then, as the second step, we can determine if our rights or preferences are worth fighting for.

Asserting our opinions, feelings, and arguments does not have to be the last word. Sharing our thoughts may lead to appropriately winning over our partner. Likewise, we should be open to relinquishing our position when we realize it doesn't hold much weight.

After moving above the horizontal line of 50/50 effort, many more possibilities open up. The willingness to invest more time on the issue affords husband and wife peace and a freedom to pursue a win-win solution. When acting in love, choosing solutions to the left or right of the midline becomes a possibility, without losing fairness. The next two chapters will explore in more detail the merit of choosing seemingly unfair solutions.

For Reflection

1. Each conflict might require a unique resolution style or at least a unique path to reach resolution.
2. The path to a win-win requires both individuals to articulate their position clearly.

3. What happens when you win and your partner loses? If you lose and your partner wins?
4. When do the needs of the one outweigh the needs of the many?
5. When do the needs of the many outweigh the needs of the one?
6. Do you utilize a different approach to conflict resolution inside and outside your marriage? What does this tell you about your priorities and values? How do you treat family differently than you treat others?

Next Steps

- When you are not sure where to start, evaluate the impact of all five options. Starting with option one, determine the pros and cons of each solution, discuss them, and then choose the one that works best for this particular situation.
- For more complicated decisions, ask God for His input. If you and your partner hear the same direction from God, you may not need to discuss it further.
- Considering the five options:
  - Analyze past conflicts to identify which style you and your partner tend to use most. How often were you clearly using a less than optimal style?
  - Resolve a currently unresolved argument using this new information.
- Take the *Thomas-Kilmann Conflict Mode Instrument* (kilmanndiagnostics.com) to learn more about your preferred conflict resolution style.
- Review these resources:
  - Movie: *Pride and Prejudice (2005)*
  - Book: *Marital Counseling* (particularly Chapter 11) by H. Norman Wright
  - Site: cppblogcentral.com/cpp-connect/tennis-balls-hula-hoops-conflict-modes
  - Site: emotionalcompetency.com/conflict.htm

Blueprint Space

Chapter 34

Pursuing the Win-Win

But God has put the body together, giving greater honor to the parts that lacked it, so that there should be no division in the body, but that its parts should have equal concern for each other. If one part suffers, every part suffers with it; if one part is honored, every part rejoices with it.
—1 Corinthians 12:24b–26

When husband and wife do not cheerfully agree, they should slow down the decision making process, otherwise they may create an even bigger problem: unnecessary, painful, and relationship-threatening division.

Division Slowly Kills a Relationship

If we do nothing else while resolving conflict, we should do everything to keep unity with our partner. Nothing unifies a couple faster than having their eyes wide open to the harsh consequences of division. Usually division doesn't happen overnight. Contention followed by small steps away from our partner slowly diminishes the sense of relationship over time.

Nothing divides a couple faster than keeping secrets. But couples avoid speaking the truth all the time. For people-pleasers, the habit of making up the difference between other's expectations and their reality is hard to shake. To the degree we accept too much responsibility in our relationships (with parents, peers, or partners), we lose a part of ourselves. But whatever we choose to keep secret or separate from our partner creates a division. Typically this shows up as withholding negative feelings from our partner, which only builds resentment. Instead of bringing the truth out into the open, we hide our unhappiness from our partner.

In addition to keeping secrets (not wanting to hurt with the truth), division can result from:
- Favoring and remaining loyal to other relationships and responsibilities;
- Feeling obligated to please or submit;
- Rigidly adhering to our ideas out of fear;
- Lacking an understanding and experience of oneness;
- Fearing being taken advantage of or treated unfairly; or
- Pursuing individual needs apart from our partner's knowledge.

Fully on Board

A win-win solution eliminates pretending to be happy with a solution. Hiding disappointment is deceptive—it keeps distance in place rather than closeness and, in the long run, benefits no one. When considering various solutions, we can either:
1. Accept our partner's idea (say yes) and genuinely have nothing to complain about.
2. Decline our partner's idea (say no) and offer reasons why.

Complaining after accepting someone's offer is a passive-aggressive response. Our goal should be to live out of our true identity, not a false passive-aggressive identity. Consider Dave and Samantha who are deciding their vacation plans:

- They vacation at the same spot every year;
- Dave enjoys the mountain resort they visit; and
- Samantha hides her dislike of mountains and puts on a happy face.

There are several problems with this recurring situation:
- The relationship is robbed of its mutuality and equality when Samantha creates an imbalance by withholding information;
- They lose the synergy of making a joint decision; and
- Eventually Dave will find out Samantha is unhappy.

An optimal solution means finding a creative way so both are pleased with the solution. When husband and wife are on the same team, one winner and one loser is not possible. How do they go about finding a win-win?
- They should be aware of needs and ask for them. Samantha should communicate her dislike of the mountains.
- They shouldn't break loyalty by keeping secrets or finding substitutions. After Dave discovers the truth about how his wife feels, he should not angrily pursue activities with others apart from her.
- Dave should be fully transparent by communicating his reality to Samantha to ensure she is on board. They should discuss their feelings and decide together how to resolve the situation. For example, maybe Dave can go skiing in the mountains without Samantha but with her blessing.
- If Samantha is distressed by Dave's activities (traveling without her), they should address this vulnerability before pursuing a course of action.

If our partner is not fully on board with what we want to do, something is wrong and needs to change. *Fully on board* means approving a course of action, not necessarily that our partner would do it exactly the way we'd do it.

Develop a Secure and Flexible Connection

We can be rigid or flexible in pursuing a resolution, however, the fears that lead to division cause us to be rigid. A typical couple can find themselves in one of three degrees of flexibility based on their relationship experiences:
1. Frozen: stuck in a position of insisting life goes exactly their way;
2. Flexible: able to successfully pursue win-win scenarios;
3. Free: solutions do not have to be balanced when a couple fully grasps oneness.

Level One is essentially "my way." Level Two is "our way." These levels focus on an external fairness more than an internal reality. But Level Three could be called "God's way" because that kind of security only comes from meaningful experiences with Him.

Requiring an equally balanced solution can be worse than an imbalanced one. A boy who must have his cake cut exactly even has not yet internalized a secure love. He lives in fear of being treated unfairly because when he receives a smaller piece, he believes he is not valued as much as others. When he grows up and marries, he believes, "My feelings have never been fully considered so I need everything to happen my way in my marriage. Maybe I can finally be fully recognized and valued for who I am!"

But what if his wife had a similar experience as a girl? Then they are on a collision course.

Establishing a high enough level of trust to reach freedom (Level Three) takes time. But at this level, we can see issues from our partner's perspective without feeling threatened.

As long as we don't feel secure on the inside, we must rely on some form of external fairness. Early on in a relationship, a history of faithfulness doesn't exist. If this security has never been built with someone, or if our partner betrays our trust, we will likely resort to a self-protective stance.

A lack of positive life experiences makes discerning another's motives much harder. This appears to limit our options. We believe we can only adopt a "better safe than sorry" attitude or a "blindly trusting" attitude. But we can also patiently build a secure relationship.

Creating a true win-win is more a state-of-mind than a legal dividing of available options or resources. When a significant amount of trust and loyalty are established, a relationship can endure just about any shortcoming. Love always hopes, always trusts . . . (1 Corinthians 13:7).

Love is ultimately a subjective liking that does not waver in the midst of bad news.

For example, consider Dave and Samantha again. Dave wants to go to a mountain resort, but Samantha wants to go to the beach. A Frozen (Level One) approach results in a deadlocked position. They may end up cancelling their vacation, or going separate ways.

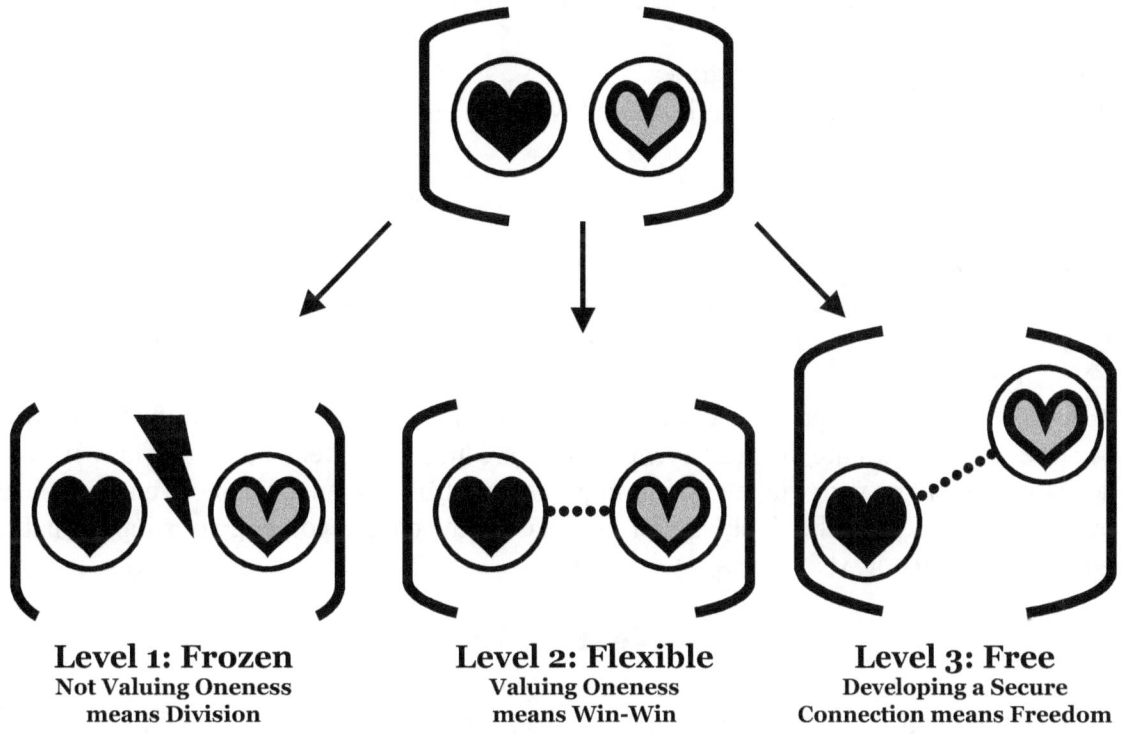

Level 1: Frozen
Not Valuing Oneness
means Division

Level 2: Flexible
Valuing Oneness
means Win-Win

Level 3: Free
Developing a Secure
Connection means Freedom

They could compromise and spend half of the time at each location, but then they must spend more time traveling. Or maybe they go to the beach this year and the mountains next year.

A Flexible (Level Two) approach provides a clever win-win solution such as finding a resort with access to both a beach and a mountain. The idea is to consider other options both can agree on so they are receiving most of what they want (or at least better than a 50/50 split). After all, 80/80 is better than 50/50.

Achieving a creative solution takes effort. To find a win-win solution, we can break down the choices into what we value. For example, instead of the demand, "I have to go to Myrtle Beach," we present, "I value sun, warmth and getting a tan." Now, the potential solution becomes finding a mountain resort also known for its higher temperatures and sunny days. But if we are stuck on the position of having to go to a specific beach, this sets up a guaranteed conflict where someone will lose.

Let's revisit Dave and Samantha's options when one or both have Level Three freedom. The context is one of prayerful consideration and a mostly positive life together. With this information, we might find them making a decision with relative ease. For example, Dave could hear from God that giving up his first choice is a good thing to do. Samantha, from a thankful heart, could offer to go where her husband will be happiest.

The difference in their attitude is obvious. These are not "fair" solutions, but they are superior. Instead of a passive resignation, each person presents an energetic offering. This kind of generous offering comes only from a heart secure in God's love, which takes time and effort to develop. At one point in time a couple can be at Level One and then years later be at Level Three, with exactly the same circumstances, yet choose a different solution.

For Reflection

1. Is fear keeping you rigid? Take a moment to consider what you are afraid might happen.
2. Are you holding onto resentment instead of being transparent about your preferences and feelings?
3. How secure are you with your partner?
4. When you are confident about yourself and who you are (as Jesus was), more room exists for flexibility.
5. When you are loyal to your partner:
   - You are willing to die for them.
   - You stick up for them against their adversaries.
   - You tolerate imbalance; life doesn't always have to be fair; you do not keep score.
   - You overlook deficiencies; you do not look down on them when they are weak.
   - You remain faithful even when they are not faithful.
6. A couple who understands fairness and flexibility can resolve conflict and feel like winners because they are secure in their identity, and are not dependent upon the fairness of the decision. Seeking a win-win resolution requires an artful mixture of objective and subjective perspectives. Look for the right way for you, the unique couple you are, not simply what feels good individually or what others say is right.

Next Steps

- What can you do to increase the level of security with your partner?
- How can you shift from "you versus me" to "you and me versus the problem"?
- What if failure was not an option for your relationship?
- Write out your process for finding your "best way."
- Review these resources:
  - Movie: *Apollo 13*
  - Book: *Getting to Yes* by Roger Fisher and William Ury
  - Site: marriagebuilders.com

Chapter 35

Embracing Conflict Realities

Blessed be the God and Father of our Lord Jesus Christ, the Father of mercies and God of all comfort, who comforts us in all our affliction, so that we may be able to comfort those who are in any affliction, with the comfort with which we ourselves are comforted by God.
—2 Corinthians 1:3–4

In marriage, ideally we contribute 100% of what we have. When we hold back a reserve, this alters the outcome and we will never know what could have been. Dividing everything in half is necessary at times, but it is also a sign of low levels of trust and security. You'll be better off if you invest your energy into building trust rather than arguing about what is fair.

Overcoming the Myths of Conflict Resolution

If we find we are in a relationship where the individual issues win considerably more than the relationship, or one person consistently votes for the relationship and the other for their issue, then potential exists for painful division. Partners benefit greatly when both value the relationship at the same time. But this is no easy task.

Resolving conflict is difficult because of all the emotions involved. When we have principles to guide the process, it goes much smoother. Knowing the myths of conflict resolution allows us to lower our expectations for a perfect solution.

Myth #1: The Perfect Solution must be Equally Balanced

Reality: Most solutions will not be perfectly balanced 50/50. But after brainstorming all reasonable possibilities, we can choose the best one. Reaching a solution both husband and wife are happy with is different from an objectively fair solution, which may not be practical, possible, or even preferred.

We can let fairness be subjective. We can decide what we are happy with even if outsiders cry foul. Why would we do this?

- Each couple is unique with differing values. What totally satisfies one couple might not satisfy another. Take advantage of this! If both husband and wife are satisfied, outside opinions don't matter.
- This is a three-legged race, not a four-legged one. We will come out ahead by seeking the best overall solution as a couple, not only what works for one partner. Giving to our partner does not take away from us. In fact, it usually results in an increase for us, too.
- God is the great balancer. He can make a good situation out of a bad one. His primary goal is to supply us with His love so we can supply others.

In general, the longer we are in a relationship, the less we care about having to have our way for negotiable issues. We are pleased to spend time together and enjoy our partner's company. We know our partner well enough that we trust the give-and-receive of the relationship.

When our longings for worth are met, we feel acceptable and confident. Agreement becomes easier. We feel a fullness about who we are, so we no longer need to place a heavy demand on the relationship. We don't look primarily to the relationship to validate our worth.

Less pressure to have our way equals a higher likelihood of enthusiastic agreement even when the solution is not objectively fair. Often, talking through the dilemma is enough to remove significant threats. What at first was considered unfair is no longer relevant.

Myth #2: The Perfect Solution Means Both Get Everything They Want

Reality: Solutions are rarely 100% win / 100% win. Realistically, to reach agreement, we will not get everything we originally wanted. But with determined brainstorming we can find the most optimal imperfect solution. Often the final solution is much better than our original idea because the solution incorporates both hearts' desires.

Myth #3: The Perfect Solution Means Doing Everything Together

Reality: Some optimal solutions will result in each partner doing their own thing. Emphasizing separateness in the relationship is sometimes okay as long as the individual pursuits don't crowd out togetherness.

If we have placed a low value on building the relationship, we probably need to emphasize togetherness, which banks deposits for the relationship. If we choose too many individual solutions, we could devalue the relationship to the point we no longer want to stay in it. Be sure to find enough ways to feel connected and develop the relationship.

The win-win solution assumes the issue is negotiable. If our partner wants to steal some money, we should say no and not offer any compromises. Yet, even in this situation, a legitimate desire is likely present within an illegitimate one. If the issue is money, a win-win might be taking out a loan or picking up extra work. Love should never force the other person to compromise their values just for the pleasure of the other.

The potential for a real conflict and a real fight exist when issues are more important than the relationship. But this might be okay. Some issues **are** more important than the relationship. When the individual concern is more important, we need to develop tolerance for the differences of opinions.

Some seasons of life legitimately require more individual focus than relationship focus. When this is true, pursue the individual efforts in such a way that they do not damage the relationship. When a person marries young, they may need to spend extra time finishing school or learning how to be appropriately independent. These activities invest in a stronger relationship. An older person might sense a calling to return to school. This shouldn't be a cause for alarm, provided other responsibilities are not neglected.

Over time, a couple can relax in the security of the bond they've established. This opens up many more possibilities for them. What is practically impossible at one point in a marriage might become a valid option later. The difference is the amount of trust banked with each other.

As we age, our emotional needs are felt and met in different ways. The first years of marriage might require more focus on a perfect balance (preserve "I" through compromise). Middle years tend to be defined by focusing on an established pattern of fairness (discover "Us" through win-win). Later years tend to offer even more flexibility in roles and pursuits (accomplish something beyond "Us" which requires going beyond fairness). The critical remaining factor is not only communication but communion with each other.

Myth #4: The Perfect Solution Means Giving Up My Desires

Reality: Our desires add flavor to the relationship and cause more harm when left out. If giving up our desires means giving up our right to have our opinions and preferences considered, then we should never do this. We must relate to others while being true to ourselves. God does not want us to compromise our unique identity.

We should not have to take actions that harm our conscience. Since we have to live with the consequences of our decisions, we should make wise choices. When we really believe in something, we should stand up for it as long as it does not compromise our partner's integrity.

The key is a willing heart that is open to learning how to love better. If we pray for nothing else, we should pray sincerely, "God help me love my partner better."

Myth #5: The Perfect Solution Means Not Changing What's Been Working

Reality: The way we've been doing life is not going to be sufficient for future challenges. A conflict might have nothing to do with our partner or us. Rather the problem might be the change we initiated by choosing marriage. Marriage inherently means change. For example, we can no longer only go to our own parents' home for Christmas. Accepting the reality of change is not only necessary, but also good, normal, and natural. Grieving our old, favored ways and accepting new ones is a necessary part of growth.

Myth #6: The Perfect Solution Will Come Without Struggle

Reality: A struggle usually means growth and growth resolves many problems. We must devote ourselves to pursuing growth. The perfect solution is often a struggle that results in a permanent change that makes life much easier. We must become comfortable with sacrifice. We need to grow so we don't feel threatened by giving up our desires for others.

Myth #7: The Perfect Solution is a Repeatable Formula

Reality: Finding the right way to resolve a conflict using a formula is not usually possible. A formula is not much different from a 50/50 compromise, which is usually too rigid. Structure can help but we create the best solutions with flexible guidelines and wise principles such as:
- Engaging your heart;
- Deciding from a solid identity;
- Loving unconditionally;
- Developing flexibility; and
- Trusting God is in control.

How This Works

Let's look at one more example. Emily wants to visit relatives and her husband Josh wants to stay home. Josh values the rare opportunity to spend time alone to recharge his batteries. Emily values time spent with family, including her husband. Note that Josh wanting time alone doesn't mean he doesn't want to spend time with Emily.

How could there be a win-win? Who stands to lose the most or win the most by the identified options? If both stay home, how good is that for Josh and how bad for Emily? If both go, how are each affected?

Different couples will legitimately choose different solutions. The same couple may even choose a different option on different days. All of these could be win-wins depending on the particular needs and attitudes of the couple:

- They stay home together because Josh really needs the rest and Emily doesn't want to go alone.
- They travel together but cut the trip shorter than originally planned.
- They travel together because Emily really needs the time of connection, but Josh spends a sizeable amount of time by himself.
- Josh stays home and Emily travels.

Whatever they choose, any one decision doesn't have the power to destroy the relationship. The pattern over time is what determines the fate of the relationship. If either person consistently values their own desires above the relationship, the relationship will suffer. For the relationship to thrive, the sense of being on the same team needs to strengthen over time. Maintaining a sense of mutual importance is the surest way to a satisfying marriage.

For Reflection

1. Over time the sense of "couple identity" grows to where the couple thinks in terms of "We do it this way" instead of "I do it this way and you do it that way."
2. Oneness issues involve the broad definition of marriage while individual issues involve specific decisions. An important part of marriage is spending quality time together. But this does not mean you cannot spend time apart pursuing your own interests. Using money as an example, the oneness issue would be treating any money as belonging to both, and the individual issues would be allowing for some portion of the budget to be spent on individual interests.
3. If you still have two separate bank accounts ("mine" and "yours"), you are failing to understand and experience oneness. This rigid approach might be okay if there is low trust in your relationship. But are you doing anything to increase the level of trust over time?
4. When in doubt choose options that say yes to as much as possible. Let your default be yes, but don't be afraid to use no.

Next Steps

☐ Which myths do you believe and how have they been creating problems?
☐ In your relationship, which issues are oneness issues? Which issues are individual issues?
☐ Practice brainstorming win-win solutions in the face of conflict.
☐ Review these resources:
  ☐ Movie: *Yes Man*
  ☐ Movie: *Joy Luck Club*
  ☐ Book: *Rescue your Love Life* by Cloud and Townsend
  ☐ Site: DaveWillis.org

Chapter 36

Biblical Conflict Resolution

What causes quarrels and what causes fights among you? Is it not this, that your passions are at war within you. You desire and do not have, so you murder. You covet and cannot obtain, so you fight and quarrel. You do not have, because you do not ask. You ask and do not receive, because you ask wrongly, to spend it on your passions.
—James 4:1–3

Repay no one evil for evil, but give thought to do what is honorable in the sight of all. If possible, so far as it depends on you, live peaceably with all. Beloved, never avenge yourselves, but leave it to the wrath of God, for it is written, "Vengeance is mine, I will repay, says the Lord."
—Romans 12:17–19

If anyone says, "I love God," and hates his brother, he is a liar; for he who does not love his brother whom he has seen cannot love God whom he has not seen.
—1 John 4:20

Bad conflict has at its roots a wrong heart-attitude toward God. If we cannot relate rightly to our partner, how can we say we are at peace with God?

God First, Partner Second

God created everything, including our partner. So whenever we have something to reconcile with our partner, we have something to reconcile with God first. A complaint with our partner is ultimately a complaint to God such as, "Why did you make him that way?" Or, "Why are you allowing her to treat me this way?"

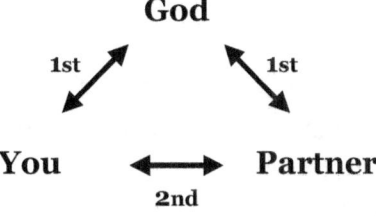

In resolving conflict, God asks us to be aware of our heart's motives. To determine our motives, we should always first open our heart and ears to God (Psalm 139:23–24). This should lead to answers to these questions:

- In what ways is my heart unclean (Luke 6:45)?

- What is the appropriate response to a sin or offense?
- Should I exercise a right to enforce a consequence?
- Should I step away completely, trusting God with all justice?

God never wants us to retaliate with revenge. He strictly denounces bringing further harm to make a point or to make us feel better (Romans 12:17–19). Others might go so far as to say we are not allowed to assess any form of consequence for another's sinful behavior. For example, David didn't take Saul's life even though he had the chance more than once and those close to him encouraged it (1 Samuel 24). We can best handle these kind of situations with discernment and wisdom on a case-by-case basis.

One key determining factor appears to be the Holy Spirit's prompting. David did not feel comfortable serving justice to Saul and, since God didn't command him, he was right to save his conscience. At other times, the Holy Spirit uses others to pronounce judgment and even carry out the sentence. For example, Moses executed the disobedient among Israel (Exodus 32).

If our motive is to bring harm or destruction to someone, then our heart is not right. However, allowing others to face the natural consequences of their actions is not evil. In fact, it will often, though not always, be the most loving thing to do.

Preparation for a Request

When conflict remains unresolved after our best efforts, a more structured approach will help. In the Bible, the book of James presents one easily understood model for resolving difficult conflicts.

James says negative conflict is the result of faulty desires. Whenever we have conflict with someone, we first need to consult with God, the one who ultimately meets our desires. Before attempting to resolve conflict with your partner, use the following steps to understand your internal conflict.

1. Stop and examine yourself (James 1:19).
    - What desires are battling within you (James 4:1)?
    - How angry are you that you are not getting your way (James 4:2)?
2. Determine your motives (James 4:3).
    - Do you know clearly what you want and why you want it?
    - Do you desire only what is for your earthly comfort (James 4:4)?
3. Believe God gives you what you need (James 1:17).
4. Ask God for wisdom (James 1:5).
5. Submit yourself to God (James 4:7).
6. Draw near to God (James 4:8).
7. Repent (James 4:8–9).
8. Humble yourself (James 4:10).
9. Don't speak negatively against your partner (James 4:11–12).
10. Classify your desire's primary significance level as 1, 2, or 3.
    - Level 1: Eternally significant reasons;
    - Level 2: Meets your earthly needs;
    - Level 3: Meets your earthly wants, preferences, or personal desires.

You could place any given desire at different levels depending on your motives. For example, a husband wanting his wife to spend more time exercising with him could be 1, 2, or 3 depending on his primary reason for wanting this.

11. Considering all three levels, ask God for what you want. Give priority to the eternally significant desires (Matthew 6:33).

Now that you have an eternal perspective, you can go to your partner and ask them for what you want. After listening to you, they will likely want to go through their own self-examination process before they can respond appropriately.

Preparation for a Response

In addressing a request, we want to respond, not react. Usually a quick response will be a sinful reaction rather than a well-thought-through godly response. These steps should help organize a response:

1. Stop and consider the desires within you.
2. What is your initial response, and what motives drive this response? Here are some questions to help you examine your heart:
   - Are you able to be a cheerful giver?
   - Do you feel compelled to give?
   - Any fears if you say yes? Any fears if you say no?
   - Do you feel angry about being asked for this?
   - Do you sense defensiveness?
   - Do you want to say no just to retaliate or be spiteful?
3. Ask God for wisdom.
4. Ask God for the eternal perspective on what is being asked of you. Consider the sacrifice of Isaac (Genesis 22). You can offer God what you have in faith, trusting He will provide.
5. Will your response be all of the following?
   - Honest
   - Thought-out
   - Realistic
   - Prayed over
6. Possible Responses (let your yes be yes and your no be no).
   - Agreement: Yes, I can do that;
   - Contingent Agreement: Yes, I can do that as long as . . . or I need more time . . .
   - Incapable: No, I don't think I'll ever be able to achieve your request;
   - Undesirable: No, I don't want to do that (only as a last resort).

Evaluation: Resolution or Recourse

After following these steps, determine if:
- You have reached resolution (you're done!);
- Further iteration will be worthwhile (start again from the beginning with the new knowledge you have); or
- A stronger solution is needed (intensify the intervention by including more people and/or more consequences if resolution is not reached).

A couple may become stuck even with both husband and wife fully seeking God. When this happens, following these guidelines may resolve the problem.
- As long as you both sense a cooperative spirit, discuss the situation in light of what you already know.

- If you face an impasse and both agree your concerns do not involve sin, then take more time to pray, cycle through the process, do further brainstorming, and involve trusted advisors and counselors.
- If you believe the other person is responding sinfully, read Psalm 37. Focus on controlling what you can control and accepting what you cannot control. Demonstrate love to your partner.
- If your partner is involved in a detrimental sin and refuses to respond to you, you must escalate your concern. Use Matthew 18:15–17 as a model. Involve your pastor. Increase consequences, but keep your motives pure. The next chapter explains how to handle these escalating situations in more detail.

The desired result is a win-win situation. We may never find a perfect solution, but we can find an optimal solution that moves us forward without resentment or remorse.

For Reflection

1. Some requests are thinly-disguised complaints or criticisms or are full of contempt. See if you can tell the difference between the three.
   - A complaint is a statement of how your partner's behavior has impacted you. Complaints usually imply a request and action to repair the problem. They involve using an I-statement coupled with sharing your feelings. For example, "I am upset because you didn't mow the lawn this week."
   - A criticism moves beyond a complaint by painting the situation in a negative light that begins to move against your partner. The language starts to suggest something is happening that cannot be undone. For example, "Uhhg! You forgot to mow the lawn again. I guess I'll have to do it like I've done all summer!"
   - Contempt focuses almost exclusively on character assassination. Hate, anger, bitterness, rage, and despair all fuel nasty verbal attacks meant to harm your partner. For example, "You never remember to mow the lawn! You are as worthless as you are lazy!"

Next Steps

- ☐ Apply biblical principles to your communication:
  - Hear your partner's heart, and consider your response before speaking into their life (James 1:19; Proverbs 15:28; Proverbs 18:13).
  - Be concerned about your partner's interests (Philippians 2:4).
  - Speak the truth, but only in love (Ephesians 4:15).
  - Don't escalate angry communication. Speak directly to the issue but without venom that will only incite a reaction (Proverbs 15:1).
  - Don't engage in endless unproductive cycles of quarreling (Proverbs 17:14).
  - When you are wrong, admit it (Proverbs 28:13; 1 John 1:9).
  - Don't repay evil for evil. Bless instead of curse (1 Peter 3:9).
- ☐ Review these resources:
  - ☐ Movie: To End all Wars
  - ☐ Book: The Seven Principles for Making Marriage Work by John Gottman
  - ☐ Site: gottmanblog.com/2013/04/the-four-horsemen-recognizing-criticism.html

Chapter 37

Biblical Confrontation

If your brother sins against you, go and tell him his fault, between you and him alone. If he listens to you, you have gained your brother. But if he does not listen, take one or two others along with you, that every charge may be established by the evidence of two or three witnesses. If he refuses to listen to them, tell it to the church. And if he refuses to listen even to the church, let him be to you as a Gentile and a tax collector.
—Matthew 18:15–17

Brothers, if anyone is caught in any transgression, you who are spiritual should restore him in a spirit of gentleness. Keep watch on yourself, lest you too be tempted. Bear one another's burdens, and so fulfill the law of Christ.
—Galatians 6:1–2

Anatomy of an Offense

Since God holds believers to a different standard than non-believers, Scripture gives us a godly process for confronting a Christian partner.

When another offends us, we are naturally hurt and usually angry. Anger can be positive in that it protects us from being vulnerable to repeated offense. Anger also lets us know we are expecting some kind of repayment because the offender owes us. Our initial reaction to hurt is usually some form of self-protection or payback. Without mercy, we will attempt to control the offense and punish the offender. But revenge without restraint ultimately ends up in destruction—the elimination of the offender.

We can choose to temper anger with mercy instead of opting for punishment or revenge. However, when we choose to neither punish nor forgive, we leave the relationship on hold indefinitely.

Forgiveness should occur as soon as we are able, but the next best time is right now. Provided the offender is repentant, forgiveness makes reconciliation possible. We surrender our desire for a destructive revenge in favor of a kindness-based revenge. This godly approach encourages the offender's repentance.

Failure to Repent

We must take seriously severe matters that threaten our personal safety, such as ongoing addiction, abandonment, adultery, or abuse. Yet even within these issues, longsuffering may bring about repentance. Therefore, no sin should ever result in an automatic divorce. We never know how quickly and sincerely our partner might repent (for example, consider Jonah).

However, if your partner refuses to repent of behavior that is destroying the marital relationship, you must respond proactively. When all else fails during conflict resolution and reconciliation, the right thing to do biblically is to escalate your concerns. Matthew 18:15–17 outlines the confrontation process in four steps:

1. One-to-One: Speak directly and only to your partner about their sin. Don't gossip or tell others about the matter. However if you believe your life is threatened, move to step two immediately. Don't risk further danger.
2. Few-to-One: Include a small group of trusted personal advisors and close friends. If possible, they should know both of you equally well so they are unbiased. Choose people that can be firm against the behavior but gentle with your partner. Your supporters shouldn't embarrass your partner but have a heart for restoration.
3. Church Community-to-One: Make a unified decision (with your advisors) to communicate with the appropriate spiritual authority in your partner's life. You should not have to bear the burden of a serious confrontation on your own. The authorities might need to pursue formal consequences.
4. Change your Strategy: Stop relating to your partner as if they are a sincere Christian with an active spiritual life. Love and pray for your partner, offer witness to Christ in your life, but recognize that trusting your partner would be foolish. Cease any and all protection that prevents your partner from facing consequences for their actions. Let God deal with your partner. "[D]eliver this man to Satan for the destruction of the flesh, so that his spirit may be saved in the day of the Lord" (1 Corinthians 5:5).

If you've spent an adequate amount of time on one step with no results, then move on to the next step. Some sins we tolerate because no one is perfect (including ourselves). Some sins are small enough that step one is the furthest we should progress. Steps two through four are for the most serious sins.

The Bible doesn't direct us to move through all four steps in as short a time as possible. Love is patient. Give your partner multiple opportunities to repent. Be extremely cautious, prayerful, and intentional before moving on to the next step. Delay permanent decisions to the end.

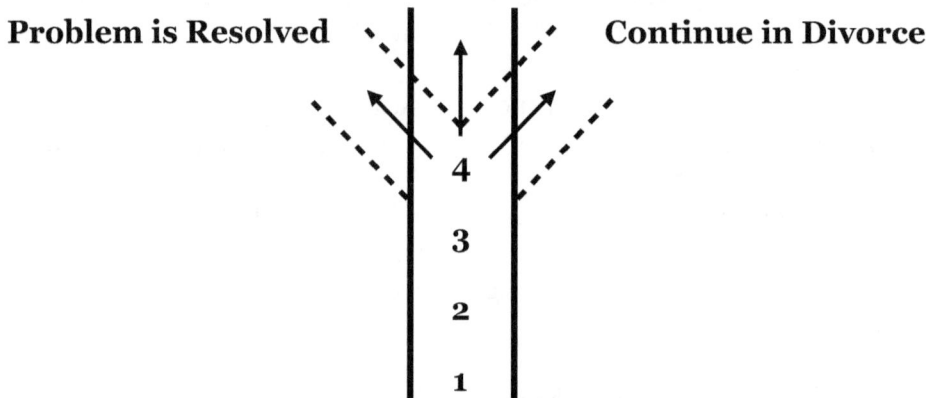

How to Restore your Partner

The purpose of confrontation is to regain our partner. Therefore, the correct heart-motive is to seek restoration, not to serve some form of punishment. Sometimes we accomplish restoration though kind but direct words. Other times, stronger medicine is required. When our partner exchanges the right path for a wrong one, sometimes we wait for them to return and at other times we must proactively find and confront them. When intentional action is warranted, this is the right time to carefully speak the truth to them in love.

We must confront in the least damaging way possible. The goal is to put an end to sin, not inflict additional and permanent harm. Yet, we must also increase the strength of the medicine when our partner is unresponsive. Note the principle:

Use the least strength of medicine possible to cure the disease.

The only way to accomplish this is to start with the least potent medicine and if our partner does not respond, increase the potency.

When our partner repents, the issue is resolved. If they don't, we must escalate the confrontation. To threaten divorce when they come home late is to act out of proportion to the offense. But what if coming home late turns into a habit? A stronger confrontation is required. What if our partner starts coming home drunk every night? An even stronger intervention is required. As their destructive behavior continues or escalates, so should our attempts at restoration.

We are to restore others with a spirit of gentleness (Galatians 6:1) so the first confrontation should be as casual and non-threatening as possible. However, if our partner does not respond to gentleness, we have a loving obligation to confront more vigorously in an attempt to win over their heart. Even so, once enough time has passed, we can declare our partner unreachable and move forward. This does not necessarily mean separation or divorce but certainly means investing our energies elsewhere until they are ready to repent.

The offended partner should set appropriate boundaries to prevent further harm but postpone making any permanent decisions. If your partner is determined to sin and your boundaries keep you safe from further harm, let your partner be the one to initiate divorce (if they so choose). Then this decision will not be on your conscience.

Being patient gives the offender an opportunity to repent, just like God is patient with us (2 Peter 3:9). Anyone acting in haste with the marriage escape clause is not acting in God's love nor in God's will. Reconciliation should always be attempted before any knee-jerk reactions. When a partner is remaining in sin, loving them will not be easy, but it is the right thing to do.

For Reflection

1. Try informally pursuing these steps for less serious circumstances.
   - You might increase the number of advisors you have without necessarily needing to confront the offender.
   - A partially cooperative partner might volunteer to pursue increasingly stronger remedies. For example, in addition to individual counseling, your partner pursues group counseling.
   - You can talk to your pastor without having to start a formal discipline process.
2. The steps are best followed from a place of forgiveness. When possible, don't wait until your anger is so great that you desire revenge more than restoration. However, you can start confronting even if you have not fully forgiven yet.
3. What warrants moving from step one to step two? Step three? Step four?

Next Steps

- ☐ If your partner is refusing to listen to you, don't hesitate to include trusted advisors. The whole point of the biblical process is to take advantage of strength in numbers.
- ☐ For step two, consider professional counseling as an option.
- ☐ Seek professional help not only for your partner's emotional health, but for yours too. This is especially needed if you struggle with codependency or haven't confronted serious sins.

☐   Use your Blueprint Space to plan your intervention. What can you delay until later without compromising your safety? You don't have to solve the whole problem in one intervention. But do something, then evaluate. Has your situation improved? Be willing to make drastic changes if needed. Be willing to give up something of lessor value than marriage. As long as something is changing, you will gain more perspective and therefore be making more of an informed decision.

Blueprint Space

Chapter 38

Deep Betrayal

He who commits adultery lacks sense; he who does it destroys himself.
—Proverbs 6:32

"You have heard that it was said, 'You shall not commit adultery.' But I say to you that everyone who looks at a woman with lustful intent has already committed adultery with her in his heart.
—Matthew 5:27–28

Roommates can live separate lives without consequence. But marriage partners must frequently and consistently connect in order to develop and remain as one, and live in sync with each other.

Disclosure and Shock

Brittany engages her husband Chris in an open conversation:

Brittany: "Is everything okay? You seem different . . . more distant lately."

Chris: "I'm fine. Work is more demanding now. I told you that already."

Two months later

Brittany: "We aren't as close anymore. How about we plan on spending some quality time together this weekend?"

Chris: "Sorry, can't happen. I have to work this weekend. Maybe next month."

Two more months go by

Brittany: "I found this receipt for a restaurant. It's a sizeable bill. What's it for?"

Chris: "I had a lunch meeting with people from the office."

Brittany: "On a Saturday at four o'clock? What's really going on?"

Chris: "Yeah, we got started late."

Brittany: "Well, I also found a number on the receipt and called it. I know what you've been doing."

The next several months are extremely difficult for them. Chances are Chris will deny the extent of wrongdoing until he absolutely has to confess to everything.

To the unfaithful person living in sin, disclosing and confessing the truth is hard. However, once the secret is out, Chris feels like a great burden has been lifted. Meanwhile, Brittany, as the victim, experiences extreme emotional shock from the disclosure. Given the revelation, she must reorient her understanding of all past related events.

Good sense makes one slow to anger,
and it is his glory to overlook an offense.
—Proverbs 19:11

Most of the time, it's not the offense that is so offensive. We can overlook offenses because they are individual incidents. But the pain it causes should not be overlooked. The heartache comes from the abrupt realization of an alternate reality. One troubling question calls out to the victim:

What is the *meaning* of this offense?

Brittany experiences retroactively the betrayal, deceit, and lies as ongoing and constant in the present moment. The disclosure is so intense because the previously unknown personal history comes to bear on one moment in time. She feels threatened by the question, "How could my husband lie to me for so long?"

Betrayal is a traumatic experience. The painful disorientation needs time and the right environment to heal fully. The pain comes from:

- The nagging feelings of suspicion prior to finding out the truth;
- Trying to resolve the hurt all at once;
- The lost closeness with our partner;
- The realization that our partner is not who we thought they were;
- Feeling overwhelmed at the amount of work needed to make repairs;
- Grieving because the relationship will never be the same.

Normal responses to shock include:

- Moving between denial and the reality that the offense really happened;
- Riding an emotional roller coaster of peace one moment and intense anger or sadness the next;
- Feeling a need to desperately grasp for control;
- Blaming oneself for what might have caused it;
- Feeling unsafe, overwhelmed, fearful, or anxious;
- Feeling disconnected or numb;
- Confusion, difficulty concentrating, and obsessing over the meaning of the offense;
- Difficulty sleeping, fatigue, agitation, aches and pains.

Why?

Affairs happen primarily when one or both partners cannot be themselves with the other. Chris, the unfaithful partner, has thoughts before, during, and even after his betrayal, such as:

- "I am not happy with my marriage, but I need to suffer patiently as a Christian."
- "I cannot tell Brittany because the pain will be too much for her."
- "I am too ashamed to tell her."
- "My marriage is empty, and I feel alive again with the other person."

Even though hiding avoids the pain, this kind of thinking only increases the pain to be experienced in the future.

The Healing Begins

Healing cannot fully begin until the offender makes a full disclosure of his betrayal to the victim. Total confession purifies any infection. God says when we confess our sin, He is faithful to forgive us (1 John 1:9). During the first few weeks after disclosure, I recommend the following to make the most of a strenuous time.

Be Patient

Be patient with yourself. Seek support from trusted others, but choose people who are in a position to remain unbiased (counselors, pastors, and mature friends). Family members are not a good choice because they are usually biased toward their own kin. In addition, they may develop a personal negative view of your partner. Limit sharing to one or two people at first.

Don't Make it Worse

Don't make matters worse by wounding each other in negative fighting. Certainly do not continue in the betrayal, and do not retaliate by committing additional sin.

Have Fun Too

Don't spend all your time focusing on what happened. This problem won't be solved overnight. Pace yourselves. Spend focused time talking about the issue, but also spend focused time having fun and participating in light-hearted activities.

Decide How Much Detail

How much does the victim want to know about the unfaithfulness? How much about future relapses? Decide together how much detail will be disclosed. At a minimum, include enough detail to describe the problem. After that, reveal as much detail as the victim desires to know.

Confess Everything

Once disclosure has started, it's best to finish without interruption. Stay focused on one step of healing at a time. Don't try to apologize during a confession. Don't hold back some information for later. If you believe you have too much to say at one time, at least prepare your partner by saying something like: "I have more to tell you that you aren't going to like, but I've said enough. You are already overwhelmed right now." Then set a specific date and time to disclose everything. If necessary, disclose information in the presence of a counselor or other objective witness.

Sort out Responsibility

The victim can share the responsibility for the overall marital conditions that led to the betrayal. However, the offender must bear the full responsibility for their unfaithful acts.

Hope is Alive

With God, hope is always alive. He is always making things anew (Isaiah 43:19). The offender may fall into sin or even intend evil, but God can bring good from either (Genesis 50:19–20). A broken bone, when properly set, actually mends stronger than before it broke. The experience of healing deep hurt builds a nearly invincible strength.

This is the message of the gospel. Christ's death and resurrection defeated death, giving us invincibility (1 Corinthians 15:54).

What does this mean for us? With God, our deepest wounding is also the place of deepest healing and restoration.

For Reflection

1. Attempting to control a betrayal cannot resolve it. The only way to heal the pain is to:
    - Go through it, not around it;
    - Discover why it happened and what it means;
    - Accept what happened but reject allowing it to define who you are;
    - Determine what you can do to move forward in the best way possible.

2. Unfortunately, betrayal is not usually an isolated incident. Marriages likely have multiple betrayal-type wounds. While one betrayal does not excuse another, unresolved emotional pain coupled with the weakness of the flesh may have led to the current betrayal. Without healing the source of the pain, history may repeat itself.
3. Betrayal comes in all shapes and sizes. If you haven't searched through your life to find and heal emotional wounds, chances are you have at least one festering wound.
4. Imagine how your life would be if you allowed Christ to heal you at your place of deepest wounding.

Next Steps

- ☐ Look beneath the surface to root causes. The unfaithful partner should write a comprehensive description and timeline of their unfaithfulness and complete sexual history (if applicable):
  - Consider the document will be a full confession, but also a healthy and normal history.
  - Start with puberty or first sexual experiences, whichever is earlier.
  - Include all sexual experiences. Summarize repetitive experiences.
  - Include frequencies and enough detail to communicate the significance of each event.
  - Include for example: all degrees of sexual intimacy with others, masturbation, lustful thoughts, use of pornography, and other paraphernalia.
- ☐ Both husband and wife can graph a timeline of the highs and lows in their marriage.
- ☐ Review these resources:
  - ☐ Movie: *The Incredibles*
  - ☐ Book: *Unfaithful* by Gary and Mona Shriver
  - ☐ Book: *Torn Asunder* by Dave Carder
  - ☐ Site: helpguide.org/articles/ptsd-trauma/emotional-and-psychological-trauma.htm

Blueprint Space

Chapter 39

Restoration

*When I am afraid,
I put my trust in you.
In God, whose word I praise,
in God I trust; I shall not be afraid.
What can flesh do to me?*
—Psalm 56:3–4

Complete restoration requires multiple activities, each of which we should handle separately. Forgiveness and repentance come first and we must achieve these independently from each other. Reconciliation brings forgiveness and repentance together, making trust possible in the future.

Hopeful Restoration

Does a sheriff lock up a victim and criminal in the same cell? How ridiculous! Can betrayer and betrayed share the same bed and live to tell of their reconciliation? As strange as it sounds, yes. God has a different strategy for marriage.

God binds husband and wife together so they can work through their ill behaviors. Marriage restoration is excruciatingly difficult because escape is not a viable option. Second only to our relationship with God, marriage requires our utmost loyalty.

When our partner hurts us, we suffer loss. Usually, we can easily replace material losses. Intangible losses of broken trust cause the most distress. They are elusive and intensely troubling. Yet, small losses over a long period can be just as debilitating. "I can't believe you're going to be traveling on my birthday again. You've been away the last five years. Your work is more important to you than I am!"

Betrayal leaves us open to gut-wrenching disappointment. Often our partner cannot even grasp how we are hurting. We suffer at the hands of our partner but suffer more when we can't go to them for comfort. All relationships face disbelief and the utter shock of betrayal. "How could *you*, the one who is supposed to have my back?"

When we hurt our partner, we suffer, too. At first, we hide in shame and shield ourselves from the truth. But eventually, with God's help, we feel our guilt, sinfulness, and brokenness. We see the betrayal in our partner's face. We come face-to-face with our failure to love. We begin the quest to be contrite, hopefully in earnest and without self-condemnation.

Bad shame does not bring healing, only self-absorbed chastisement. "I am a horrible person because of what I did. I deserve to die." Shame without hope is pure abandonment. But God does not abandon us.

Good shame, also called conviction, has a healthy serving of hope mixed in, which leads to godly repentance. "I know I was wrong, but I have hope for my recovery." God turns up the heat in a positive way, melting away resistance and defensiveness in order to transform us into a better man or woman.

Our trust and hope must be in God. Otherwise, we are indulging in misplaced trust. Whether we betray our partner, or our partner betrays us, our suffering highlights the fact that we have nowhere to go except to God. Depending on our partner for our healing won't ultimately help and may destroy us. Betrayer and betrayed equally need God's help.

Restoration Overview

Complete restoration involves consideration of past, present, and future behaviors. The offender and victim have different roles in restoration.

	Past	**Present**	**Future**
Offender	Repents	Reconcile	Grows
Victim	Forgives		Trusts

The three parts (past, present, and future) to restoring a relationship are best implemented as three separate tasks. They can overlap, but we must implement them in a specific order. We must examine past behaviors before reconciliation makes sense. We must start reconciliation before we can restore trust.

We address past behaviors independent of our partner. For example, repentance is possible without first securing forgiveness. The offender repents in order to grow and change behavior. Likewise, forgiveness is primarily for the victim and is possible without first securing repentance. We cannot change the past, only forgive it, and the offender's participation is not required.

For the victim, forgiveness is primarily an internal grieving process:
1. Identify what was lost along with its significance.
2. Figure out how to let go of what cannot be changed.
3. Walk in freedom by canceling the debt and keeping the lesson learned.

Reconciliation can only progress to the degree the husband and wife have separately completed the hard work of repentance and forgiveness. The reconciliation conversation brings the past and future together into the present moment as the couple negotiates the necessary terms to resume a trusting relationship. The victim shares their hurt and then offers forgiveness. The offender shares their apology, including the details of failure and the depth of regret, and then accepts forgiveness.

The couple also discusses what the future will look like. The possibility of growth keeps hope alive for their future together. With hope generated by the commitment to grow, trusting again is possible. Trust involves what the victim will risk in the future. Renewed trust always involves some risk, but the risk is minimized to the degree the offender chooses new and better ways to behave.

Restoring Your Marriage

In the midst of restoring a relationship, remembering the way of love is essential. Love is risky. When we love, we are not acting out of fear, and we will not unnecessarily guard our hearts. For the victim, part of the restoration process is seeking enough strength to love. For the offender, the way of love is leaving behind harmful behaviors and being patient while the victim learns to trust again.

Healing can't be forced or rushed. We can take the needed time to clean out the infection from the relationship. However, realize that we can drag out the whole restoration process by not being intentional. Life is short, and time is of the essence. We should make amends as quickly as possible. God has further plans for us when we are ready.

For Reflection

1. Trust is not ruined by the failure to be perfect—trust is ruined by the failure to repair what is broken.
2. When trusting in others, wisdom suggests, "trust but verify." When trusting in God, wisdom suggests, "lean on God, not your own understanding."
3. What can you glean about restoration from this quote attributed to Thomas Paine?

> *The harder the conflict, the more glorious the triumph. What we obtain too cheap, we esteem too lightly . . . I love the man that can smile in trouble, that can gather strength from distress and grow.*

Next Steps

- ☐ Read Psalm 56 substituting "hope" for "trust." How are you placing hope in your partner that is meant for God? How does this approach change everything? How would your life be different if you could fully lean into God during times of betrayal?
- ☐ Review these resources:
  - ☐ Movie: *The Interpreter*
  - ☐ Book: *Boundaries Face to Face* by Cloud and Townsend
- ☐ Use your Blueprint Space to draw a picture of your struggle. Sort out what has transpired into past, present, and future to help you know what to do with each part.

Blueprint Space

Chapter 40

Repentance

---

*Create in me a clean heart, O God,
and renew a right spirit within me.
Restore to me the joy of your salvation,
and uphold me with a willing spirit.
The sacrifices of God are a broken spirit;
a broken and contrite heart, O God, you will not despise.*
—Psalm 51:10, 12, 17

*True repentance hates the sin, and not merely the penalty; and it hates the
sin most of all because it has discovered and felt God's love.*
—W.M. Taylor

Genuine Repentance

Jesus defeated Death and Sin by providing His perfect sacrifice. As believers, we have salvation and a new heart but at times struggle in our flesh. God won the war, yet we battle with sin. God remade us perfect, but we are still capable of choosing wrong behaviors.

When we sin, we lose sight of the victory we have in Jesus. But with our new hearts we can grieve our dysfunctional behavior. God provides repentance for correcting the dysfunction and restoring the joy of our salvation. Repentance is agreeing with God that our behavior is sin and trusting He will cleanse us from all unrighteousness. We cannot truly repent without the work of the Holy Spirit in our heart.

Trust, the lifeblood of all relationships, is ruined by our failure to repair what is broken, not by our failure to be perfect. God desires our heart to be soft and open to His correction, not hardened and self-sufficient. A broken and contrite heart is capable of genuine repentance.

The seven Rs of repentance are the necessary steps to repair what is broken. Repentance is an inward-to-outward journey, from repairing everything deep within our heart to making amends with the victim of our sin.

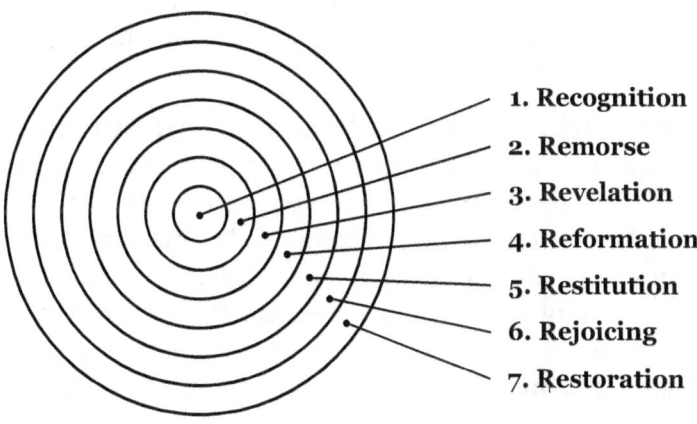

1. Recognition
2. Remorse
3. Revelation
4. Reformation
5. Restitution
6. Rejoicing
7. Restoration

Recognition: Identifying Sin

The first step of repentance is being aware we have chosen a wrong path. Identification of the true sin of the heart is limited to the work of the Holy Spirit. We identify the letter of the law and bring guilt and condemnation, but only the Spirit can identify the motive of the heart and bring conviction and healing.

Remorse: Godly Sorrow

After God places His finger on the problem, godly sorrow can begin. He helps us see that the problem is a problem. Feeling the pain of our mistake turns up the temperature enough to achieve the desired transformation in our hearts. The sorrow is like the unpleasant itch of a wound slowly healing. We want to interfere (scratch), but it is better to allow God to complete His work in us.

Revelation: Confessing Wrong Behavior

Confession is agreeing "out loud" with God that our behavior is wrong. Confessing our sin completes our responsibility in the healing—enabling God to perform His delicate surgery on our heart. Seeing God's heart of loving restoration gives us courage to admit our failure. As appropriate, we disclose our sin to the victims (if to their benefit) and to a recognized authority for accountability (if to our benefit).

Reformation: Improving Behavior

As our bodies thrive physically without cancer, so we thrive emotionally and spiritually without sin. After we've addressed the sin in our hearts, we are empowered to stop bad behaviors. True repentance makes way for establishing new habits. If we aren't growing, we might not be experiencing a deep enough healing. Starting new habits can be difficult, so sometimes we need multiple opportunities to fully replace a sinful pattern. Repentance might involve an immediate course correction, but it always involves a believable commitment to change for the future.

Restitution: Making Right When Possible

Restoring what is lost is sometimes easy, sometimes difficult, and sometimes impossible. Part of repentance is a heart willing to return the victim as closely as possible to the pre-offense state. For example, we can replace material possessions.

Emotional problems heal more quickly through counseling. Accordingly, we can mend broken trust more quickly by listening with an attitude of acceptance and understanding. We cannot change the past, but we can be patient with our partner in the present moment.

Rejoicing: Moving on in Freedom

When we've confessed all we've done and done all we can to correct any damages then, because of Christ, there is nothing left to do. We are right to stop recalling our sin. When God fully releases us from our sin, our natural response is joy. If we aren't experiencing joy, we probably haven't fully completed the previous steps.

Restoration: Continuing the Relationship, If Mutually Agreeable

With complete repentance, nothing (of the current offense) remains in the heart of the offender to fester and prevent trustworthy behavior. We are open to restoration, but at the same time, we realize variables remain beyond our control. Though we've made complete restoration with our partner possible, we must give up any desire to control the reconciliation with our partner. We shouldn't force or demand our own way. Forgiveness has its own timetable.

Achieving full repentance is difficult because it requires relentless pursuit of a clean heart. Even when we achieve it, we must humbly accept we are capable of relapse and repeating our mistakes.

This highlights even more how trusting God for His work in our hearts is essential to our well-being. With God all things are possible.

Repentance and Marriage

A genuinely repentant partner needs grace and time to make the necessary changes. Failure to change can be for different reasons, for example, lack of commitment or lack of skill.

The attitude of the heart is more important than the outward appearance. We are better off being with a known imperfect sinner than a partner who feels compelled to present a clean image but has no real intention to change. This partner's goal is to avoid being exposed rather than working towards lasting change.

Any repentance worth the effort must produce positive and lasting change. We are better off with a partner who makes realistic, permanent changes than someone who overcompensates by being superman for a few months but slowly returns to the old way of doing things.

The Holy Spirit is the one who enables enduring change. He helps us grow internally so we can choose more godly behavior. True repentance is a journey down a one-way street and leaves no breadcrumb trail back to the wrong behavior. As we travel through the doors of change, they close behind us permanently. We will have no other option but to make a new path forward.

Example of Repentance

Nicole and Ryan have been married for ten years. Nicole developed a friendship with a man at work. She thought, "There's nothing going on, so I don't need to mention anything to Ryan." Eventually the friendship became a problem.

1. Recognition: I'm feeling closer to this other man than to my husband. My pride got in the way. I failed to foresee something like this could happen. I was in denial.
2. Regret: Telling Ryan isn't going to be fun. He'll be hurt because of my prideful mistake. Telling him about this upfront would have been much easier and probably would have prevented the problem.
3. Revelation: I need to tell Ryan that my feelings crossed a line. I wasn't expecting this to happen. I was too proud to tell him upfront. I was in denial that too much distance existed between us.
4. Reformation: Nicole and Ryan develop a policy of always keeping each other informed of the time they spend with others. Nicole works on recognizing other ways she is too self-reliant or prone to denial.
5. Restitution: Nicole dotes on Ryan more, goes to counseling, and goes on dates with Ryan every week. But she needs to pace herself for the long haul. Taking on a ridiculous amount of tasks out of guilt is not a result of a clean heart.
6. Rejoicing: With a new path set before her, Nicole pursues a realistic future with enthusiasm and hope.
7. Restoration: Nicole probably won't end up divorced over this mistake, but Ryan probably won't trust her around other men for some time. Eventually he should trust her as he sees she understands the value of a no-secrets marriage.

For Reflection

1. What benefits does the repentant person receive according to James 4:8–10?

   Draw near to God, and he will draw near to you. Cleanse your hands, you sinners, and purify your hearts, you double-minded. Be wretched and mourn and weep. Let your laughter be turned to mourning and your joy to gloom. Humble yourselves before the Lord, and he will exalt you.

2. A change in behavior is external and a change of heart is internal. Complete repentance involves both. How exactly do you define a change of heart? How is a change of heart important to genuine repentance?
3. What is the difference between godly grief and worldly grief?

   For godly grief produces a repentance that leads to salvation without regret, whereas worldly grief produces death.
   —2 Corinthians 7:10

4. Have you confessed your sins appropriately? Are you feeling cleansed from all unrighteousness?

   If we confess our sins, he is faithful and just to forgive us our sins and to cleanse us from all unrighteousness.
   —1 John 1:9

5. Can you fully receive forgiveness if you haven't fully repented? Can you think of any circumstances in which this is possible?

Next Steps

- ☐ Read Psalm 51 and allow its truth to lead you as deeply as you need to go into repentance and restoration.
- ☐ Identify any ways repentance is incomplete in your life.
- ☐ Review these resources:
  - ☐ Movie: *Island of Grace (2011)*

Chapter 41

Finding Complete Healing

*He heals the brokenhearted
and binds up their wounds.*
—Psalm 147:3

*O LORD my God, I cried to you for help,
and you have healed me.*
—Psalm 30:2

*God wants us to find healing through restoration. To experience restoration
we must make an account of the past and reconcile our experience with the
truth of the Scriptures.*

Healing, Then Forgiveness, Then Healing

Which comes first, forgiveness or healing? We may say forgiveness comes first, but what if we are too traumatized to think about the offender?

We don't preach forgiveness to a severely injured car accident victim. However, we often preach forgiveness too quickly to the emotionally wounded even when they are too weakened to do anything more than receive care. Many times we cannot start, let alone complete, the forgiveness process without first receiving a significant dose of healing.

Our need to forgive our partner is directly linked to where our partner wounds us. A deep wound is personal to our identity. This is why forgiveness is so difficult—any significant emotional injury cuts to the core of who we are. While healing and forgiveness are two different processes, they are unavoidably linked together.

Healing encompasses basic recovery, forgiveness, and deep healing. Basic recovery has nothing to do with the offender but everything to do with our basic needs for security and safety. Where strength was taken, it must be restored. After we are stable, we can work at forgiveness so further healing isn't hindered. Forgiveness opens the door allowing God to come into the wound. Then we are prepared for God to provide deep healing.

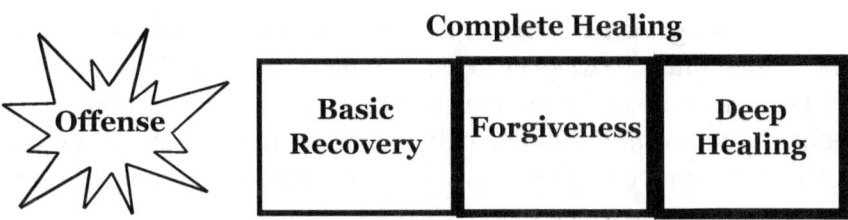

Basic Recovery Before Forgiveness

A victim needs some amount of recovery before forgiveness is required. Experiencing loving care reassures us that we will make it through the pain—and also gives us the strength to pursue forgiveness and even deeper healing. Thus, healing must start before forgiveness.

But healing can only begin when we are ready to identify the damage done. We cannot fully forgive someone until we understand and face what we've lost. Any expectation to forgive should only come from God. He knows when we are ready.

Forgiveness is a great emotional struggle because the loss and pain are real. Though God commands us to forgive, He also knows the limitations of our heart. Complete forgiveness is ultimately a work of the Holy Spirit in our lives. In order to heal, we must entrust ourselves to God's care.

Before forgiveness can start, we need to feel reasonably cared for, safe, and secure. This includes:
- A physical environment which feels comfortable and is free from reminders of the trauma;
- A community of safe people to provide support strong enough to significantly reduce the likelihood of being retraumatized;
- Spiritual attention to restore and nurture our connection with God.

After someone sins against us, we should monitor our sense of spiritual safety. God is our only hope of recovery. Blocking Him out is the most crippling action we can take. These questions help identify any problems:
- Are we still connected to Jesus?
- Do we continue to believe Jesus is for us and not against us?
- Do we trust God is our stronghold, an ever present help in our time of need?
- Can we look to Jesus to meet what is unmet in our life (including the damage from this most recent offense)?

If so, we are in a good place to forgive our offender. By moving our attention away from our offender and onto God, we cast away any anxiety caused by looking to our offender for healing. Then, when we are strong enough, we can extend forgiveness and offer reconciliation as appropriate.

The health of our marriage is dependent on our ability to find and maintain our spiritual safety with God. Waiting on our partner to make up for their shortcoming is a mistake. Our life could be on hold for a long time. We should ask ourselves if we are looking to our partner for what only God can provide. Is what we want from our partner more important than our connection with God? God does not give us everything we want, but neither does He limit our spiritual security with Him. When we ask for good things, God gives generously. We can never go wrong by asking:
- Help me love my partner.
- Help me forgive my partner.
- Help me be more loving, joyful, peaceful, patient, kind, honest, faithful, gentle, and self-controlled.

Forgiveness Before the Deepest Healing

God is a part of the entire healing process, but the deeper healing is especially personal, spiritual, and even supernatural. Offenses are usually personal, so the healing needs to be personal. Part of deep healing is transcending the negative meaning thrust upon us by the offense. Only God's touch upon our life can accomplish this. When God heals us emotionally, we end up stronger than we were before the trauma.

At some point in the healing process refusing forgiveness is counter-productive. Forgiveness and healing are inseparably dependent on each other. If we haven't completely forgiven, we cannot say we are completely healed because we remain in waiting for payment of a debt. The longer forgiveness is incomplete, the more likely bitterness will take root. Who can say, "I'm healed," while holding a grudge?

Stages of Emotional Recovery

Recovering from emotional trauma is not much different than recovering from physical trauma. After an accident, we experience shock and the need to stabilize (stage 1). We work to accept and recover from our losses (stages 2–3). And, we figure out how to return to our best productive functioning (stages 4–5).

Stage 1: Ambulance, Surgery, and Intensive Care

Goal: Stabilize and prevent further decline and/or death.
Functioning:
- Incapacitating emotional pain, shock, numbness;
- Confusion and denial about what's happened;
- Not-fully-present or unconscious;
- Helpless and out-of-control;
- Has no choice but to accept help—cannot function without assistance.

Expectations for Productivity: None.

Stage 2: Hospital Room

Goal: Identify and accept impact of trauma.
Functioning:
- Increasingly able to understand the repercussions of what's happened;
- Anger and hopelessness;
- Resistance to recovery—may stubbornly refuse assistance;
- High potential for irrational behavior (such as suicide);
- Believes nothing good can come from this.

Expectations for Productivity: Minimal.

Stage 3: Intensive Rehabilitation

Goal: High motivation and participation in recovery.
Functioning:
- May still be upset and overwhelmed by discovering new perspectives on what's happened;
- Increasingly accepting of new reality;
- Strong appreciation for the help of others;
- Painful process of failure and success;
- Many positive days, but has the potential to move in reverse some days;
- Concludes better days are ahead, but must fight vigorously to stay determined to recover.

Expectations for Productivity: Moderate.

Stage 4: Back to Normal Functioning

Goal: Function at similar levels of productivity as before the trauma.
Functioning:
- Less focus on healing and more on productivity;
- Occasional setback from a bad day is short-lived;
- Stability, consistency, and trust are all regained;
- Confidence about the future;

- Potential for relapse increases if not careful to maintain self-awareness.

Expectations for Productivity: High.

Stage 5: Exceed Previous Functioning

Goal: Function at all-time highs and work to prevent relapse.

Functioning:
- Healthy understanding of limitations and capabilities;
- Sees the potential for regression and relapse;
- Mood is frequently grateful and thankful;
- Works proactively to stay healthy and grow;
- Able to care for self and others in similar situations.

Expectations for Productivity: High.

For Reflection

1. Healing is a process of emptying yourself of pain and bitterness to make room for God to restore and fill you as He determines.
2. Consider the story of Stephen (Acts 7:55–60). How was he able to forgive so quickly?
3. Are you trying to forgive before you have properly regained your strength?
4. Are you claiming to be fully healed yet still harboring bitterness toward your offender?
5. God can heal a broken heart, but He has to have all the pieces.

Next Steps

☐ To what degree are you safe spiritually (connected to and trusting in Jesus Christ for your wellbeing)?

☐ Review the Stages of Emotional Recovery. Familiarize yourself with them so you can set realistic expectations whenever you experience emotional trauma in your marriage.

☐ Meditate on 1 Peter 5:6–10. How does it feel to know that God has plans to restore, confirm, strengthen, and establish you?

> *Humble yourselves, therefore, under the mighty hand of God so that at the proper time he may exalt you, casting all your anxieties on him, because he cares for you. Be sober-minded; be watchful. Your adversary the devil prowls around like a roaring lion, seeking someone to devour. Resist him, firm in your faith, knowing that the same kinds of suffering are being experienced by your brotherhood throughout the world. And after you have suffered a little while, the God of all grace, who has called you to his eternal glory in Christ, will himself restore, confirm, strengthen, and establish you.*
> —1 Peter 5:6–10

☐ Review these resources:
  ☐ Movie: *Spiderman 3 (2007)*

Chapter 42

Surviving an Offense

For if you forgive men when they sin against you, your heavenly Father will also forgive you. But if you do not forgive men their sins, your Father will not forgive your sins.
—Matthew 6:14–15

When we fully understand how much we have been forgiven, we should not have reason to hesitate to forgive anything and anyone else. I don't know the actual meaning of maturity, but for me, maturity is when a person hurts you and you try to understand their situation rather than hurting them back.
Author Unknown

Responding to Offense

When our partner offends us, we have two considerations:
1. The debt resulting from the offense (the sinful behavior).
2. The status of our relationship with our partner before God.

The offense results in a debt that interferes with the relationship. To restore the relationship, we must first figure out what to do with the debt. To what degree should we serve justice and collect the debt?

A right attitude must be cultivated before we respond to an offense. Our attitude should be filled with grace and truth—the very essence of Jesus. In the new covenant, we lead with grace and mercy because that is how God treats us. Mercy triumphs over judgment (James 2:13). This does not mean we should ignore the debt. Ignoring the problem does not support the teachings on repentance.

God is all-powerful and full of mercy, but He does not force us to accept His forgiveness. In fact, His forgiveness is worthless to us if we don't receive it.

Our partner might or might not wish to repent, forgive, or reconcile. Either way God calls us to love our partner. Love covers over a multitude of sins. In loving concern, we pray for our partner's heart to soften and receive whatever else they seem to need to be able to draw closer to God. The correct attitude acts for our partner's benefit, not with selfish or ulterior motives.

In our attempt to reconcile with our partner, we can focus not only on forgiving what cannot be repaid, but also on repentance and restoring the relationship in fairness.

To survive the offense, we can ignore, judge, or forgive the offensive behavior, and we can keep, abandon, or destroy the relationship. Overall, this leaves us with four practical responses depending on whether we respond to the sin with grace (or not) and with truth (or not).

I respond:	Without Truth	With Truth
Without Grace	**Abandon** The Relationship	**Destroy** The Relationship
With Grace	**Preserve** The Relationship	**Reconcile** The Relationship

Preserve

Responding with grace and forgiveness preserves the relationship. But forgiveness does not avoid, approve, excuse, justify, pardon, deny, forget, or minimize the offense. If we ignore the offense, we remain vulnerable and set ourselves up for unnecessary hurt. Our partner will lack an incentive to improve their behavior. Minimizing and/or denying the offense may help us to avoid the pain, but it is grace without truth. We shouldn't maintain the peace of the relationship at the expense of the truth.

Abandon

If we ignore the offense and abandon our partner, we give up on the relationship. In our weakness we withdraw passively from our partner in order to insulate ourselves from further pain. Passively holding onto a grudge avoids confrontation but despises the relationship. The resulting "peace" only mimics forgiveness. Abandoning relationships in bitterness is the opposite of forgiveness. This option offers neither grace nor truth.

Destroy

Aggressively seeking justice without mercy is foolish vengeance. Revenge attempts to harm or destroy the offender and can include gossip or ill-speaking. Whole-hearted forgiveness eliminates the need to speak ill of the offender. When speaking truth without grace, we might serve justice but only at the expense of the relationship.

Reconcile

An offense can leave our heart in a bad state, but we are supposed to forgive the debt and work to keep the relationship. Forgiveness prepares our hearts for restoring the relationship with our partner by expressing mercy before judgment occurs. As a loving attitude of the heart, forgiveness:
- Benefits us as much or more than our partner;
- Wishes the best for our partner, not destruction;
- Seeks fairness in reconciliation; and
- Confronts sin with loving intention.

Forgiveness starts as an act of the will but finishes with peace in the heart. It begins with facing the offense and the offender and ends by looking to God for healing. The right attitude prevents bitterness, seeking control, illness of the heart, evil, revenge, destruction, and generalization (such as "all men are evil"). However, forgiveness does not:
- Provide automatic or instant healing;
- Eliminate the desire for fairness or justice;
- Eliminate the need for restitution or consequences.

Recovering from an offense is hard work. We need to be patient with ourselves. Forgiveness is both work to be done immediately after an offense and an attitude to cultivate throughout our entire life.

Forgiveness in Marriage

Marriage might be the one place where forgiveness is needed an unlimited number of times a day to maintain the relationship in good working order. Half-done forgiveness leaves bitterness to fester. God wants us to put aside destructive anger. We need to deal with whatever surfaces in our marriage and put it in its place. When done right, this can be exciting as we participate in restoring a valued treasure to health. After we deal with any issues, we need to move on to the positive.

When husband and wife forgive thoroughly, they can move on unhindered by problems. Love doesn't keep a record of wrong. The debt must be released permanently, and the repentance must be sincere. This doesn't mean the same or similar issues won't surface again. But when they do, there shouldn't be venom from previous sin to poison the reconciliation.

For Reflection

1. Only after we feel the hurt is fully healed will we **feel** like forgiveness is complete.
2. Are you aware of any inexcusable behaviors for which you have not received God's forgiveness?
3. Can you recall any inexcusable behaviors for which you received God's forgiveness but find you still struggle with your partner's inexcusable sins? Can you pinpoint exactly what these are?

Next Steps

- Meditate on God's forgiveness of you. Pay attention to your attitude towards God and others who have offended you. What makes forgiveness easier or harder for you?
- Review these resources:
  - Movie: *Braveheart*
  - Book: *Total Forgiveness* by R.T. Kendell
  - Book: *One Small Step* by Yvonne Dolan
- In your Blueprint Space, make a list of offenses you find in your heart that you have yet to release. Quantify each offense on a scale from one to ten, ten being the most bitter. If your bitterness is four or below "let it go;" if five or above "speak in love."
  - Make a list of safe ways to be angry.
  - Write down your thoughts, questions, impressions, hopes, dreams, anger, feelings, etc.
  - Write four letters (do not actually send them): 1) to your offender about how angry you are 2) their response 3) to your offender about letting it go 4) their response.

Chapter 43

A Forgiving Heart

"If your brother sins against you, go and tell him his fault, between you and him alone. If he listens to you, you have gained your brother."
...
Then Peter came up and said to him, "Lord, how often will my brother sin against me, and I forgive him? As many as seven times?" Jesus said to him, "I do not say to you seven times, but seventy-seven times."
...
And in anger his master delivered him to the jailers, until he should pay all his debt. So also my heavenly Father will do to every one of you, if you do not forgive your brother from your heart.
—Matthew 18:15–35

Not forgiving is like drinking poison and expecting the other person to die.
Author Unknown

Four Attitudes of Biblical Forgiveness

I am convinced that forgiveness is first and foremost an attitude of the heart. We bring our heart-attitude into relationship with others. When repentance is genuine, forgiveness holds nothing against the offender and leaves us ready to reconcile. Four attitudes are necessary for forgiveness.

	Forgiving Heart	Bitter Heart
1	Desires to restore the relationship	Seeks to eliminate or destroy the offender
2	Trusts God for healing	Abandons the relationship by withdrawal, avoidance, or self-protection
3	Offers mercy	Repays evil with evil by intentionally inflicting pain on the offender
4	Seeks justice without destruction	Believes that retaliation is serving justice

Desire to Restore the Relationship

Christian brothers and sisters should be willing to stay open to the relationship and even endure pain during the reconciliation process. The heart like God's grieves the loss of relationship and does whatever the relationship needs to restore it to good standing. Do we have a heart that truly desires reconciliation to make a relationship possible again?

We first need a desire to eliminate the barriers to continued relationship. This requires us to directly confront our brother (Matthew 18:15) and expose the breakdown in the relationship. Holding a grudge against our partner without communicating the problem only promotes division and strife.

If our brother is open to working out the problem, we are required to forgive him. If he is not open, then God wants us to persist in our desire to reconcile until the situation becomes completely hopeless (he refuses to repent after following the procedure in Matthew 18:15–35).

Some people will not want to speak with us or will deny any wrongdoing. When this is the case, we can't do anything about the problem. Jesus tells us to move on with our lives at this point.

Trust God for Healing

Healing is a separate process from both forgiveness and repentance. While forgiveness is essential for complete healing, it is not essential to start healing. Forgiveness begins with an act of the will, but healing begins when we look beyond the offender to God. While we are still looking to the offender for healing, forgiveness is delayed and usually impossible.

Focusing on the offender misses the opportunity to address our wound with God. When we experience sin, unfair treatment, and evil behaviors, we have the potential to receive a soul-withering message. Our vulnerabilities leave us susceptible to believe lies such as:

- We are worthless because we've been treated as if we are worthless;
- God doesn't care about us or about justice because He allowed us to be hurt **and** did not make the offender repay the debt;
- Serving justice upon the offender will resolve our pain.

To truly forgive, we must have a relationship with our advocate, Jesus. He offers more than an offender could ever take from us. Ultimately, forgiveness is the process of negotiating a loss with the offender before Jesus. Forgiveness is possible because we can turn to our advocate to heal the wound.

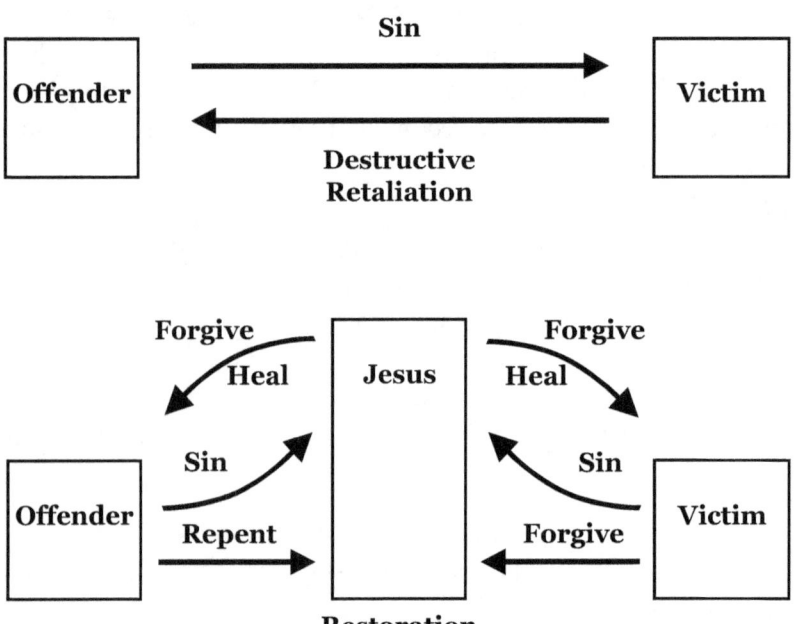

Forgiveness is complete when we no longer feel entitled to demand the offender to make up the loss. Jesus stands with us to make up for our loss. Because of His protection and power, we have the ability to offer forgiveness and comfort to the offender (Genesis 45). If this were not the case, there would be no incentive to do anything but seek our own protection and gain. What others do to us does not limit us in the least.

Offer Mercy

Pride and hypocrisy keep us from forgiving. In the parable of the unforgiving servant, the servant repents superficially and fails to appreciate the king's mercy. We know this because after the king forgives him more than he can ever repay, he immediately demands payment for a debt from his peer. The king shows him great mercy, but he shows no mercy to his friend. This kind of prideful attitude will keep some from entering Heaven (Matthew 6:14–15; Matthew 18:35).

Without mercy we choose to remain focused on the offender until we've either received payment-in-full or eliminated the offender. This gives control to the offender as we become sinfully preoccupied with the offender's failure to treat us well. Even when we avoid the offender, he remains too important in our minds and hearts, and our total freedom is blocked. No offender can ever fully restore what was lost. In reality, all of us are dependent on Jesus (the advocate) for true forgiveness.

When our brother responds to us with repentance, we should be prepared to whole-heartedly forgive him (Luke 17:3–4; Matthew 18:21–35). This means we are prepared to forgive even before the offender repents because we have cultivated a merciful heart. Jesus forgives us so much more than we can ever repay. When our partner has failed us, the appropriate response is to pass on the mercy we've received with genuine acceptance and understanding.

God commands us to get rid of bitterness, anger, and vengeance. Instead we are to speak kindly to our brother and forgive him as Christ has forgiven us (Ephesians 4:31–32). Jesus forgives others often before they are aware they need forgiveness. This clears the way for Him to be primarily concerned about whatever stands in their way of a deeper relationship with Him. In the gospels, we find Jesus displaying compassion for the hurting and confronting the lost with reality. Whatever Jesus does, He does to reveal more of God to each of us.

Seek Justice without Destruction

The best attitude tempers the desire for justice by making mercy a priority. This is exactly what God does for us. His mercy and forgiveness allow us to approach the throne of grace and offer our repentant hearts. When we repent of our own sin, we fully receive forgiveness and are able to show mercy to those indebted to us. After our heart is filled with mercy, we can confront our partner and seek to regain the relationship.

We can be merciful and let the offender face the consequences if that is deemed in the best interest of the offender. But in seeking justice, we need to be sure we are not taking the place of God. We should never seek the destruction of our partner. We need to execute justice on our level, and leave God to execute justice on His level. We know from the parable of the unforgiving servant that God sets severe consequences (Matthew 18:33–35). At the very least, we need to be patient with the brokenness of others.

We know repentance is important because Jesus praised Zacchaeus for his repentance and offer of restitution (Luke 19:9). We can be prepared to forgive, but we cannot complete reconciliation until our partner is prepared to repent. Careless forgiveness would not respect the relationship. Moving forward, both partners need to feel the resolution is equitable.

We might decide to soften or remove consequences when we sense genuine repentance, but without repentance, we don't have to. We can forgive, love, and refuse bitterness but hold our partner accountable for their behavior. This approach is loving.

For Reflection

1. Consider this list of synonyms for advocate: champion, proponent, backer, benefactor, counselor, intercessor, and supporter. Do any of these positively alter your understanding of forgiveness? How about the role of the Holy Spirit in forgiveness?
2. How does the word "if" influence the meaning of Jesus' words?

> *"Pay attention to yourselves! If your brother sins, rebuke him, and if he repents, forgive him, and if he sins against you seven times in the day, and turns to you seven times, saying, 'I repent,' you must forgive him."*
> —Luke 17:3–4

Next Steps

- ☐ Read the parable of the unforgiving servant in context (Matthew 18:15–35).
  - What do you notice about forgiveness?
  - What feelings surface for you?
  - Identify ways in which you have been shown mercy, yet have been unwilling to cancel your partner's debt.
  - Identify ways you have done wrong but have not truly repented and experienced godly sorrow.
  - What fears stand in the way of your brokenness over the matter?
  - Can you develop the ability to live with an imperfect self, an imperfect partner, and an imperfect marriage?
- ☐ Read about the Year of Jubilee (Leviticus 25:8–22). All relationships will incur debt over time. Forgiveness restores equality to the relationship. How does the Year of Jubilee help with your marriage?
- ☐ Review these resources:
  - ☐ Movie: *Les Misérables (2012)*
  - ☐ Book: *Living With Your Dreams* by David A. Seamands

Blueprint Space

Chapter 44

A Reconciling Heart

So if you are offering your gift at the altar and there remember that your brother has something against you, leave your gift there before the altar and go. First be reconciled to your brother, and then come and offer your gift.
—Matthew 5:23–24

It is not good that the man should be alone . . .
—Genesis 2:18

Without forgiveness, healing, repentance, and faithfulness, we cannot reconcile; without reconciliation, we cannot trust; and without trust there is no us.

Reconciliation Requires Forgiveness and Repentance

Reconciliation is bringing all we have into play to restore our relationship. When a victim is able to forgive and an offender is able to repent, this lays the foundation for reconciliation. The Bible teaches that the purpose of forgiveness and repentance is reconciliation. If we are worshiping and have a gift for God, He prefers first to receive the gift of reconciliation between His children.

Our attempt to reconcile is the decisive moment because it tests how thoroughly we completed the work of forgiveness and repentance. Working through forgiveness and repentance brings us to the proper heart-attitude and allows reconciliation to work. Once in a great while, we need to do no further work to benefit from the work already done. But usually a couple finds they have more to negotiate to make the relationship right again.

Reconciliation can stall for at least two reasons. Is the problem the offender's lack of trustworthy behavior, the victim's lack of healing, or some combination of both? Finding areas that need more work during reconciliation may seem discouraging but is actually a blessing. Proactively discovering problems is always better than stumbling upon them at the wrong moment.

Reconciliation Builds Trust

Some say trust, once broken, can never be the same. I agree. It won't be the same; it can be even better!

We can completely restore broken trust and then some. Trust is not ruined by the failure to be perfect but by the failure to repair what is broken. The process of discovering and working through weakness strengthens the relationship—the sense of us—and this is exactly what builds trust! When done successfully, reconciliation is part of the healing.

At the point reconciliation is complete, the foundation is laid for trust. Desiring to trust again should be a no-brainer (see Chapter 45). However, we should have a clear understanding of the appropriate amount of risk to take to trust again.

Reconciliation is a priority for God. Those with a heart open to reconciliation do not have to be concerned with the details (following the letter of the law) because they are already doing what God wants (following the spirit of the law).

If we struggle to trust, then we usually have no problem being trustworthy. We would not want to put another through the same pain. The inability to trust results from being burned too many times by seemingly trustworthy people. Those who lie frequently struggle to believe others are trustworthy. Their inability to trust is mostly their own fault! Fear destroys our ability to trust, but trusting in God helps us to alleviate this fear.

A genuine attempt at trusting again does not expect or demand perfection in the future. Anyone who has lived a while knows not to expect perfection on the first try. Our choice to trust again is sensible if we can see genuine effort and progress in our partner. Growth creates hope, and hope provides a reason to trust again.

Pursuing the Joy of Joint Effort

Joint activity done in a spirit of teamwork and appreciation of the other is as good as it gets. God made Adam and Eve to experience the blessings of an all-in relationship. For example, playing tennis with a partner who plays with the same effort is the most fun. Both players end up playing better and enjoying the game regardless of who wins. The game is much more fun to watch than when one player has lost heart.

Sin, a lack of repentance, and a lack of forgiveness all cloud (and sometimes poison) the water. In marriage, we need a clean slate completely unhindered by resentment, disappointment, negativity, bitterness, frustration, anger, and rage. Snuffing out these joy-killing attitudes is always time well spent. We need to ruthlessly and relentlessly pull these weeds from the marriage garden. Stay vigilant. Focus on keeping a meticulously maintained marriage. Make this your highest priority, and you will reap a hundred-fold reward.

Enduring the Loneliness of Solo Effort

What happens when one partner tries and the other doesn't? They won't have nearly as much fun as other couples who are equally matched by their love of the game and the effort they put forth. Maybe our partner refuses (whether consciously or not) to repent or forgive, and we hear statements like:

- "For the hundredth time, I'm sorry! Why can't you get over it already?" This doesn't sound very apologetic.
- "I forgive you, but I don't love you anymore." But forgiveness is supposed to make love possible again.

A partner who continues in reckless behavior is different from one who honestly struggles to completely forgive or repent. We need to escalate consequences with the one but patiently persevere with the other.

A partner who doesn't try or persists in doing their own thing creates one of the most lonely and painful scenarios in all of life. Being bound to a partner in a lifelong commitment when the partner keeps you at arm's length is challenging at best and tortuous at worst.

Our partner, if they wrong us, is supposed to work on rebuilding trustworthiness so that we can trust again. To reconcile, they must be willing to work out their character defects to reduce the possibility of re-offending.

Likewise, when we wrong our partner and repent, they are supposed to forgive us and work at restoring the relationship. To reconcile, they must be willing to risk being hurt again.

Unfortunately, we are not guaranteed cooperative effort. Even well-intentioned partners lack appropriate effort for a variety of reasons. Real change from the inside out is not possible without God's help. And God may have his own timetable with respect to change. But expecting our partner to take the need to grow seriously and work at it as a priority in their life is reasonable.

Trusting With Christ

When we attempt to trust without Christ, we will fall when our partner becomes untrustworthy. With Christ to lean on, we might stumble, but we won't fall (Psalm 37:23–24).[13]

Trust without Christ   **Trust with Christ**

If there is no trust, there is no "Us." But if there is no "Us," there will be no trust. The right amount of effort results in freedom to enjoy life, even when our partner is not cooperative. When rebuilding trust, remember to:
- Lean on Christ;
- Be prepared to reconcile and increase joint activity with your partner;
- Love God and your partner;
- Live in freedom; and
- Pursue your activities while waiting and hoping for your partner to join you.

For Reflection

1. What would reconciliation look like without forgiveness?
2. What would reconciliation look like without repentance?
3. Imagine your partner says, "Trust me." Now describe how you feel inside. How does your answer change if you imagine someone else saying those words? Who is easier/harder to trust? Why is that?

Next Steps

☐ How much is your relationship a solo effort? Talk to God about any sadness from the unfairness. If you tend to be passive, try speaking up more and asking for what you need from both God and your partner. If you tend to be aggressive, find ways to love and serve your partner without the usual demands for attention. Hold to your value of marriage, but also don't put your life on hold when your partner is not cooperative. Pursue your activities and dreams, but also be prepared to re-engage your partner when they are ready.

---

[13] Trust with Christ cross concept originally from Eric Sweitzer; The illustrations are mine.

- ☐ Try these suggestions for building trust with your partner:
  - Risk being more transparent;
  - Be clear about who you are, and encourage your partner to do the same;
  - Don't make sudden moves away or toward your partner;
  - Look and see the positive—believe in your partner even when you cannot trust them;
  - Don't expect you will never get hurt or will never be disappointed; and
  - Find your optimal balancing point for time together and time apart.
- ☐ Sometimes the problem is a distorted view of God. The God you are afraid to trust is a false god created by you. Because of our distortions, we can end up blaming God for our problems. But this only leads to more distance from God and more distortion. For each statement, consider the problem created by believing it is truth, then modify it so it is true.
  - God will never let anything bad happen to me.
  - God makes sure life is fair.
  - Christians will always feel peace.
  - God will fix any problem I have.
  - God doesn't really care about me.
  - If I am obedient, I can avoid pain and problems.
  - If I am obedient, God will give me what I want.
- ☐ Find Scriptures to support your newly modified statements. For example, John 16:33 works for the first one.
- ☐ Thomas Merton was an American Catholic monk and a writer. He wrote a book called, *Thoughts of Solitude*. In it, he has a prayer about trusting God which begins, "My Lord God, I have no idea where I am going. I do not see the road ahead of me." Find this prayer online or in print and read it. How does it help you build trust?
- ☐ Review these resources:
  - ☐ Movie: *Take the Lead*
  - ☐ Book: *How to Act Right when your Spouse Acts Wrong* by Leslie Vernick
  - ☐ Book: *Wounded* by Terry Wardle
  - ☐ Group Counseling: *Healing Care Group* by Terry Wardle

Chapter 45

A Trusting Heart

When I am afraid, I put my trust in you.
—Psalm 56:3

Insecurity originates within an individual, but it affects both husband and wife. When a husband or wife places their insecurity fully on the other, it is enough to totally crush and suffocate the relationship. Insecurity obstructs communication and weakens trust. Overcoming insecurity means learning to trust others according to who they are, not for who we want them to be.

Different Responses to Wounds

Recovering our ability to trust is an essential part of the healing process. Each of us has a preferred pattern of response to ways others have failed us. The four responses to offense in Chapter 42 correspond to four approaches to trust.

Having trust issues means trusting when we shouldn't (blind trust), refusing to risk again (passive mistrust), or coercing others to meet our needs (aggressive mistrust). All three are maladaptive ways to cope with the uncertainty of relationships. Those who respond blindly or passively desire peace with others but go about it differently. Those who respond aggressively disregard others while reaching for their goals. To improve our ability to trust, we need to identify patterns in our approach.

The fourth approach is the healthy response to potential disappointment. We love others freely but understand the limits of trust (perceptive trust).[14]

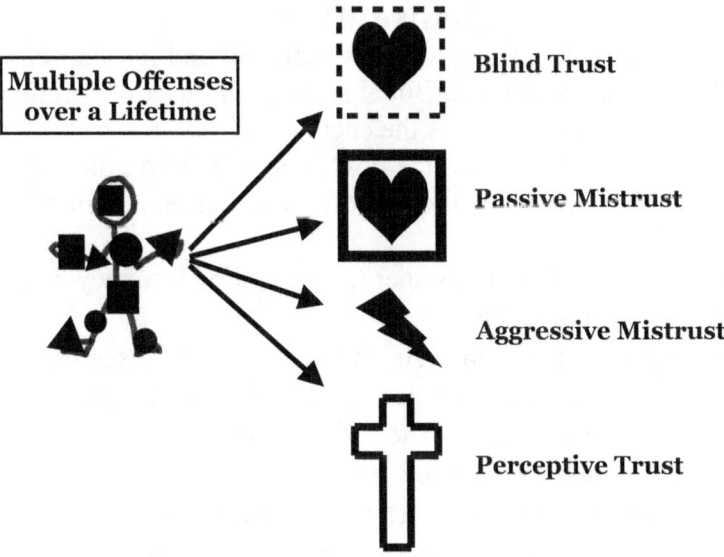

---

[14] The four kinds of trust found in *Trusting* by Pat Springle; also adapted from Terry Wardle's Healing Care Groups.

When our partner hurts us but repents, then ideally we can gradually move forward in trusting them again. When we are willing to trust again, we open ourselves up to the possibility of being hurt again. Foolproof guarantees don't exist. But in wisdom, we can discern appropriate risk. In trusting again, the goal is to give our partner the benefit of the doubt but in a calculated way to prevent being taken advantage of unnecessarily.

The amount we trust should be in direct proportion to the reliability of our partner. Trusting too much too quickly could result in them lacking incentive to continue corrective changes. For trust to work, we must sense reasonable safety before we will be honest about how we feel.

No matter how cautious we must be with respect to the area of offense, maintaining the relationship in non-risky areas is important. Having fun together by emphasizing the positives will lead to a sense of normalcy in the rest of the relationship.

Blind Trust

Blind trust gives unconditionally without discernment or question. This approach has the best prognosis for recovery because it works moderately well when our partner also blindly trusts. Eventually, though, the obligation to give proves to be a trap. Discrepancies in effort create a crisis in the relationship often resulting in extreme anger and disappointment. Childhood neglect can create a desperation for relationship that leads to blind trust.

Blind trust often leads to a classic codependent relationship where we attempt to have our needs met by meeting our partner's needs. When we are caught up in blind trust, we:

- Attempt to have our needs met by trying to make others happy;
- Preserve "Us" at the expense of "I";
- Give to get (risk too much expecting a payoff);
- Obligate our partner to meet our needs when we try hard enough or give enough;
- Need to achieve and be a hero (to feel appreciated and needed);
- Control by seeking to create obligation through vulnerability;
- Allow persistently weak boundaries for self and expect them in others; and
- See promises from God where none exist then justify our anger and disappointment.

Passive Mistrust

Passive mistrust is refusing to trust by quiet withdrawal and resistance. This approach works well to the degree isolation is therapeutic. But at some point, lack of communication undermines the relationship. Ever increasing distance is the enemy.

We choose passive mistrust to survive the downside of relationships by avoiding our partner altogether. On some days, our choice is the peaceful one, but on others it is cowardly. When we passively mistrust, we:

- Control by moving away from our partner (avoid risking intimacy and vulnerability);
- Preserve "I" at the expense of "Us";
- Self-protect by seeking peace at all costs, thus avoiding the discomfort of conflict;
- Believe avoiding others is better than risking to make ourselves known to others;
- Want persistently thick boundaries for self and others;
- Rely exclusively on ourselves and rarely on others;
- Feel safer in isolation even though this causes greater loneliness;
- Internalize or ignore anger and hurt; engage in morbid introspection and analysis; and
- Superficially engage people while over-connecting with activities, animals, etc.

Aggressive Mistrust

Aggressive mistrust is refusing to trust by coercing others to meet our needs. This approach works by using our partner, at their expense, to gain what we need. Left unchecked, aggressive mistrust is hurtful to all involved. We need to recognize this pattern of behavior and learn to accept others' boundaries. If we don't, hopefully our partner will figure out what is happening and form stronger boundaries without being forced to abandon the relationship.

We choose aggressive mistrust when we believe we are better off taking matters into our own hands to ensure our needs are met. When we aggressively mistrust, we:

- Control by moving against others;
- Express "I" at the expense of "Us";
- Demand others give to us (eliminating risk);
- Want persistently thick boundaries for self and weak boundaries for others;
- Feel safe when we have power even though this can result in alienating others;
- Use our position of authority to get our way;
- Blame others and attack their weaknesses while denying our own weaknesses;
- Dominate to avoid our own hurt; and
- Believe our partner is at fault for the poor relationship.

Perceptive Trust

Perceptive trust is the healthy form of trust. In all three of the less-than-ideal options, we over-compensate by exerting some form of control to minimize the pain of having our needs go unmet. Perceptive trust is the ideal approach because it balances out the needs of "I" and "Us."

Those having perceptive trust generously love others without enabling them to remain immature. When we trust perceptively, we:

- Are initially open to a relationship by testing another's trustworthiness;
- Trust others' words and actions because, for a trustworthy person, these will line up;
- Have the courage to take educated risks;
- Keep hope alive by frequently risking to trust slightly more than another's trustworthiness;
- Give up control by loving unconditionally;
- Adjust boundaries depending on who we are with;
- Discern others' behaviors and respond accordingly;
- Seek mutual agreement whenever possible but are comfortable with disagreement;
- Give cheerfully what we have decided we want to give and also receive graciously;
- Recognize that only Heaven is totally safe and only God is totally trustworthy;
- Avoid black-and-white thinking (such as my partner is all good or all bad);
- Give each new person a chance by not making unilateral vows (such as "all men are untrustworthy"); and
- Do not interfere with others' growth for our benefit.

Genuine trust always takes time to develop—not simply because we don't know our partner, but as much because we don't know ourselves. We need to understand our vulnerabilities, and we should trust more cautiously in areas where we've been bruised the most. No one benefits if we carelessly allow ourselves to be reinjured. But with God's help, we can find the path forward.

For Reflection

1. Answer the following questions after reading each saying.
   - What does it communicate about trust?
   - Do you agree or disagree? Why?
   - How do you feel?
   - Are you encouraged or discouraged? Why?

Healthy trust puts love first. We can always love, but trusting is not always the prudent option.

We are better off trusting someone who has the ability to make an error and admit it, rather than someone who believes he is superman.

When you fully trust someone without any doubt, you finally get one of two results: A person for life or a lesson for life.

Trust must diminish with every mistake because we must use it like an eraser to correct the error.

If you over-trust you might be hurt. However, if you fail to trust enough, you will miss out on the best a relationship has to offer. All relationships require risk. Minimize the risk, but don't surrender the opportunity to love and be loved.

---

2. What does it mean to perceptively trust by loving others freely while understanding the limits of trust?

Next Steps

- ☐ Which of the four responses most accurately fits with your attitude about trusting others?
- ☐ Imagine your partner has to cross a bridge to get to your heart. Design a bridge that represents your ability to trust. What will this experience be like for both of you?
- ☐ What steps are you willing to take to improve your ability to trust perceptively?
- ☐ Will you come to God, asking that He help you to unconditionally trust Him and perceptively trust others?
- ☐ Review these resources:
  - ☐ Movie: *The Lord of the Rings Trilogy*
  - ☐ Book: *Trusting* by Pat Springle.

Chapter 46

Divorce Prevention

> *"If anyone comes to me and does not hate his own father and mother and wife and children and brothers and sisters, yes, and even his own life, he cannot be my disciple. Whoever does not bear his own cross and come after me cannot be my disciple. For which of you, desiring to build a tower, does not first sit down and count the cost, whether he has enough to complete it? Otherwise, when he has laid a foundation and is not able to finish, all who see it begin to mock him, saying, 'This man began to build and was not able to finish.'"*
> —Luke 14:26–30

> *The question is asked, "Is there anything more beautiful in life than a young couple clasping hands and pure hearts in the path of marriage? Can there be anything more beautiful than young love?" And the answer is given. "Yes, there is a more beautiful thing. It is the spectacle of an old man and an old woman finishing their journey together on that path. Their hands are gnarled, but still clasped; their faces are seamed, but still radiant; their hearts are physically bowed and tired, but still strong with love and devotion for one another. Yes, there is a more beautiful thing than young love. Old love."*
> Author Unknown

Commitment Makes a Marriage

After we understand the beauty of marriage as God created it, we desire to participate in it wholeheartedly. Wanting the benefits of such a rich life experience, we commit to live with another person for the rest of our lives. But to prevent divorce, we can't stop here. A complete understanding of marriage leads to a commitment which leads to ownership, which leads to investment. The decision process looks like this:

1. Understanding: I value marriage as God designed it.
2. Commitment: I vow to live according to my understanding.
3. Ownership: I accept responsibility for the quality of my marriage.
4. Investment: I invest in its success.

Marriage fails when our reasons for it are no longer valid. If we are only committed to a partner who loves, provides, and serves us, then we can "fall out of love" when our partner does not love, provide, or serve. If we "fall out of love" this is a sign we've become addicted to positive feelings and validation.

Feeling in love can be such an overwhelmingly enjoyable experience. Does our partner have to demonstrate love and validation for us to feel positive about ourselves? Definitely not. But when our partner affirms us, not much else compares.

The Forces Against Commitment

The decision to divorce is not a simple "yes" or "no" dilemma. At least three options exist:
1. Stay together and be miserable;
2. Divorce and possibly be happier, but maybe not; or
3. Stay together in commitment to improve what we can and be content with what we can't.

Options one and two are not biblical solutions.

If marriage was easy, no commitment would be required. Passion and time together would carry us along in never-ending bliss. But there are real forces at work against intimacy.

Some forces are internal:
- Impatience and unrealistic expectations;
- Selfishness and jealousy;
- Fear and insecurity.

And some forces are external[15]:
- Loss;
- Trauma;
- Health problems.

We know marriage is difficult (or the divorce rate would not be so high and marriage counselors would not exist). Without a strong commitment, these internal and external forces pull a marriage apart. For example, getting married primarily because we want to share our life with someone is probably not reason enough to overcome the negative forces. While it is better to understand our motivations before marrying, we can discover the deep reasons for getting married no matter how many anniversaries we've celebrated.

Understanding the Reasons for Commitment

Marriage is not the problem. Marriage only reveals the problem within ourselves. We don't need to shoot the messenger.

Anything difficult and important benefits from commitment. As a tool to organize and direct our efforts, commitment promotes success rather than failure. But it is devastatingly weakened when it's not based on convincing reasons. Without understanding why our goals are important, we have little incentive to stick with them. When we believe something is important, we commit to it by solidifying the reasons ahead of time.

> **A commitment is only as good as the reasons you have for keeping the commitment. A commitment without solid reasons is easily broken.**

A real commitment is one that inspires us to press on no matter the circumstances. A complete commitment:
- Directs you back to the purpose of the commitment;
- Helps you identify and accomplish what is most important;
- Protects from catastrophic loss (losing your marriage/family);
- Encourages focus ("I'll find a way or die trying");
- Inspires and motivates us to keep going when the work is exhausting or mundane;
- Increases efficiency and clarity so that energy is not wasted on indecisiveness; and

---

[15] For a more complete list see Chapter 51 on grief.

- Provides incentive to grow and to develop character.

The road to accomplishing great things for God has many distractions. Without a commitment, the distractions win and you lose what could be. Have you ever started a large project and become bogged down with all the details? In the midst of changing diaper number 1272, deep thoughts come to mind:
- I've got better things to do with my time besides changing diapers.
- This really stinks!
- Why did we decide to have another child?
- Why did God make raising kids so difficult?

Have you ever done something risky and dangerous? Would you go mountain climbing without a safety line? If you are committed to reaching the top, then you pack that safety line. Failure to plan is planning to fail. Coming to the realization that failure is not an option changes everything.

Covenant Commitment

God created marriage as a covenant, not a contract. A covenant is best characterized by:
- Commitments as permanent promises;
- A focus on protecting the other;
- God's unconditional love (1 Corinthians 13);
- Using confrontation, repentance, and forgiveness to preserve the covenant; and
- Including God as the third person.

A postmodern marriage is best represented by a contract. A contract is best characterized by:
- Lasting for a limited period of time;
- A focus on specifics and contingencies;
- An "If you . . . , only then will I . . . " mentality;
- A focus on self-protection; and
- Planning for termination by allowing for a way out.

Ownership and Investment

Investment in marriage involves:
- Finding the potential in our partner that no one else can see; and
- Incubating the potential until it bears fruit.

Stopping by the supermarket and picking up the latest healthy marriage is no more possible than buying a healthy body. A better marriage can only be home-grown—acquired by real sweat equity. A home-grown marriage requires putting ourselves into it, owning it, valuing it, improving it, caring for it, etc. No one else can strengthen our marriage for us.

What if a potential husband grasped this concept? He would grow his own marriage and be willing to pay for the outcome he desired, rather than try to get something for nothing. In some cultures present and past, when a man gains a wife, he compensates the bride's family for their loss. Similarly, God paid a price to gain His bride (1 Corinthians 6:19–20).

Often we think of ourselves as less than God does. In our own eyes we might depreciate in value if we do not perform well. But we must value ourselves according to the value God places on us. Our value is fixed; we do not depreciate in value in God's eyes. A hundred-dollar bill is worth a hundred dollars no matter how dirty or how abused.

What if a man marries a woman who has horribly low self-worth? She believes she is nothing special and she walks with her shoulders hunched and her head down. She belittles herself and avoids relating to others. She desperately needs self-confidence.

What if a man pays a high bride-price for his wife and treats her according to the high value he sees in her? If she is open to the truth, her low estimation of herself will eventually increase to her full potential according to God's design. She will be poised and confident and her countenance will portray her true beauty. Others who haven't seen her since she married will hardly recognize her.

When a husband only sees his wife as who she is today, he misses who she really is. Viewing her this way drains the marriage of hope. He contributes to how she views herself. If he treats her poorly, he works against her and hinders her from realizing her potential. But when he sees her fullest potential and encourages her to become this, he aligns himself with God.

For Reflection

1. Without a commitment, would you finish what you started?
2. Marriage needs time to develop. If you abandon it, you will never see the beauty of its potential.
3. What are the consequences of a failed marriage (to you, to others, to God)?
4. If your marriage were to fail, what do you think would be the reasons?
5. Consider how an attitude of commitment can help you stay married for each of these:

But the trick and challenge I want to propose to you is that you set out with the goal of falling a little more in love every day. So that by the time you're eighty, you're so in love that you wobble when you walk. To do this, you have to have a plan and you have to be deliberate.

Which comes first, investment or commitment? If we are ready to commit to a relationship, then we feel a sense of ownership, so we also commit our resources to its success. However, contributing our hard-earned resources to a relationship gets our blood pumping faster than usual, dramatically increasing our interest and commitment to the relationship's success.

Without a commitment made by free choice from the heart, all words, plans, and promises can only be trusted as tentative at best.

Next Steps

- Why do you want to stay married? Read Luke 6:47–49. Are your reasons good enough to endure a torrent?
- How is a cup like a marriage? Draw a cup that has a leak. Describe what is leaking out. Draw a cup that has no holes. What does the cup store? How are you like a cup?
- What are your reasons for committing to marriage? How stable are they? Are they dependent on, or independent of, your partner?
- What is Jesus saying is the secret to commitment in Luke 14:26–30?
- Review these resources:
  - Movie: *A Vow to Cherish*
  - Story: *Johnny Lingo's Eight-Cow Wife* (find online or February 1988 Reader's Digest)

Chapter 47

Divorce Decisions

Therefore a man shall leave his father and his mother and hold fast to his wife, and they shall become one flesh.
—Genesis 2:24

So they are no longer two but one flesh. What therefore God has joined together, let not man separate."
—Matthew 19:6

We can either treat other people as if they are disposable objects, or as people that are going to be around for eternity. When our partner does not live up to our often unrealistic and selfish expectations, abandoning them for a better option is sometimes overwhelmingly tempting. When we are immature, our loyalty can change in an instant. We rationalize that since we would never marry our partner today, then it's okay to claim the original decision was in error. This causes us to separate ourselves emotionally. Then we can rationalize that since we are no longer in love, staying together doesn't make sense. Then we can focus on our partner's faults to justify our behavior and put off any guilty feelings. This happens all the time when we place our immediate happiness at the top of our list of values. Should happiness be the supreme value above others such as love, understanding, acceptance, mercy, grace, patience, and perseverance?

God's Heart

God designed marriage so that husband and wife are one for life. He joins a man and woman together as one flesh for purposes of modeling His image and for godly offspring. A Christian marriage has three people involved. By joining a man and a woman, God is personally involved in marriage. What God joins together, man should not put asunder. When speaking of marriage and divorce, Jesus proclaimed that divorce was not an original part of God's plan (Matthew 19:6–8).

God is love. When marriage experiences a fracture, His heart is for reconciliation and restoration. Christ sacrificed Himself for his bride, taking away her sin. He has no plans to abandon her. As Christ is faithful to us in the midst of our wrongdoing, so we should be to our partner.

God's patience is extreme. Divorce is truly a last resort and a merciful option in place of stoning, the Old Testament consequence for adultery. When God divorces an idolatrous Israel, He does not discard her for another nation but confronts her and waits in anticipation of repentance. The purpose of divorce is not to "get out of marriage" but to promote reconciliation by bringing awareness to the wayward partner that they are sinning.

Reasons for Divorce

When we are in significant emotional pain, we naturally want to end the suffering. If we believe our circumstances are hopeless, our thoughts might turn to suicide. If we believe our circumstances will improve if we are no longer married, our thoughts may turn to divorce (marital suicide).

If we've come to the point of seriously considering divorce, we should examine whether our desires are biblical. Where the Bible is clear on marriage, the task is easy. However, some grey areas exist that make the process difficult. Dividing the possible reasons for divorce into three categories helps us identify our heart-motives for divorce:

1. Biblical: we do not sin.
2. Extreme: our partner's sin is destructive but does not qualify directly for divorce.
3. Non-biblical: cases when it is a sin to initiate divorce.

Biblical Reasons

God does not want divorce (Malachi 2:13–16). However, the Bible directly mentions three scenarios, and implies a fourth, which legitimately release us from marriage:

1. Our partner dies (Romans 7:1–3; 1 Corinthians 7:39–40).
2. Our partner is a non-believer and no longer wants to be married (1 Corinthians 7:15–16).
3. Our partner commits sexual sin and refuses to repent (Matthew 5:32; Matthew 19:9). The Greek word for this sin is *porneia* which means illicit sexual intercourse.[16] *Porneia* has a connotation of an ongoing pattern of behavior.
4. Based on number 3 and Deuteronomy 24:3–4, we can infer that we are also released when our partner divorces us and marries someone else.

Extreme Reasons

Sometimes life is messy, resulting in grey areas. God desires us to uphold marriage, but He also wants us to live in peace and freedom. Concerning divorce, the Bible does not specifically mention extreme, ongoing, unrepentant behaviors. However, divorce might be the right action within the context of a church community confrontation process. Certainly, divorce is not an option if our partner is struggling but repentant (see previous chapters on forgiveness and repentance). Behaviors like the following require wisdom and discernment:

1. Addiction: pornography, alcohol, drugs, gambling, food, sex, etc.
2. Abuse: physical, emotional, verbal, sexual, etc.
3. Abandonment: moving out but not divorcing, refusing sexual intimacy, refusing forgiveness, refusing emotional intimacy, etc.

Non-Biblical Reasons

Except for the reasons already listed, all others are illegitimate reasons for divorce. Depending on the heart-motives involved, even some of the legitimate reasons can be wrong to pursue. If we consider divorce for our own selfish reasons, we lack the love described in 1 Corinthians 13:4–7:

1. We sin, our partner has a forgiving heart, but we are not repentant. Love is humble, not arrogant (v. 4).
2. Our partner repents, but we don't want to forgive. Love is forgiving (v. 5).
3. Our partner sins, doesn't repent, but we don't confront them biblically. Love rejoices with the truth (v. 6).
4. We decide being married to our partner is too hard, and we no longer want to be married. Love bears and endures all things (v. 7).

---

[16] biblehub.com Thayer's Greek Lexicon

Deciding What to Do

If you are contemplating divorce you should know whether your reasons are Biblical, Extreme, or Non-biblical. You might feel like you have two or even all three reasons at the same time! Now what? How do you move forward?

Vows must be taken seriously even when infidelity is involved. By itself, "I'm suffering!" is not a valid reason for divorce. Before you act on your desire for divorce, consider:

- Is the sin serious enough? To qualify, the sin must be ongoing and unrepented.
- Have you biblically confronted your partner in an attempt to restore your marriage? Are you considering divorce as strictly a last resort to save your marriage?
- Have you told trusted advisors your situation as objectively as possible? Do they all agree you should consider divorce? Have you allowed enough time for repentance and forgiveness? You should allow for accountability because two or three together can render a true judgment (Matthew 18:18–19).
- If you've been unfaithful, are you asking these questions objectively without the interference of an attachment to the person with whom you were unfaithful?

The following table provides an overview of what you should do, depending on your reasons:

Actions to Take	Biblical Reasons	Extreme Reasons	Non-biblical Reasons
Seek Reconciliation?	If applicable	Yes, to the degree partner is willing	Yes! Reconciliation should be the primary focus
Confront Biblically?	Not necessary except for the case of sexual sin	Yes, intensive process of humbly setting firm boundaries and seeking repentance	Not needed, unless you want help to repent of your desire to wrongfully end your marriage
Utilize Counseling?	Not necessary, except if you need support and help adjusting to the change	Yes, to help set boundaries and heal from partner's sinful behaviors	Yes, significant help is needed to discern unmet needs and pursue emotional maturity
Church/Pastoral Involvement?	Not necessary except for the case of sexual sin	Yes, highly involved in a likely difficult, biblical confrontation process	Not needed, unless want to accept help to: 1) Restore marriage 2) Repent of sin
Okay to Divorce?	Yes, but not required	Maybe, but only with permission from church authority	No, but some do anyway
Okay to Remarry?	Yes, but not required	Probably, but only after healing so mistakes are not repeated	No, but maybe yes depending on fullness of repentance and healing
How long before dating again?	1–3 years	2–4 years	3–5 years

Discerning Heart-Motives

When in doubt, always return to the heart and spirit of the matter. Check the motives of your heart against God's standard of love and forgiveness. The default and best path is to keep your marriage. Before you marry, choose wisely. After you marry, stay together as you are one.

- Jesus came to reconcile us to God so our attitude must always be to reconcile with others to the best of our ability.
- The purpose of any legitimate exception to staying married is not to provide greater license for those looking for an easy way out of a difficult marriage. If you are looking to the Bible for an escape clause, your heart is likely not in the right place. First seek reconciliation no matter how your partner behaved.
- The purpose of the Matthew exception is to allow for hardness of heart: unforgiveness and refusal to choose love. The first objective is to find a way for love to prevail. "I'm no longer in love!" is not a valid reason for divorce. Love can revive in our hearts.
- In our brokenness and immaturity, we don't often choose this way of love. But this is exactly why God made marriage a lifelong commitment—so enough time exists to grow out of immature love and into committed, sacrificial love. Working through the disappointments in marriage causes us to grow our ability to love.

Feeling wronged does not justify divorce. The truth is, we can justify divorce in our minds through all kinds of rationalization. Likewise, we can bring a spirit of legalism to the Bible and misinterpret it in this extreme too. In final analysis, we need to base our decisions on a general examination of our hearts instead of a narrow look at an exception clause. Anyone considering divorce first needs to examine their heart and be clear the divorce is in the best interest of their partner, not simply for their own selfish gain.

Both Licentious and Legalistic attitudes miss the heart and, therefore, miss God's intentions for us and marriage. Matthew 23:25–26 cautions against legalism, and Galatians 5:13–15 cautions against license.

Signs of a Licentious Heart

- Use of Scripture to justify action without considering the whole context of Scripture;
- Emphasis on grace to the point that any suffering is wrong;
- The truth is not explored deeply enough;
- Our heart is left mostly unexamined because relief is the priority;
- The purpose of our life becomes instant gratification.

Signs of a Legalistic Heart

- Loss of the truth that everyone sins and everyone falls short;
- Emphasis on suffering to the point that our partner has to "suffer for their mistakes," often to the fullest interpretation possible;
- Inability to accept sin as in the past even after our partner has moved on;
- Our heart is left mostly unexamined because correct behavior is the priority;
- The purpose of our life becomes proving ourselves to be perfect.

Chapter 47 - Divorce Decisions

For Reflection

1. Some say we should interpret *porneia* in its strictest sense—that in the context of Matthew it refers only to pre-marital fornication and does not include adultery after marriage. What do you think about this idea?
2. If you are the one who has sinned, your marriage is the legitimate relationship. Even if you currently feel closer to the other person, break all ties and seek reconciliation with your partner.
3. Some say if a partner breaks the covenant for any reason, then you are free to divorce. But this opens the door too wide. We are called to take the higher ground in relationships, not exact an "eye for an eye." Patience is needed to provide room for repentance.
4. Divorce is not required in the case of sexual sin. Just because you have a legitimate reason to seek a divorce does not mean you should. Forgiveness leading to reconciliation is a better option.
5. In the Old Testament, divorce was allowed as a compassionate alternative to stoning the unfaithful person.
6. God remained faithful to Israel. Jesus remains faithful to us, His bride. Allow these examples to encourage you to grow in faithfulness.
7. In what ways are you making happiness your supreme value? How should it fit on the list of values?
8. Ending a marriage because you've fallen out of love is like blaming your refrigerator for running out of food.
9. Our greatest weakness lies in giving up. The most certain way to succeed is always to try just one more time. — Thomas Edison

Next Steps

- If you are contemplating divorce, have you examined your heart to identify its true motive? What motive do you find in your heart?
- Stir some peanut butter and honey together. Can you easily separate (divorce) them again?
- If you are single and have any doubts about the person you are marrying, it's better to talk about it first. If an imbalance exists between the two of you, where one of you feels superior or inferior, work through this before getting married.
- Review these resources:
  - Movie: *The Vow* (2012)
  - Book: *Divorce Dilemma* by John MacArthur
  - Book: *Marriage, Divorce, and Remarriage in the Bible* by Jay E. Adams
  - Site: donjosephgoewey.com/wired-to-love
  - Site: carm.org/what-does-bible-teach-about-divorce
  - Site: comereason.org/new-testament-contradictions.asp
  - Site: mikeharderministries.com/2011/12/divorce-and-remarriage
- Divorce is not all black and white. Use your Blueprint Space to write out your beliefs about divorce to help the issues become clearer in your mind.

Chapter 48

Divorce Recovery

To the married I give this charge (not I, but the Lord): the wife should not separate from her husband (but if she does, she should remain unmarried or else be reconciled to her husband), and the husband should not divorce his wife.
—1 Corinthians 7:10–11

A wife is bound to her husband as long as he lives. But if her husband dies, she is free to be married to whom she wishes, only in the Lord. Yet in my judgment she is happier if she remains as she is. And I think that I too have the Spirit of God.
—1 Corinthians 7:39–40

People get divorced. You might be divorced. Now what do you do? You can deny what has happened or you can accept your circumstances and grow in spite of your divorce. Surviving divorce means going through the stages of loss: shock, acceptance and grief, then recovering and redefining who you are.

Healing What Breaks

Divorce is a process of breaking a divine bond between husband and wife. Recovery requires us to experience the healing of our ability to seek and form intimate relationships. We should spend time reflecting on how we ended up divorced to reduce the chances of it happening again. Here are three typical mistakes a person makes after their divorce:
1. Finding a replacement partner too soon.
2. Seeking revenge with their ex-partner.
3. Denying the reality that they are divorced.

Accepting that the marriage is over is the best medicine. Focus first on acceptance instead of revenge or remarriage. If your marriage is truly over, you've probably lost significantly more than the marriage. You may have lost a sense of your identity, which you desperately need to regain.

When a marriage breaks apart, many types of relationships are affected. Divorce affects how the world views marriage, and how we see our relationship with others.
- A child must consider how they relate to father, mother, authority figures, and God.
- A wife must consider how she relates to men and God.
- A husband must consider how he relates to women and God.

The Impact of Divorce

Divorce is not an unforgivable sin, but we must take it seriously because it comes with many emotional, relational, spiritual, and financial consequences. Whether your divorce is final or you have an opportunity to prevent it, recognizing the impact of divorce is critical. Children are more vulnerable than adults, so we can see the impact on them the easiest. However, divorce affects the parents in many of the same ways.

Judith Wallerstein, author of *The Unexpected Legacy of Divorce,* followed children from divorced families for 25 years. She concluded that divorce significantly and negatively affects a child's life long-term. A child's life is unquestionably set on a different course because of divorce. Adult children of divorce struggle with whether or not they should risk marrying and having children of their own.

From a child's perspective, divorce rarely makes a bad situation better. Usually just the opposite is true: it makes a bad situation ten times worse. Divorce causes a deep rift in the stability and security of a child's life. Children of divorce need to invest extra time to recover a sense of well-being about life.

Because of divorce, children are:
- No better off even if parents are happier;
- More sexually active;
- More aggressive toward authority figures;
- Less frequently married and more frequently divorced; and
- Significantly more likely to need therapy for depression and other problems.

Children lose emotional and financial security. They likely will have to work harder to achieve the same or even worse levels of functioning. They will lose relational contact time with at least one parent (usually the father). The losses and new family structure produce stress and may trigger a crisis. Divorce can destroy the network of family and friends. Children may lose the ability to see some relatives and their friends.

Both parents need to communicate directly to their children about the divorce. The children need to hear that the divorce is not their fault and their parents still love them. Understand that children need **extra** patience and attention—likely more than they've been getting—to recover from the loss.

When You Are Divorced

Before you are divorced, seek to stay married. After you are divorced, seek recovery. The recovery process, which shouldn't be taken lightly, takes significant time and effort. It's purpose is to carefully wash away any existing emotional residue from your marriage and divorce. To divorce is difficult and heart-breaking on its own, but to bring the same problems into another marriage is foolish.

Consider the following general principles to assist in recovery:
- Are you sure your marriage is over? As you go through recovery, you might find healing to restore your marriage (provided your ex-partner is open to this). Be open to the possibility of righting what you did wrong and reconciling with your ex-partner (provided they are also open to righting their wrongs).
- If your marriage is ending or has ended, don't seek to be in another relationship until your recovery is complete. Date again only after a season of singleness. Depending on specific circumstances, the season could last anywhere from one to five years. If you are dating while married or too soon after being divorced, chances are you are using romantic relationships to avoid dealing with your emotional pain.
- Spend time considering your contribution to the atmosphere of your marriage (even if you did not commit the big and final sin).

- Remember, the goal is to gain closure from your divorce so you can move forward without any baggage (to the best of your ability and knowledge).
- Join or put together a support community to help you with recovery. Work at learning how to relate again to others without the pressure and complexity of a romantic relationship.

Can I Marry Another?

In light of grace and Jesus' sacrifice, you can eventually remarry if you want to. However, there must be a prudent period of waiting so you can understand what went wrong in your marriage, recover from the difficulty, and enter into a new relationship without unnecessary baggage. To rush carelessly ahead will likely cause more harm, if not sooner, then later. Don't make the same mistake twice.

Not My Fault or Biblical Reasons

If your partner breaks your marriage and abandons you, the ultimate reason for the divorce is not your fault. However, you must still consider what is necessary for you to recover before marrying another. You might need significant time to heal depending on how badly you are hurting. For example, the betrayal from repeated infidelity can be extremely emotionally draining. You are free to remarry after you've taken the appropriate time to recover.

My Fault or Non-Biblical Reasons

Divorce for non-biblical reasons requires genuine repentance. Although you might not want to face natural consequences for your actions, such as working through emotional baggage, to do otherwise is irresponsible. Your obligation remains to repent, receive forgiveness, and seek the restoration of your marriage if possible (1 Corinthians 7:10–11).

Whether your marriage can be salvaged or not, the most honorable way to move forward is an extended time of singleness. You might not need this time to recover emotionally, but instead it can help you develop a respect for all that marriage is. If you take marriage this seriously after a divorce, my opinion is that because of God's forgiveness, you can choose to marry again. Again, if realistic, your first choice needs to be to reconcile with your partner.

Like the decision to divorce, consider remarriage only within an appropriate authority and/or accountability relationship. This helps eliminate any blind spots you might have. God says what two people agree on will be bound in Heaven (Matthew 18:18–19).

The journey to prepare your heart for being married again should be done under the authority of someone objective who can claim you are ready to consider remarriage. Find someone, such as a pastor or counselor, who can vouch for you and your recovery. While you may need only one authority, more than one accountability person will likely be helpful.

Place a premium on a clean slate before entering into another marriage. Follow a restoration process so you can move on with your life. Consider what a gift this will be both to yourself and to a future partner.

For Reflection

1. What is done is done. Repent and receive forgiveness, then move forward with integrity and uprightness.
2. Do you have any hesitations or fears in seeking accountability for your recovery? Facing weakness is not easy, especially if you anticipate condemnation. With the right person, you will experience what is in your best interest: firmness, support, grace, and healing.

Next Steps

- Take time to identify what you can own from your marriage. What are you responsible for, and what is your partner's responsibility?
- Attend a support group for those going through divorce. Try finding a local DivorceCare group.
- Review these resources:
  - Book: *Growing Through Divorce* by Jim Smoke
  - Book: *The Unexpected Legacy of Divorce* by Judith S. Wallerstein
  - Site: divorcecare.org

Chapter 49

Is My Partner Abusive?

"Thus says the LORD of hosts, Render true judgments, show kindness and mercy to one another, do not oppress the widow, the fatherless, the sojourner, or the poor, and let none of you devise evil against another in your heart." But they refused to pay attention and turned a stubborn shoulder and stopped their ears that they might not hear.
—Zechariah 7:9–11

The US Department of Justice defines domestic violence as a pattern of abusive behavior in any relationship that is used by one partner to gain or maintain power and control over another intimate partner. This can be physical, sexual, emotional, economic, or psychological actions or threats of actions that influence another person. This includes any behaviors that intimidate, manipulate, humiliate, isolate, frighten, terrorize, coerce, threaten, blame, hurt, injure, or wound.
justice.gov/ovw/domestic-violence

How to be Safe

Vulnerability is required for a close intimate relationship. An abusive person maintains a pattern of harmful behavior against their partner which takes advantage of this vulnerability. One incident of violence toward an intimate partner counts as domestic violence or abuse but doesn't necessarily mean the person is abusive.

Within intimate relationships, abuse can be hard to identify and stop because of our desire and responsibility to love, forgive, and be loyal to our partner. An abusive person uses the relational bond to perpetuate the abuse. Because abuse is personal, the abusive partner can consistently take advantage of their partner's natural desire for a loving relationship.

God's Perspective on Abuse

God is strongly against anyone who would take advantage of someone's vulnerability (Matthew 18:1–6). An abusive person lacks the ability to see the other person as valuable. Who harms what they consider valuable?

God is valuable and He made us in His image. Losing sight of this is a first step to becoming abusive. One flesh means when one person suffers, the other person suffers too. When one person benefits, the other also benefits.[17]

Am I a Victim?

A victim is defenseless against attack and has their vulnerability exploited by someone else with an advantage. If you do not have the ability to prevent your partner's harmful behavior, then you are a victim. All of us have been victims at one time or another. Even a mature, responsible

---

[17] Review Chapter 30 for more details.

adult can be temporarily defenseless as trust can be betrayed in an instant. There should be no shame in this because no one can remain perfectly guarded and safe.

Legitimate victims have a real disadvantage. Others may be stronger (able to physically overpower) or more experienced (able to exploit naivety). Others may have the element of surprise or have control over the finances.

Victims, after becoming aware of abusive behavior, have a choice. They can either take steps to prevent abuse, or do nothing and resign themselves to an inferior status. To choose to do nothing means they are no longer victims but have become co-dependents. By refusing to embrace their true value, co-dependents choose to remain helpless. This only makes the problem worse for everyone involved.

How to Assess the Situation

You have more to gain by assessing yourself before you assess your partner. Ask yourself these questions to determine the strength of your position:
- Am I able to defend myself emotionally (I am not easily weakened)?
- Am I knowledgeable about domestic violence?
- Am I able to objectively evaluate my partner as either relatively harmless or dangerously abusive?

If your answers lean towards "no," then you should immediately seek support (friends and family) and other objective help (pastors and counselors). Your primary goal is to make sure you are safe. Then, once you are safe, you can evaluate your partner's behavior.

First ask, "Am I safe?" Then ask, "Is my partner abusive?"

When you don't understand your position, you will be unclear how to act. Being confused in a potentially abusive situation is not a position of safety and strength. But this doesn't mean a dramatic scene is necessary. Your goal should not be to stir up your partner's anger by accusing them of being abusive, nor should you put down your partner in the eyes of your supportive friends and family. Your partner could be relatively harmless, so don't bring unnecessary harm to them through doubtful accusations. But do seek safety and answers.

A "Blind" and unaware partner is relatively harmless. They may be hurtful, and occasionally seriously so, but they don't have evil intention to bring you harm. On the other hand, an "Exploitative" partner is dangerously abusive. The degree of harmful intent must be evaluated on a continuum.

	More Likely Blind	More Likely Exploitive
Degree Behavior is Intentional	Lacks insight and understanding into actions; Can be impulsive	Chooses harmful behaviors; Can be manipulative
Degree of Control Behavior	Possible to leave without worry of retaliation; Financial resources are available	Attempt to leave is met with more severe abuse; Financial resources are not available
Severity of Behavior	Mild to moderate	Moderate to severe
Pattern of Behavior	Infrequent and no clear pattern	Frequent or regularly repeating even if periods of absence
Context of Behavior	Occurs in the context of a temporary problem like an acute life stressor	Can occur at any time for seemingly no reason

Insight and Repentance	Hurtful person is genuinely sorry, admits to error, and works to correct behavior	Hurtful person is unwilling to seek help and denies any wrongdoing
Balance of Power	When the balance is disrupted, it is restored relatively quickly	Hurtful person maintains power and control that is not needed

How to Respond

Whether behavior is outright abusive or unintentional or circumstantial, our overall goal should be to stop all harmful behavior. The main question becomes, what happens to the relationship during these attempts at proactive growth?

As victims, we are often in a double bind. We are supposed to be able to trust our chosen lifelong partners to bring us good. But what do we do when they are abusive?

If you are being abused and you sense the threat of retaliation if you become a whistle-blower, you are excused from sincere and honest communication with your partner. Involve others until you are safe and strong enough to prevent further abuse. Abusive behavior requires intentional, evasive action on your part. Do what you must to escape and find safety with friends, family, or the legal system.

Otherwise, with a "Blind" partner, focus more on developing assertiveness skills and speaking up when you feel unsafe, and focus less on labeling your partner's behavior as abusive. Communicate and enforce boundaries, and be patient and tolerant with your partner. When you disagree over what constitutes abuse, seek the help of a third party who can look at your relationship objectively.

After you have a basic idea of how to proceed, you can develop a long-term plan to manage your situation (see Blueprint Space).

For Reflection

1. How does Zechariah 7:9–11 address abuse? Does any of your behavior upset the balance of power in your marriage?
2. Read Ephesians 5:28–29 and 1 Peter 3:7. God intentionally made women more vulnerable than men. Sensitivity is not a defect, but a reality to embrace. How does God expect a husband to live with his wife?
3. Only God is all good, and only Satan is all bad. The rest of us are somewhere in between. Just because a behavior is perceived as abusive doesn't mean it is abusive.
4. Ask yourself the purpose behind labeling specific behaviors as abusive. If you are genuinely trapped as a victim, or even in doubt, seek immediate assistance! Otherwise, be sure you aren't avoiding your responsibility to be assertive.

Next Steps

- ☐ Review these resources:
  - ☐ Movie: *Shattered Dreams*
  - ☐ Book: *The Emotionally Destructive Relationship* by Leslie Vernick
  - ☐ Site: ovw.usdoj.gov/domviolence.htm
  - ☐ Site: gotquestions.org/Bible-abuse.html
  - ☐ Site: drmichele.org/think-like-victim-overcomer
- ☐ Use your Blueprint Space to determine your position and follow-up actions.

		My Partner is Primarily:	
		Blind	Exploitive
I am Primarily:	Confident and Discerning	My position is **Strong** 1) Confront 2) Find Support 3) Stay with Partner 4) Find Training	My position is **Isolated** 1) Find Support 2) Confront 3) Avoid Partner 4) Find Training
	Fearful or Defenseless	My position is **Undeveloped** 1) Find Training 2) Confront 3) Find Support 4) Stay with Partner	My position is **Trapped** 1) Flee Partner 2) Find Support 3) Find Training 4) Confront

Blueprint Space

- ☐ **Strong**: Trust your judgment; Perceptively trust your partner; Engage and confront your partner.
- ☐ **Undeveloped**: Trust your judgment in moderation; Delay trusting your partner; Seek assertiveness training to move to Strong.
- ☐ **Isolated**: Trust your judgment; Don't trust your partner; Seek strong support; Confront when you have strength in numbers.
- ☐ **Trapped**: Don't trust your judgment or your partner; Flee your partner; Seek strong support; Seek assertiveness training.
- ☐ **Abuser or Hurtful**: Make amends by:
  - Offering freedom to your partner, not more controlling behaviors.
  - Seeking help, repentance, and forgiveness.
  - Looking deep into the emotional reasons why you struggle to value, protect, and empathize with others.
  - Finding positive ways to meet your needs instead of exploiting others as a means to an end.

Marriage thrives when you understand what it is like to walk in your partner's shoes and know in your heart that your partner's feelings matter as much or more than your own.

Chapter 50

Is My Partner Addicted?

"You have heard that it was said, 'You shall not commit adultery.' But I say to you that everyone who looks at a woman with lustful intent has already committed adultery with her in his heart. If your right eye causes you to sin, tear it out and throw it away. For it is better that you lose one of your members than that your whole body be thrown into hell.
—Matthew 5:27–29

Sexual addiction is an intimacy disorder. Addicts prefer false intimacy on their terms over true intimacy with a real person. They pursue a life that avoids vulnerability with their partner and others. One of the first steps in recovery is confessing to trustworthy and supportive people.

What is an Addiction?

Addictions are no different from adultery in their potential to disrupt and destroy marriages. However, we should not take addictions personally. To the addict, as deceived as they can be, God is not enough. So how can marriage or a partner be enough? An addict falls into the snare that feeling good now, in this particular moment, is superior to real emotional intimacy.

All of us struggle at times with keeping God first in our lives. For addicts, the struggle is chronic and debilitating. Addicts experience shame more intensely than non-addicts. They trade their attachment to God for an addiction to false gods. An addiction creates an unhealthy idol out of something created rather than worshiping the Creator.

What do we worship?

True worship doesn't involve praising God because He is worth it in theory. We worship the God of our experience. As we connect with our Creator by the power of the Holy Spirit, we experience His love and acceptance. Worshiping God is difficult if we don't see Him as positive. Our heart aches for a love which feels unattainable.

Intermittent reward is one of the main causes of addictive behavior. The reward is soothing enough to keep us interested but not enough to be a permanent solution. The addict's lack of lasting satisfaction and the guilt of giving oneself over to the addiction make for a death-grip of a downward spiral.

We are addicted when all of the following are true:
- We engage in a behavior that causes significant problems;
- We are usually aware the behavior is unhealthy;
- Often we don't want to continue the behavior; and
- We have tried to stop, but cannot, so we eventually return to our addiction.

The Co-Dependent and the Addict

When we choose an addiction, we leave our own identity behind and identify more with the addiction of choice. We also reject our relationship with our partner for a relationship with our addiction of choice. This leaves behind a vacuum.

We call the partner who takes over management of the addict's life the co-dependent. Similar to the addict, the co-dependent can become addicted to attempting to control the addict's life. However, when a partner attempts to manage the addict's life, the addict cannot experience their emptiness enough to drive them back to God. In the worst case, both the addict and co-dependent separate equally from their identity.

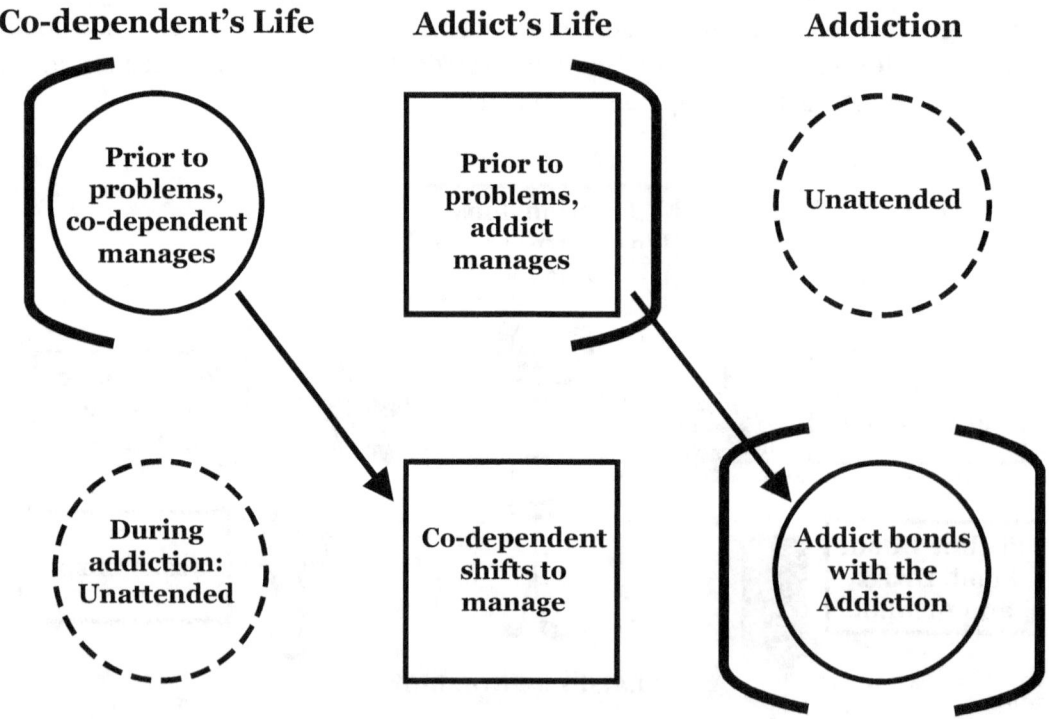

Recovery Planning

We become addicted when we attempt to fulfill our God-given desires with our addiction of choice instead of allowing Him to meet our longings. The process of allowing God to meet these longings is a journey of faith and greater intimacy with Him.

Successful recovery from addiction requires both tactics and strategy. Tactics are the short-term plan we must implement immediately to "stop the bleeding." For example, a tactical maneuver for pornography is installing internet accountability software.

However, simply stopping the addiction is not enough. We need to replace the addiction with positive behaviors. Strategy is the long-term plan we must implement to improve skill and execution so we can prevent "another horrible accident." A strategy for pornography, for example, is seeking to understand our unmet core longings so that we can seek to have them legitimately met.

Each of the four categories of addiction corresponds to one or more of our core longings (identified in Chapter 13):

Addiction of Choice	Core Longing Found in Christ
Relationships, Love, Pornography, and Sex	Unconditional Love and Connection
Performance, Achievement, and Fame	Significance
Possessions and Money	Security
Feeling Good, Food, Drugs and Alcohol	Hope

To be free, an addict needs grace, confrontation, and accountability. Some partners of addicts focus more easily on grace; they need to be prepared to set firm boundaries. Other partners are more naturally truth-tellers; they need to remember that addicts need love and support. Ultimately, we all need to find ways to experience Jesus as He meets our core longings.

Escalation Levels

When seeking to be free of addiction, we need to increase the strength of treatment until we extinguish the addiction (Matthew 5:27–29). Here are eight levels of increasingly stronger interventions:

1. Self-care: accountability with family and friends;
2. Pastoral-care: confession and counseling with pastoral staff;
3. Individual Counseling: professional counseling with a specialist;
4. Group Counseling: support in a community of other addicts;
5. Marriage Counseling: interventions focused on confrontation to eliminate denial;
6. Intensive Outpatient Services: local intensive treatment;
7. Intensive Inpatient Services: national long-term treatment (up to three months);
8. Permanent Living Services: live onsite long-term (up to one year).

If self-care is not enough to stop and prevent an addiction, add pastoral care. If pastoral care is not enough, add individual counseling, and so on. The partner of the addict needs to be prepared to initiate increasing the level of treatment. We can start with level one and move to the next level after a reasonable amount of time has passed. Some levels work well together, such as levels four and five.

Addiction is Distraction

As Christians, we have an enemy whose goal is often to simply distract. Addiction is both a perfect distraction and a perfect trap. The real problem is the couple's lack of an affectionate bond.

The prognosis for recovery is much higher for the couple who does not allow addiction to overshadow their connection.

While being addiction-free is important, sin removal as a primary and only goal is less efficient than focusing on the marital bond. Jesus already solved the sin problem. Instead, the greatest success will come by forgiving the sin, implementing tactical strategies to prevent further sin, and strategically increasing the degree of affectionate connection. This requires humility on the part of both husband and wife.

Genuine intimacy with God and our partner is the antidote. A couple with strong affection for each other and for God will endure just about any degree of addictive behavior long enough for their marriage to heal.

For Reflection

1. Watch out for relapse when you are HALTSB (Hungry, Angry, Lonely, Tired, Stressed, or Bored).
2. An addict needs both time to let go of the negative (the "addiction of choice") and time to embrace the positive (what replaces the "addiction of choice").
3. Whether you are an addict or the partner of one, are you willing to escalate the treatment all the way to the most intense treatment?

Next Steps

- ☐ Read 1 Timothy 5:1–2. Use this Scripture as a constant reminder of who they, the opposite sex, are to you as fellow Christians.
- ☐ Read John 8:1–11. Use this Scripture as a constant reminder that we all need mercy, not condemnation.
- ☐ If you or your partner is addicted, what escalation level are you using? How is it working? Do you know when you need to escalate further?
- ☐ Write a timeline of your ups and downs over the years. How do these correlate with any addictions you've had? How about the ups and downs of your marriage?
- ☐ Write a detailed history of your addictive behaviors (see Chapter 38 for a detailed exercise). Share it with your partner.
- ☐ Review these resources:
  - ☐ Movie: *When a Man Loves a Woman*
  - ☐ Book: *From Bondage to Bonding* by Nancy Groom
  - ☐ Book: *The Search for Significance* by Robert McGee
  - ☐ Book: *Healing the Wounds of Sexual Addiction* by Mark Laaser
  - ☐ Book: *Out of the Shadows* by Patrick J. Carnes
  - ☐ Book: *No Stones: Women Redeemed from Sexual Addiction* by Marnie C. Ferree
  - ☐ Book: *The Complete Works of Walter Trobisch* by Walter Trobisch
  - ☐ Book: *False Intimacy* by Harry Schaumburg
  - ☐ Book: *Wired for Intimacy* by William M. Struthers

Chapter 51

Grieving Traumatic Loss

"Blessed are those who mourn, for they shall be comforted.
—Matthew 5:4

Bear one another's burdens, and so fulfill the law of Christ. For each will have to bear his own load.
—Galatians 6:2, 5

Sadness and grief do not indicate weakness. Grieving is necessary for emotional, physical, and spiritual health. When we have taken the risk to attach to others and we lose them, deep sadness is normal. When grieving becomes difficult don't stop in the middle of it. As best as you can, provide enough structure in your life so you don't become trapped. The only way out of grief is to keep moving through it.

The Grieving Process

Life is unpredictable and often hard. What we depend on one day may be gone the next. A traumatic loss can devastate a marriage, but we can survive the loss if we learn how to adjust to life changes. We must grieve all losses.

Grieving is an open-ended process that ends when we conclude we are done. A scientific process cannot tell us when that will happen because grieving is so subjective. In some ways, the process never ends. Experiencing loss from a trauma usually involves some or all of the following responses:

- Shock: an automatic, negative, emotional reaction to the trauma;
- Denial: refusing to acknowledge the trauma;
- Awareness: recognizing and feeling the pain of the trauma;
- Anger: rebelling against God by asking "Why me?";
- Depression: resigning to the worst of the trauma;
- Acceptance: ready to move forward again in the new reality;
- Hope: reframing the past so it doesn't restrict the future; and
- Reconstruction: building a better future.

Sources of Loss

With any significant loss, the danger exists to wrongly attack or blame our partner for life's misfortune. We can also become severely depressed. If the loss sufficiently distracts us, our marriage suffers. Unresolved grief can lead to acting out in inappropriate ways such as addictions, adultery, fighting, and abandoning each other. Acting out only perpetuates a negative cycle of grief.

Any of the following life events, or ones like them, can result in significant burden to an individual and a marriage:

- Miscarriage or other death of a child
- Infertility
- Coming to terms with childhood wounds (abuse and neglect)
- Health changes (including hormonal changes)
- Life-changing accident
- Addiction
- Adultery
- Death of parent
- Empty nest
- Loss of job
- Business stress
- Severe debt or bankruptcy

Carrying Loads and Bearing Burdens

God doesn't intend for us to manage the burdens of life alone. In Galatians 6:1–10, the Greek word for burden is *baros*, which means heavy, crushing, or troubling loads.[18] However, the Greek word for load is *phortion*, which means something personal that an individual must carry.[19]

Believers have both an individual responsibility and a corporate responsibility. The first ten verses of Galatians 6 contain several examples of both kinds of responsibility.

Individual responsibilities include:
- Watch yourself;
- Test your own actions;
- Carry your own load;

Corporate responsibilities include:
- Restoring another gently;
- Carrying each other's burdens; and
- Doing good to all people, especially believers.

Whenever we are carrying a burden, we need to determine its "heaviness." We might be able to carry it, and we might need help. The same applies to marriage. An individual's burden may not only be too much for the individual, but also too much for the marriage. We learned in Chapter 4 that God is our ultimate source. God gives us a whole community of people within the church with whom we can share our larger burdens.

If we are not sure if we need help, we probably need help. At least we need to ask an objective person their opinion. Every married person could use a reliable confidant outside the marriage. The person should be of the same gender and able to keep confidences. Your partner needs to approve of your selection. If your partner protests your selection, find someone else.

---

[18] biblehub.com Thayer's Greek Lexicon
[19] biblehub.com HELPS Word-studies

Getting Through Grief

When we've already suffered a loss, the last thing we need is to make it worse by abandoning or attacking our partner. After a trauma, the pain of life may be too overwhelming for the marriage. What was acceptable and tolerable before the loss may be a real problem for the survival of our relationship. We need to be willing to find additional help.

Every person grieves differently, even husband and wife. Acknowledge and embrace this sober fact. Your partner may cry a lot while you shed few, if any, tears. Give space for each of you to grieve in your own way. Don't assume the other wants to talk, but don't assume they don't want to talk either. Certainly do not pretend everything is fine when it isn't. However, keep balance in your life. Enjoying the part of your life that you can is okay even while you are still grieving.

Most trauma is not resolved by fighting against it—that usually makes it worse! Instead, we have to find a way to go through it.

For Reflection

1. Nothing is wasted. Anything we go through, as horrible as it is, has purpose and meaning because God is not careless.
2. Life is hard. But it is only one night when compared to eternity. When you are ready for hope and encouragement, read Psalm 30.

For his anger lasts only a moment, but his favor lasts a lifetime; weeping may remain for a night, but rejoicing comes in the morning.
—Psalm 30:5 NIV

---

3. Read 1 Peter 5:1–11. Your enemy may seek to devour you. God doesn't promise you won't suffer, but He promises to restore, confirm, strengthen, and establish you.

Humble yourselves, therefore, under the mighty hand of God so that at the proper time he may exalt you, casting all your anxieties on him, because he cares for you.
—1 Peter 5:6–7

Next Steps

- ☐ Read Job 1–3 and Job 38–42. What did you learn about grief and God?
- ☐ Go through the Sources of Loss. What part of each one is a "load" and what part is a "burden"?
- ☐ Consider the ups and downs of your life to date. Identify your life-altering losses. How did you or how can you recreate yourself to move forward? Perhaps your difficulty will move you in the direction needed to pursue a greater life calling. Every change closes a chapter in your book of life, but it also allows for writing a completely new chapter.

- Review these resources:
  - Movie: *Lorenzo's Oil*
  - Movie: *Ordinary People*
  - Movie: *Bridge to Terabithia*
  - Site: recover-from-grief.com
  - Site: tolovehonorandvacuum.com/2013/11/miscarriage-affects-marriage
  - Site: http://en.wikipedia.org/w/index.php?title=Kubler-Ross_model&oldid=634772322
- Using your Blueprint Space, draw a symbol of your loss. Ask God to give you a corresponding symbol of hope, then draw it.

Blueprint Space

Chapter 52

Time to Endure and Enjoy the Journey

Then God said, "Let us make man in our image, after our likeness. And let them have dominion over the fish of the sea and over the birds of the heavens and over the livestock and over all the earth and over every creeping thing that creeps on the earth."
So God created man in his own image,
in the image of God he created him;
male and female he created them.
And God blessed them. And God said to them, "Be fruitful and multiply and fill the earth and subdue it, and have dominion over the fish of the sea and over the birds of the heavens and over every living thing that moves on the earth." . . . God saw everything that he had made . . . was very good.
—Genesis 1:26–31

Marriage is God joining together a man and a woman, loyal to each other for life, who each contribute distinct but equally important abilities towards the completion of a fruitful mission greater than can be accomplished apart.
Chapter 18

Dominate

God created the first marriage and instructed Adam and Eve to have dominion over His Creation. To have dominion means to rule by power and authority.[20] As God's stewards, we need to understand fully the awesome responsibility He gives us. With authority over the physical and spiritual realms, we can bring order to Earth. This is God's first commission to us.

Find your Direction

God sets our journey before us. Throughout this book, we've learned its basic framework. We know we don't start at our full potential, but we come to understand our true identity over time, in steps and stages. God has a long-range vision for us as a Christian community and equally for you as an individual. He has in mind both your activities for today and your potential into eternity.

God provides us purpose and significance. We must hold onto God's big picture perspective, and trust Him for the details. If we focus on the details too much, we may forget why we are here. Without a vision, we may lose our direction. Then, when marriage becomes a struggle, we will lack a reason to persevere. God never runs out of energy. His understanding is beyond us, but we are totally within His grasp. God will not abandon you amidst your journey (Isaiah 40:27–31)!

Direction is more important than position and resolve more important than appearances. If you must lose position to gain a better direction forward, go for it! If your resolve makes you look foolish in others' eyes, dare to look foolish!

---

[20] yourdictionary.com/dominion

Balance Work and Play

Life has a rhythm—its ups-and-downs. There is a time to be content (to accept where we are in life) and a time to grow up (to move on in life). There is a time to enjoy marriage as it is, and a time to work hard to move it to the next level.

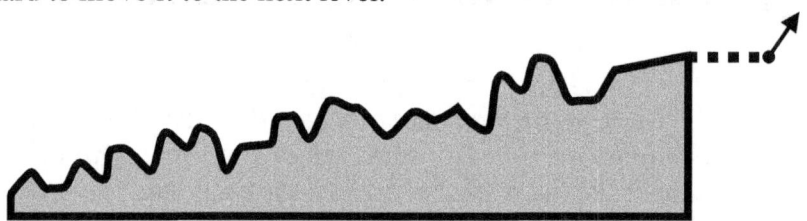

A journey without various stops along the way to enjoy the scenery doesn't pass time well. After all, we only get to live each moment once. Either work or enjoyment may be emphasized over the other depending on the stage you are in and other life circumstances. However, we need a balance between work and enjoyment for fruitfulness.

If we don't invest enough time to work on the relationship, it will suffer from being overgrown with thorns and weeds. If we wait too long to work on the relationship, we will end up spending the majority of our life in a dysfunctional relationship. By the time we figure things out, our life might be over (though it is never too late to begin).

If we don't invest enough to enjoy the relationship, we fail to drink deeply of the riches that God provides for us. Failure to grow in intimacy means we don't risk life becoming messy with someone else. Intentionally or conveniently stuck, we avoid the risk of moving forward. If we don't enjoy the journey, we might cease to care why it matters. And that's the danger. We must never lose touch with why the journey matters.

Spend Your Time Wisely

Our journey will be more enjoyable when we rest in the truth that God has our journey planned (Ephesians 2:10). Moses lived in Egypt for forty years, then he lived away from Egypt for another forty years before God called him back as His chosen instrument to save Egypt (Acts 7:23, 30). When God appears not to be using us, He is only preparing us for the right moment in time for which He created us. Roots grow deep so the plant can endure, mature, produce fruit, and be around for seasons to come (Psalm 1:3).

God has chosen us as His allies against evil. He provides the pathway and establishes our steps (Proverbs 16:9). From our perspective, we make up life as we go. But as we realize God knows our steps, we can participate and fully engage in life with less fear.

In the movie *The Fellowship of the Ring*, Frodo fully engages by volunteering to destroy the evil ring. If someone didn't destroy the ring, it would end up destroying all he knew to be good, including his home, The Shire. Frodo didn't understand why such evil existed in his lifetime. Gandalf, Frodo's trusted adviser, encouraged him by pointing out that none of us can choose our time in history. God chooses many things for us such as our identity, our family, our birthday, and our time of death. But God also gives us the power to choose what to do with our time.

We must choose what to do with the limited time God gives us. Will we waste it or spend it wisely? What have you decided in your heart is worth fighting for? Once you know this, you will know your direction.

In the movie *Braveheart*, William Wallace says, "Every man dies, but not every man lives." We need to make sure we are living for the important reasons, those that are of utmost value to God, but also to us.

Make a Better World With Your Marriage

Marriage is not for making up lost time from your childhood but for sharing your life with someone else. Your partner is a witness to your life: contributor, empathizer, adviser, confidant, and *partner*. But your partner is not Mom, Dad, Son, Daughter, or God.

Be willing to fully engage God's truth and fully experience His truth with your partner. You are on this journey together. By making today a little better than yesterday, you will save some room for tomorrow to be a little better than today.

Marriage is a journey with a purpose. You are here to make the world a better place by your love, by your unique gifts and abilities, and by your marriage. Now go and fulfill God's commission by being all that God made you to be!

For Reflection

1. Being together all the way is more important than your individual choices along the way.
2. Life is a journey with problems to solve, lessons to learn, and experiences to enjoy.
3. Life is a journey during which you learn to freely give and receive love.
4. During the busy seasons of life, having children, establishing careers, etc., take time-outs to pursue life with intention. Enjoy yourselves often by having fun with each other throughout your marriage.
5. Commitment allows you to achieve your goals, but more importantly, it allows you to become the person God intends you to be.
6. Marriage proves to be both a challenge and an opportunity. We must figure out how to love someone when they don't deserve it. When we can do this, everybody wins.
7. We might regret not taking action toward our dreams twenty years ago, but we don't have to make the same mistake twice.
8. Reflect on this quote:

Nothing in the world is worth having or worth doing unless it means effort, pain, difficulty . . . I have never in my life envied a human being who led an easy life. I have envied a great many people who led difficult lives and led them well.
—Theodore Roosevelt

Next Steps

- ☐ Review these resources:
  - ☐ Movie: *Mr. Holland's Opus*
  - ☐ Movie: *Gladiator*
  - ☐ Poem: *Birth is a Beginning* by Rabbi Alvin Fine found online.
  - ☐ Site: blueletterbible.org/Comm/guzik_david/StudyGuide_Psa/Psa_1.cfm
  - ☐ Site: kevinmartineau.ca/life-is-a-journey

☐ Use your Blueprint Space to reflect on the legacy you want to leave. Plan for it now. As your 90-year-old self, write a letter to your present-day self. Talk about what you are satisfied with, what you regret, and what you don't want to later regret. What is of utmost value to you?

Blueprint Space

Supplemental Material

More Help for Your Journey

Appendix A   **Cinema Therapy**

Selected Bibliography

Index of Scriptures

More Help for Your Journey

By faith Abraham obeyed when he was called to go out to a place that he was to receive as an inheritance. And he went out, not knowing where he was going. By faith he went to live in the land of promise, as in a foreign land, living in tents with Isaac and Jacob, heirs with him of the same promise. For he was looking forward to the city that has foundations, whose designer and builder is God.
—Hebrews 11:8–10

We never know for sure when God will choose to act. But look out when He does! Hang in there even if your marriage is difficult right now. You don't want to miss what God is going to do.

Individual and Marital Checkup

Return at least once a year to this book for a Marriage Checkup. We all tend to drift off center when we take our eyes off the goal. During your checkup, review the past year, then plan for the next year. These questions will help with that process.

In the past year, with respect to your individual and marital growth, what were your:
1. Top accomplishments?
2. Major difficulties or challenges?
3. Unexpected blessings?
4. Most significant things you wanted to accomplish but didn't?
5. Most significant things you learned about yourself and about your partner?

For next year, with respect to your individual and marital growth, what are your:
1. Top five goals?
2. Top five obstacles to these goals?

Review the Next Steps questions from Chapter 24 for additional questions.

Further Study Resources and Help

MarriageFromRootsToFruits.com
- Bonus material specifically for this book.

ChristianConcepts.com
- Additional material about individual and marital growth;
- Opportunity to ask questions and post comments; and
- News about upcoming products and resources.

NewReflectionsCounseling.com
- Coaching, counseling, and other more intensive help.

Comments

Direct your comments to mpavlik@nrcounseling.com, or visit one of the websites above for contact information.

Appendix A – Cinema Therapy

This is a list of the movies found in each chapter. For each movie I've included a few words to describe its theme and any cautions. The ratings span from G to R. Most of the R movies are rated this way because of the intense violence or trauma necessary to tell the story. However, some movies have offensive material. I approach such material with discernment. Some movies may not be for you. If you have concerns, research the movies before you watch them.

Use these questions to help you organize your experience into a plan for growth.
1. What are the main themes and principles of the movie?
2. With which character do you identify most? Least?
3. How does the movie support the current chapter you are reading?
4. How does this movie speak to the reason you are reading this book?
5. How has your outlook on marriage changed?
6. In what ways did the movie inspire you?
7. Develop a plan for growth based on what you learned.

Chapter	Movie	Themes	Rating
1	The Notebook	Knowing what you want; persevering, maturing love	PG-13
2,3,4	The Passion of Christ	Jesus' life and sacrifice	R; graphic depiction of crucifixion
5	The Truman Show	Confidence vs self-doubt	PG
6	Life is Beautiful	Self-sacrifice to make life better for others; positive attitude	PG-13
7	The River Wild	Priorities and values	PG-13
	Jerry Maguire	Priorities and values; some positive marriage modeling	R; strong sexual content
8	Back to the Future Trilogy	Confidence vs self-doubt; self-control	PG
9	Groundhog Day	Self-awareness; growth is fun	PG
10	Butterfly Circus	Overcoming limitations	NR
	Slumdog Millionaire	Growing up without parents; perseverance	R; graphic pictures of abuse and neglect
11	Curious George	Innocence; attachment	G
12	Spiderman (2002)	Responsibility	PG-13
13	Simon Birch	Purpose; significance	PG
14	Ragamuffin	Inadequacy; addiction	PG-13
	A Beautiful Mind	Sorting fact from fiction	PG-13
15	The Lion King	Finding your identity	G
16	Remember the Titans	Teamwork amidst diversity	PG
17	Into the Wild	Need for relationships	R; language, some nudity
18,35	The Joy Luck Club	Growing up, boundaries, leaving parents; fairness	R; some boundary setting doesn't prioritize marriage
19	Cinderella Man	Honesty; integrity	PG-13; language
	You've Got Mail	Timing/patience in dating	PG
20	Evan Almighty	Leading, following; faith, trust	PG
21	The Four Seasons	Adjusting to change	PG

22	*Miracle*	Forming a team	PG
23,27	*Shadowlands*	Opening to love means being vulnerable to sorrow and pain	PG
24	*Up*	Enjoying the moment you have; no regrets	PG
	The Story of Us	Relationships and family are worth saving	R; language, brief sexuality
25	*Good Will Hunting*	Giftedness; recovery from abuse	R; language, sexuality
26	*The Horse Whisperer*	Trauma, communication	PG-13
27	*Beauty and the Beast (Disney)*	Intimacy; beauty is not skin deep	G
28	-		
29	*Fireproof*	Resolving conflict; addiction	PG
30	*Marriage Retreat (2011)*	Teamwork; communication	NR
31	*The Thing About My Folks*	Separation; expectations; communication	PG-13
32,52	*Gladiator*	Fighting for what is important; self-sacrifice; legacy	R; war violence
33	*Pride and Prejudice (2005)*	Choosing a life partner	PG
34	*Apollo 13*	Failure is not an option	PG
35	*Yes Man*	Openness to new experiences	PG-13
36	*To End all Wars*	Forgiveness; freedom	R; war violence
37	-		
38	*The Incredibles*	Preventing infidelity; teamwork	PG
39	*The Interpreter*	Mercy, forgiveness	PG-13
40	*Island of Grace (2011)*	Repentance	NR
41	*Spiderman 3 (2007)*	Forgiveness	PG-13
42	*Braveheart*	Trust, betrayal, sacrifice	R; war violence
43	*Les Misérables (2012)*	Redemption, mercy, sacrificial love	PG-13
44	*Take the Lead*	Trust, teamwork, leading and following	PG-13
45	*The Lord of the Rings Trilogy*	Perseverance; teamwork, trust	PG-13
46	*A Vow to Cherish*	Commitment	NR
47	*The Vow (2012)*	Commitment; vow; trauma;	PG-13
48	-		
49	*Shattered Dreams*	Domestic violence, passivity	NR; priest gives poor counsel
50	*When a Man Loves a Woman (1994)*	Boundaries; addiction; separation	R; language
51	*Lorenzo's Oil*	Effects of loss	PG-13
	Ordinary People	Effects of loss	R; language
	Bridge to Terabithia	Loss	PG
52	*Mr. Holland's Opus*	Legacy	PG

Selected Bibliography

Alberti, R., & Emmons, M. (2008). *Your Perfect Right.* Impact Publishers.
Allender, D. B. (1990). *The Wounded Heart.* NavPress.
Allender, D. B., & Longman III, T. (1994). *The Cry Of The Soul.* NavPress.
Barry, S. R. (2011, March). *Eyes on the Brain.* Retrieved Nov 2014, from Psychology Today: psychologytoday.com/blog/eyes-the-brain/201103/memory-the-amygdala-and-ptsd-0
Bartholomew, K., & Horowitz, L. M. (1991, August). Attachment styles among young adults. *Journal of Personality and Social Psychology, 61(2)*, 226–244.
Benner, D. (2003). *Surrender To Love.* InterVarsity Press.
Bevere, J. (2004). *The Bait Of Satan.* Charisma House.
Calvin, J. (1845). *The Institutes of the Christian Religion.* (H. Beveridge, Trans.) Christian Classics Ethereal Library.
Carder, D. (2008). *Torn Asunder.* Moody Publishers.
Carter, L., & Minirth, F. (1993). *The Anger Workbook.* Thomas Nelson Publishers.
Chapell, B. (1998). *Each for the Other.* Baker Books.
Childerston, J. K. (2014). Beyond Chemistry. *Christian Counseling Today.*
Clarke, J. I., & Dawson, C. (1998). *Growing Up Again.* Hazelden.
Clinton, T., & Straub, J. (2010). *God Attachment.* Howard Books.
Cloud, H. (1995). *Changes That Heal.* HarperPaperbacks.
Cloud, H. (2011). *The Law Of Happiness.* Howard Books.
Cloud, H., & Townsend, J. (1999). *Boundaries In Marriage.* ZondervanPublishingHouse.
Cloud, H., & Townsend, J. (2001). *How People Grow.* Zondervan.
Cloud, H., & Townsend, J. (2003). *Boundaries Face To Face.* Zondervan.
Cloud, H., & Townsend, J. (2005). *Rescue Your LoveLife.* Integrity Publishers.
Covey, S. R. (1990). *The 7 Habits Of Highly Effective People.* Simon & Schuster.
Crabb, L. (1988). *Inside Out.* Navpress.
Crabb, L. (1991). *Men & Women.* Zondervan Publishing House.
Davis, M. W. (2001). *The Divorce Remedy.* Simon & Shuster.
Dolan, Y. (2000). *One Small Step.* Authors Choice Press.
Eggerichs, E. (2004). *Love and Respect.* Thomas Nelson.
Eldredge, J. (2011). *Beautiful Outlaw.* Hachette Book Group.
Eldredge, J., & Eldredge, S. (2011). *Love and War.* WaterBrook Press.
Erikson, E. H. (1993). *Childhood and Society.* W W Norton & Company.
Fine, R. A. (2001). Birth is a Beginning. In H. J. Fields, *B'chol L'vavcha* (p. 121). UAHC Press.
Fisher, R., & Ury, W. (1991). *Getting To Yes.* Penguin Books.
Gottman, J. (2005). *The Seven Principles For Making Marriage Work.* Three Rivers Press.
Groom, N. (1991). *From Bondage to Bonding.* NavPress.
Grudem, W. (2002). *Biblical Foundations for Manhood and Womanhood.* (W. Grudem, Ed.) Crossway.
Heller, D. P. (2014). Somatic Attachment Trainings (dianepooleheller.com).
Hemfelt, R., & Warren, P. (1990). *Kids Who Carry Our Pain.* Thomas Nelson.
Howells, M. (1894). The Difficult Seed. In *Friends' Intelligencer* (Vol. 51, p. 284). Friends' Intelligence Corporation.
Hybels, B., & Hybels, L. (1991). *Fit To Be Tied.* Zondervan Publishing House.
Johnson, S. (2004). *The Practice of Emotionally Focused Couple Therapy.* Brunner-Routledge.

Kendall, R. T. (2002). *Total Forgiveness.* Charisma House.

Kilmann, R. H. (1974). *Conflict Mode Instrument.* Retrieved November 2014, from Kilmann Diagnostics: kilmanndiagnostics.com/catalog/thomas-kilmann-conflict-mode-instrument

Laaser, M. (2004). *Healing The Wounds Of Sexual Addiction.* Zondervan.

Leman, K. (2003). *Sheet Music.* Tyndale House Publishers.

Lewis, C. S. (1960). *The Four Loves.* Harcourt Brace.

Manning, B. (2002). *Abba's Child.* NavPress.

McGee, R. (1998). *The Search For Significance.* Thomas Nelson.

Nelson, T. (1998). *The Book of Romance.* Nelson Books.

Powell, J. (1998). *Why Am I Afraid To Tell You Who I Am?* Resources For Christian Living.

Pulaski, M. A. (1971). *Understanding Piaget.* Harper & Row.

Ryken, L. (1995). *Redeeming The Time.* Baker Books.

Schaumburg, H. W. (1997). *False Intimacy.* NavPress.

Seamands, D. (1990). *Living With Your Dreams.* Victor.

Shapiro, F. (2012). *Getting Past Your Past.* Rodale.

Siegel, D. J. (2012). *The Developing Mind.* The Guilford Press.

Smedes, L. (1993). *Shame & Grace.* HarperOne.

Smith, H. W. (1994). *The 10 Natural Laws of Successful Time and Life Management.* Warner Books.

Smoke, J. (1995). *Growing Through Divorce.* Harvest House Publishers.

Springle, P. (1994). *Trusting.* Servant Publications.

Stanley, S., Markman, H. J., & Blumberg, S. L. (2001). *Fighting For Your Marriage.* Jossey-Bass.

Stanton, G. T. (1997). *Why Marriage Matters.* Pinon Press.

Struthers, W. M. (2009). *Wired For Intimacy.* IVP Books.

Thomas, G. (2000). *Sacred Marriage.* Zondervan.

Trobisch, W. (1987). *The Complete Works of Walter Trobisch.* InterVarsity Press.

Vernick, L. (2001). *How To Act Right When Your Spouse Acts Wrong.* WaterBrook Press.

Vernick, L. (2007). *The Emotionally Destructive Relationship.* Harvest House Publishers.

Wallerstein, J. S. (2000). *The Unexpected Legacy of Divorce.* Hyperion.

Wardle, T. (2005). *Wounded.* Leafwood.

Wardle, T. (2009). Formational Prayer Seminar. Healing Care Ministries (healingcare.org).

Wheat, E., & Wheat, G. (1998). *Intended for Pleasure.* Fleming H. Revell.

Wilson, S. (1992). *Shame Free Parenting.* InterVarsity Press.

Wilson, S. (2002). *Released From Shame.* InterVarsity Press.

Wolfe, J. L., & Bernard, M. E. (1993). *The RET Resource Book for Practitioners.* Institute for Rational-Emotive Therapy.

Worthington, E. (1989). *Marriage Counseling.* InterVarsity Press.

Wright, H. N. (1983). *Marital Counseling.* Harper & Row.

Index of Scriptures

Genesis
- 1:1–3 — 62
- 1:26–28 — 86
- 1:26–31 — 217
- 1:27 — 79
- 1:28 — 75
- 2:17 — 13
- 2:18 — 183
- 2:18, 24 — 42
- 2:23–24 — 75
- 2:24 — 75, 77, 195
- 2:25 — 77, 109
- 3:12–13 — 14
- 3:16–17 — 13
- 3:3 — 13
- 3:7–8 — 13
- 5:1–2 — 65
- 12:1–5 — 95
- 17:1 — 63
- 22 — 109, 153
- 22:14 — 23
- 41:41 — 38
- 45 — 180
- 50:19–20 — 161

Exodus
- 15:25–27 — 63
- 32 — 152
- 34:6 — 63

Leviticus
- 25:8–22 — 182

Numbers

Deuteronomy
- 4:31 — 63
- 24:3–4 — 196

Joshua

Judges

Ruth

1 Samuel
- 24 — 152
- 25 — 86

2 Samuel

1 Kings

2 Kings

1 Chronicles

2 Chronicles

Ezra

Nehemiah

Esther

Job
- 1–3; 38–42 — 215
- 12:12 — 43

Psalms
- 1:3 — 218
- 16 — 45
- 16:8–9 — 45
- 18 — 54
- 23 — 54
- 23:1–2 — 53
- 23:1–3 — 63
- 30 — 215
- 30:2 — 171
- 30:5 — 215
- 37 — 154
- 37:23–24 — 185
- 40 — 99
- 40:1–3 — 99
- 51 — 170
- 51:10, 12, 17 — 167
- 56 — 165
- 56:3 — 163, 187
- 56:3–4 — 163
- 71:17–18 — 42
- 78:4 — 42, 103
- 90:16–17 — 102
- 92:12–15 — 43
- 103 — 63
- 127:1a — 1
- 139 — 39, 54, 62, 63
- 139:13–16 — 61
- 139:14–16 — 62
- 139:23–24 — 37, 151
- 145:15–19 — 54
- 147:3 — 171

Proverbs
- 6:32 — 159
- 12:12 — 39
- 13:11 — 31
- 13:12 — 53
- 13:22 — 42
- 15:1 — 154
- 15:22 — 3
- 15:23 — 135
- 15:28 — 154
- 16:9 — 218
- 16:32 — 51
- 17:14 — 154
- 18:13 — 154
- 19:11 — 159
- 20:5 — 37
- 22:6 — 42
- 24:3 — 1
- 25:11 — 135
- 25:28 — 51
- 27:5–6 — 123
- 28:13 — 154
- 30:8–9 — 29

			18:15–35	179, 180, 182
31	87		18:18–19	197, 203
31:12	86		18:21–35	181
Ecclesiastes			18:33–35	181
3:1–4	89		18:35	181
3:12–13	101		19:6	195
4:9–12	42, 127		19:6–8	195
Song of Solomon			19:9	196
4:16b	115		23:25–26	198
Isaiah			25:14–28	42
40:11	63		25:14–30	63
40:27–31	217		26:41	14
40:28b–31	97		28:20	54
42:3	93	Mark		
43:1	62, 161	Luke		
43:19	161		2:41–52	41
Jeremiah			6:45	151
29:11	54		6:47–49	93, 194
Lamentations			8	79
Ezekiel			10:38–42	79
36:26	61		12:48	50
Daniel			13:6–9	21
Hosea			13:10–17	79
Joel			14:25–33	27, 28
Amos			14:26–30	191, 194
Obadiah			15:11	125
Jonah			15:11–32	54
Micah			17:3–4	181, 182
Nahum			18:1–8	134
Habakkuk			19:9	181
Zephaniah		John		
Haggai			2:1–12	79
Zechariah			3:3	15
7:9–11	205, 207		8:1–11	212
Malachi			11:25	15
2:13–16	196		12:24	95
Matthew			14:18	62
5:4	213		15:2	29
5:23–24	183		15:5	19
5:27–28	159		16:33	186
5:27–29	209, 211		19:26–27	79
5:32	196		21:20–23	44
6:7–8	131	Acts		
6:7–13	134		7:23, 30	218
6:14–15	175, 181		7:55–60	174
6:33	153		17	17
7:3–5	35		17:24–25	17
10:29–31	54		17:26	54, 64
10:30	64	Romans		
11:29–30	15		1:25	14
13:3–9	7		4:25	54
13:8	101		5:20–21	16
15:19–20a	38		5:3–5	25, 26
18:1–6	205		7	14, 196
18:2–4	62		7:1–3	196
18:15	179		8:1	36, 63
18:15–17	154, 155			

8:22–23	16	Ephesians	
8:22–25	14	2:10	54, 57, 62, 63, 218
8:23	15	3:16–20	132
8:29–30	54	4:15	154
8:31–39	127	4:31–32	181
8:38	64	5:25–32	84
8:38–39	36, 54	5:28–29	207
12:2–3	57	6:4	42
12:3	135	6:10–12	128
12:5–6	61	Philippians	
12:17–19	151, 152	1:21	43
15:5–6	97	2:3–4	83, 139
1 Corinthians		2:4	154
3:6–7	19	4:19	63
5:5	156	Colossians	
6:19–20	193	3:9–10	109
7	132	3:18–19	83
7:3–5	119	3:19	115
7:10–11	201, 203	1 Thessalonians	
7:15–16	196	2 Thessalonians	
7:32–35	81	3:3	127
7:39–40	196, 201	1 Timothy	
10:13	15	6:7	43
11:3	83	2 Timothy	
12	61	1:6–7	42
12:5–26	54	2:2	39, 42
12:21–27	69, 71	Titus	
12:24b–25	67	2:2–6	80
12:24b–26	143	2:4	115
12:31	63	2:4a	115
13	193	Philemon	
13:12	54	Hebrews	
13:4–7	54, 101, 196	3:3–4	62
13:5	121	4:15	41
13:7	145	9:25–26	16
15:54	161	11	16
2 Corinthians		11:1	132
1:3–4	147	11:6	13
3:17–18	58	11:8–10	223
4:16	43	12:1–2	25
5:17	61	13:4	121
6:18	62	13:5	54
7:10	170	James	
9:6–8	49, 134	1:2–4	93
9:7	132	1:5	152
Galatians		1:17	152
1:10	135	1:19	152, 154
3:13a	15	1:19–20	105
5:1, 13	49	2:13	175
5:13–15	198	4:1	59, 151, 152
5:22–23	35	4:1–3	151
6	214	4:1–10	59
6:1	157	4:2	123, 152
6:1–2	155	4:3	152
6:1–10	214	4:4	152
6:2, 5	213	4:7	152

4:8	152
4:8–9	152
4:8–10	170
4:10	152
4:11–12	152

1 Peter

2:5	62
3:1–6	87
3:7	85, 207
3:9	154
4:10	61
5:1–11	215
5:6–7	215
5:6–10	174
5:8	14

2 Peter

3:9	157

1 John

1:9	154, 160, 170
3:1	61, 62
4:4	15
4:19	19
4:20	151

2 John

3 John

Jude

Revelation

20:10	15

www.ingramcontent.com/pod-product-compliance
Lightning Source LLC
Chambersburg PA
CBHW060510300426
44112CB00017B/2615